That Time We Ate Our Feelings

For Jordana &
Asher
Marcia & David!
Eat, Sip, love, read!
Smargra ♥
☺

To Jordana & Asher,
Marcia & David,
Food = Love.
Always.

That Time We Ate Our Feelings

150 RECIPES FOR COMFORT FOOD FROM THE HEART

Lisa Lucas and Debrianna Mansini
With Photographs by Penina Meisels

APOLLO
PUBLISHERS

FROM DEBRIANNA

For David, with whom all things are possible.

FROM LISA

For Marija Rakela Stokov Konatich, Marija Pleše Papatone, Antica Radicić Caric, Katia Magaretich Kukurusović, Sally Marie (Caric) Lucas, Srecka Konatich, Mary Letinich Corleone, Georgia John Kitchupolos Papatone, Bortolo and Antonia (Konatich) Letinich, Francesca Sulić, Strina Bojitsa Stokov, Jelica Pleše, Mary Joan (Tudor) Caric, Millie Caric Karatan, Mae Caric Sandrini, Danica and Tony Kulisich, my dear Nana, Radoslava Ruža Konatich Pavich, and especially my beloved mother, Frances Mary Pavich.

CONTENTS

INTRODUCTION

Around March 16, 2020, Lisa had wrapped on *The Holy Word*, a clever Catholic-schoolgirl comedy short film, and was feeling generally very optimistic about the rest of 2020. Her production company, LikeMinds, had three TV series in development as well as a feature film that she and her producing partner, Sarah Gartner, had optioned and were excited about producing in late 2020. Debrianna was continuing to tour her one-woman show, *The Meatball Chronicles*, across the United States and had just learned it would be one of the inaugural shows of the United Solo Theatre Festival in London. Then all of a sudden the novel coronavirus landed in the US. There were a lot of mixed messages from the federal government regarding the virus, and they had the effect of downplaying its severity, while at the same time international coverage indicated that it was very serious. Italy, for example, was a catastrophic deathbed. But while other countries were scaling mass efforts to combat the virus, the US was not. It was more than unsettling.

There was so much chaos and no clear information about what was happening from the Trump administration. All we knew was that we were ordered to quarantine in our home state of New Mexico and "shelter in place." Panic ensued. Grocery stores had long lines out the door. There were toilet paper and disinfectant shortages. People began hoarding flour and sugar and fighting over basic home goods and foodstuffs. What was happening? It was a scary time, and no one realized how long this would go on in the US. We certainly had no idea. As friends, as artists, the only thing we knew was that it would be important to stay connected to people, and so we set about searching for coping mechanisms.

We are both entertainers. Debrianna is an accomplished theater, film, and TV actor and writer of nearly forty years, and Lisa is a two-time Emmy Award–winning writer, producer, and actor of twenty-five years. We had both settled in Santa Fe, New Mexico, to continue our respective artistic endeavors, and true to serendipitous form in the Land of Enchantment, as New Mexico is known, we met twelve years ago at a television network's "meet and greet" dinner, where we were randomly seated next to each other and all we could talk about was how bad the food was. Thus, our sisters-from-another-mother kinship was born! We both love to cook, and we both love to hang out in each other's kitchen and watch the other person cook dinner. We still don't remember exactly how we decided to start Corona Kitchen; it just happened one day when we were on the phone talking about the state of affairs. One of us said, "Hey, what if we welcome people into our kitchens to share what we are making for dinner as well as our thoughts on the ever-evolving trials and tribulations of life during the pandemic? One of us could go on Tuesdays and the other one could go on Thursdays. It would be fun, like improv!" Well, that two-days-a-week thing never happened. We set up a Facebook group named Corona Kitchen and started live streaming one day at the end of March 2020 and took turns cooking every night for literally 143 nights straight. We even created a YouTube channel on which to also air the show and archive every episode. Then we realized, *Wait, we could take weekends off and show reruns, couldn't we? We own this network!* In real-world TV terms, we'd produced enough episodes for about ten seasons' worth on YouTube.

And so Corona Kitchen was born. Today it is a weekly live streamed show on Facebook Live and YouTube where people can chat, ask questions, and hang out while we cook. Community members also post and share their own culinary creations in the FB group. The result is an organic, spontaneous, entertaining, and real conversation with each other and a live audience once a week—all while cooking and testing out fabulous recipes and never shying away from discussing the events of the day.

That Time We Ate Our Feelings is a natural progression of the live stream series. It is an introduction to this docu-experiment for those outside the Corona Kitchen social media sphere as well as a written culinary diary for our dedicated followers. We thought,

Who wouldn't want to read about two opinionated feminists who were trying to cope during a worldwide pandemic in a particularly tense election year? As a bonus, we have added some wonderfully poignant stories to accompany the fantastic family recipes we shared and "test kitchened" with viewers over the course of the quarantine. We are happy to make these scrumptious recipes available for people to enjoy and re-create in their own kitchens.

Not going to lie, we are a quirky duo: engaging and outspoken, irreverent and resourceful. We spent 2020—every episode of the show—making mention of our daily lives, current events and US politics, books, articles, movies, and media we were consuming. Valuable information sharing happened—sometimes through tears, but most times through laughter or frustration, all while watching the country burn to the ground. This has been a personal experience for us in all aspects, and our loyal audience connects with that, thank God. It has been refreshing and cathartic to hold an honest, no-holds-barred discussion every night that we hope has enlightened and entertained. It has definitely been an exercise in letting go to be in front of an audience who gets to experience us and all of our imperfections. It is reality TV as it was meant to be, real and unscripted. Even our kitchen accidents are well documented for all to see on YouTube—flying KitchenAid mixers, chef's knife and bloody finger accidents, all adding to the joyful reality of cooking for two friends.

We want to thank our dedicated fan base, which started with a handful of friends and family members and now represents over five thousand viewers (and counting) from all over the globe. It has been an honor to be here for you. We feel like the personal connections we have made via the live chats with so many people who were hurting or felt alone or perhaps needed a friend or just cooking advice have been invaluable. It was a unique situation to cook during the early days of COVID—sometimes the precise ingredients we would have normally used were not available and we were forced to "corona" the recipe, making use of alternative or second-choice ingredients—but the dishes came together. Other key features of the show that the audience loves are our inclusion of special guests, such as famous comedians, news anchors, bloggers, chefs, community activists, and entrepreneurs, and our weekly food photo contest. We especially love to support women and activists for change in whatever capacity we can on the show. Through the vehicles of food and friendship, the show created a coping mechanism for thousands of people during the darkest days of COVID, and it continues to help people today. Good food and stories are like a warm hug, and we all need to feel that now more than ever.

This cookbook was written as an extension of a wonderful online community. It contains our best recipes; our dearest family stories, influences, and inspirations; and recipes from special guests as well as our regular contributor and sister-friend, Hollie Lucas-Alcalay of Hollie's Homegrown; along with a select few culinary contributions from our viewers.

Thank you so very much to our phenomenal Corona Kitchen members, without whom we would not have written this book. Food is love. We came together online at a time when people could not come together in person. Through cooking, we managed to keep our friends, family, and ourselves sane during an insane time. When life is precarious, we turn to food for nourishment, communion, and storytelling. We are grateful for the time we have with family and friends, even when it's in little boxes on our laptop screens. And this unexpected, forced isolation had a silver lining: it taught us to reconnect with the simple pleasures of life, like a great loaf of bread or a bunch of greens freshly picked from the garden. It also created a particular bubble of introspection and self-analysis underscored by the one thing that makes us feel like it's all going to be okay: comfort food. Comfort food is calming and restorative, tasty, wholesome, welcoming, and filled with stories. Our goal with this comfort food cookbook is for it to be unintimidating and perhaps even inspire people who may never have dared to cook before. We believe that the title of Chef Auguste Gusteau's cookbook from the Pixar movie *Ratatouille* is spot on: *Anyone Can Cook.*

In good health (and with proper measuring cups),

Debrianna and Lisa

P.S. There is always a place to hang out and watch how we did it on our YouTube channel, where we have several hundred episodes, including most of the recipes in this book. Feel free to ask us any questions on our Golden Goose Kitchen Facebook page (formerly Corona Kitchen) or @thecoronakitch on Instagram. We're here for you! XO

A VERY BRIEF OVERVIEW OF OUR BASIC PHILOSOPHY ON FOOD AND LIFE

Okay, let's begin here. For us, we believe in *organic everything* for our recipes and in life. Let's keep the planet clean together! Let's also keep our ecosystems intact. GMOs, pesticides, and hybridization all contribute to the diminishing of heirloom seeds and varietals. We could go on and on. Here are some experts in these matters of our natural world who have influenced us and you may want to read or listen to: Vandana Shiva, Winona LaDuke, Jane Goodall, Michael Pollan, Mark Winne, Wangari Maathai, Rachel Carson, Al Gore, Upton Sinclair, Anna Edey, John Robbins, Marion Nestle, Maria Rodale, Bill McKibben, Bioneers, and Seeds of Change.

Whenever possible, please buy and/or grow organic/non-GMO products, especially fruits and vegetables that have no outer skin that you'd remove before using, like celery, berries, lettuces, tomatoes, etc. If you are using the peel of oranges and lemons or keeping the skins on apples or potatoes, organic is also important to reduce pesticide intake. And buy local! When you buy from a local farmers market, not only are you helping out a farmer, you are also getting high-quality produce with a low carbon footprint. When you are at the grocery store, read labels and consider the ingredients. Support sustainable family farms and fair trade growers.

It is also important to know what we are putting in our bodies. Know that there are often metals in food. We always use aluminum-free baking powder for baking, and we refrain from baking with aluminum pans, pots, and sheets. Everything we cook with is either steel or copper lined with steel.

Also, we love leftovers! Don't fear larger portion sizes; just have reusable containers on hand to preserve leftovers. There are many stretchy tops for bowls, reusable avocado tops, and other products that will help you contribute to less packaging, plastics, and fuel used for transportation. Make the effort. We're all in this together. Like Hillary said in 1996, "It takes a village." Love the planet, and it will love you back.

RULES WE LIVE BY, AND WE HOPE YOU DO TOO:

- If you live in a place where you can compost your food scraps, it's important to do so. Also keep in mind that, as Debrianna knows well, some things can be saved for soup stock, and, as Lisa discovered, you can plant your green onion tips and other bulbs and grow them again.

- Recycle everything you can. Make sure to check what your sanitation department accepts. You may also find ways to repurpose items in your own home.

- Conserve water, reducing your use.

- Go solar. Get your energy from the sun. We do!

- Food is political. Like it or not, you vote with your dollar. When you purchase food, you are making a statement about what is important to you. Make your dollar count.

- Grow your own ingredients in your backyard if you can. At a minimum, have an herb container garden or potager on your porch, balcony, or windowsill. They are easy to keep and worth the effort. Fresh herbs make all the difference.

Throughout the book, we have labeled recipes that are gluten-free, vegetarian, or vegan. Be sure to check food labels, though, to make sure there are no hidden allergens or products sourced from animals.

(GF) Gluten-free

(V) Vegetarian

(VG) Vegan

 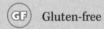

Breakfast & Brunch

FEEL LIKE A WINNER CRANBERRY COFFEE CAKE

MAKES NINE 3 X 3-INCH SQUARES

Nonstick cooking oil

1½ cups all-purpose flour

½ cup almond flour

½ cup (1 stick) unsalted butter, room temperature

1 cup granulated sugar

1 large egg, room temperature

1 teaspoon vanilla extract

2 teaspoons baking powder

1 teaspoon vanilla salt or sea salt

½ cup half-and-half with 1 teaspoon lemon juice (let sit 5 minutes) or ½ cup buttermilk

1 (12-ounce) package frozen whole cranberries (do not thaw)

1 tablespoon demerara sugar or turbinado sugar

½ cup sliced almonds

1. Preheat oven to 350°F.

2. Lightly spray a 9 x 9-inch square baking pan or 9-inch round cake pan with nonstick cooking oil.

3. In a small bowl, combine the flours with a whisk, and then set aside.

4. In a separate bowl, use a hand mixer to cream the butter and granulated sugar until the mixture is light and fluffy. Scrape the bowl to fully incorporate.

5. Add the egg and vanilla, and beat until combined. Add the baking powder and vanilla salt, and blend until combined.

6. Add half the flour mixture, and combine with the mixer on low speed. Add the half-and-half lemon juice mixture, and then add the rest of the flour mixture. Blend until the flour is fully incorporated, but don't overmix.

7. Fold in the frozen cranberries until evenly distributed through the batter. It will be thick.

8. Spread the batter evenly into the baking pan. Sprinkle demerara sugar and almond slices over the top.

9. Bake until a cake tester comes out clean, about 40 to 45 minutes, and then remove the pan from the oven and let the cake cool 15 to 20 minutes in the pan.

10. Serve while slightly warm or after cooling completely. Store the cake at room temperature in the pan covered with foil.

"No! Bridgette, pleaaaase! Not a French apple pancake! Don't you want eggs and cinnamon toast? C'mon, we can have the pancake tomorrow, I promise."

That is how we would often start the morning as we were all in a rush to get off to school. Five girls ranging in age from kindergarten to high school. Bridgette, the only towhead, was the youngest, and somehow the rule was whatever she wanted for breakfast, we had to make. And her palate by age five was a little . . . shall we say . . . too extended. Bridgette's breakfast desires ranged from cold cereal on a good day to steel-cut oats with raisins and honey, from eggs over easy and cinnamon toast to the dreaded French apple pancake.

Thankfully, our cooking ability, with my sisters and me at the top of our food chain, had become very proficient. We could whip up anything in thirty minutes, things a short-order cook would have been proud of, but if we were running late, our sales skills had to kick in and we had to redirect Bridgette's attention. If not, the scene went like this, with me barking orders like a command sergeant:

"Donna, slice the apples super thin. I'll make the batter and get the skillet going. Denice, brush her hair. C'mon, you have to—you're the only one who can put her pigtails in right! Oh, and turn the oven on first, please," and off we'd go, hoping the pancake came out in time for Bridgette to eat it before we had to make it out the door to catch the bus.

Breakfast was a mad rush, and the kink in the wheel could be a demand for gourmet delights midweek. But the weekends were different. Our mom, an immigrant from Europe, introduced us at an early age to café au lait and Nutella, and the steamy, milky coffee combined with the taste of creamy chocolate with a slight peak of hazelnut dripping off warm chunks of French baguette was a Saturday morning breakfast my childhood friends thought exotic but normal in our house.

When our mom wanted to treat us, she'd make a sour cream coffee cake on Saturday night as a special for Sunday morning. The house would fill with the smells of cinnamon and nutmeg, pastry from the ringed cake pan dripping over the edge of the pan and onto the bottom of the oven, and the crackling sound of brown sugar and nuts in the oven. Coffee cake is still a favorite of mine.

One of my favorite coffee cake recipes is made with cranberries. At holiday time, you will find me stocking my infamous freezer with bags of fresh cranberries, my heart tickled with the knowledge that they will be used for a coffee cake once the holidays are long over—a secret treat waiting to happen. And that coffee cake is divine. Just when you think a coffee cake is always just another rendition of the same, your mouth explodes with the tart and tang of a cranberry, surrounded by tender cake fallen over with brown sugar. This recipe is so easy, I often use it in a pinch for parties, because I can still bake anything in a hurry.

Debrianna's baby sister, Bridgette.

DEBRIANNA'S

Turn That Frown Upside Down Roasted Yams with Maple Bourbon Coffee Sauce

SERVES 6 TO 8, WITH ¾ CUP COFFEE SAUCE

(V) (GF)

1½ cups brewed strong coffee

½ cup maple syrup

3 tablespoons brown sugar

½ teaspoon instant espresso powder

⅓ cup bourbon

2 tablespoons unsalted butter

1 teaspoon orange zest

Pinch ground cayenne pepper

6 to 8 large organic yams

Olive oil for rubbing the yams

TO MAKE THE SAUCE

1. In a small saucepan, combine the coffee, maple syrup, brown sugar, and espresso powder over medium-high heat, and cook until it reduces by half.

2. Remove the mixture from the heat, and add the bourbon and butter.

3. Simmer until the sauce is reduced to ¾ cup, about 40 minutes. The sauce will thicken as it sets and when ready should be thick enough to coat a spoon—but not sticky.

4. Remove the sauce from the heat, and stir in the orange zest and cayenne pepper.

TO MAKE THE ROASTED YAMS

1. Preheat oven to 425°F.

2. Wash and dry the yams, and then poke them multiple times with a fork.

3. Rub the yams with olive oil, and place them on a baking sheet in the oven for 45 to 50 minutes or until a fork inserted into the yams has no resistance.

4. Remove the yams from the oven, open them in halves lengthwise using a knife, and then drizzle the coffee sauce generously over them.

TIP: If you prefer to roast the yams in chunks, coat them with olive oil and some smoked paprika. You can also serve the sauce separately and allow each person to drizzle on their preferred own amount. This sauce is so versatile and delectable, you can even pour it over ice cream.

LISA'S

Take on Dinah Shore's "'S Wonderful" Dutch Bébé

Ⓥ

SERVES 4, IF DIVIDED INTO QUARTERS.
IF YOU ARE REALLY HUNGRY, SERVES 2.

1 cup all-purpose flour

1 tablespoon ground flaxseeds

2 full dashes sea salt

1¼ cups half-and-half or whole milk

⅓ cup brown sugar

3 eggs

1 teaspoon vanilla extract

6 tablespoons (¾ stick) salted butter, melted

1 teaspoon ground cinnamon

1 cup blueberries, raspberries, blackberries, or apple slices (optional)

Maple syrup for finishing

Freshly squeezed lemon juice for finishing

1. Preheat oven to 375°F.

2. To prepare batter, mix flour, flaxseeds, sea salt, half-and-half, brown sugar, eggs, and vanilla in a large bowl until just combined.

3. Pour the melted butter into a 12-inch cast-iron skillet, and swirl until the pan is coated. Then pour the batter into the skillet.

4. Sprinkle the cinnamon on top. If desired, sink berries or apple slices into the batter.

5. Bake the pancake for 30 minutes, and then remove it from the oven. If done properly, it will resemble a sombrero—all fluffed up and looking like a "bébé" in the pan!

6. Serve portions with maple syrup and a squeeze of lemon juice over the syrup.

TIP: Additional berries, apple slices, whipped cream, and powdered sugar also work as great toppings. Serve with the maple syrup and lemon juice along with these additions, as this is the most traditional and delectable way to enjoy this.

Lisa's mother, Franny.

First things first: I need to tell you that I was born in America as a second-generation Croatian, or Dalmatinka, as women from the Dalmatian Coast of Croatia are known. There is a long history of incredible cooks and chefs in my family. As you delve further into this cookbook, I will share more of my family specialties and stories of my life and times. This recipe is my go-to on Sundays for breakfast for my kids or special brunches for friends and family.

Let me tell you a little about my mother, Frances Mary Pavich (a.k.a. Franny). She is a remarkable woman who raised my sisters and me, kept us all in line, and supported us in doing whatever it was we set our minds to. This is a woman who taught us the world is a place where it is not uncommon for someone to burst into a Broadway song and dance to express their feelings. She is only twenty-one years older than I am, and in a lot of ways I feel like I watched her grow up right alongside me. Now for her latest endeavor, she's taking on the role of matriarch of this ever-changing Dalmatian complexity that is our family. It's a role well suited for her, being a Virgo, but one that will inevitably be exasperating at times. Her daughters and nieces and nephews and grandchildren are an opinionated, loquacious, overachieving bunch of feelers and Hrvatski dance partiers—and we get loud, cut no slack, debate the issues of the day, and can stay up teary-eyed storytelling until the sun rises. So here's to the new generation, to breaking old cycles that no longer serve us and to forging new frontiers in love, life, and food. We all love you dearly, Franny, and know you are up for the challenge.

My sisters and I are truly blessed to have Franny as our mother. All her time was spent raising us, forever supporting us and believing in our dreams while forsaking her own, and managing our busy lives like a superhero mom-a-ger. Thank you, Mom, for giving us so much.

My mother used to watch Dinah Shore on TV every day in the 1970s. In 1971 Dinah's cookbook *Someone's in the Kitchen with Dinah* became very famous, and in it there was a recipe called "Cousin Selma's Pancake." Well, Franny, of course, morphed it completely into her own over the years, but the inspiration began with Dinah's version. This recipe is my mother's version of it, and it makes for a guaranteed boost of happiness when you eat it.

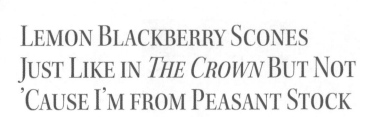

LISA'S

Lemon Blackberry Scones Just Like in *The Crown* But Not 'Cause I'm from Peasant Stock

SERVES 8

SCONES

2 cups all-purpose flour, and more for prepping work surface

6 tablespoons granulated sugar

2½ teaspoons baking powder

½ teaspoon salt

½ cup (1 stick) salted butter, frozen and then grated

½ cup heavy cream, and more for brushing the dough

1 large egg

½ teaspoon vanilla extract

Zest of 1 lemon

1 cup blackberries

1 tablespoon turbinado sugar or Debrianna's ginger-infused sugar (page 208)*

HONEY LEMON DRIZZLE

1 tablespoon honey, warmed

½ teaspoon lemon zest

1 tablespoon freshly squeezed lemon juice

1 teaspoon raspberry or blackberry preserves (optional)

* If you want some spectacular flavor for these scones, check out Debrianna's ginger-infused sugar (page 208), which she made for her Ginger Chocolate Brownie Bite Me's. Substitute that for the turbinado sugar. Mindblower!

1. In a large bowl, mix the flour, granulated sugar, baking powder, and salt together. Incorporate the butter with the dry mixture until you get what looks similar to a coarse sand consistency. Do not overmix.

2. Add the heavy cream, egg, vanilla, lemon zest, and blackberries. Mix with a hand mixer set on low speed or by hand, just enough to incorporate the ingredients.

3. Flour a work surface, and then spread the dough onto the floured surface.

4. Form the dough into a disc shape the size of a dinner plate; or, if you want your scones to be taller, make the size of the disc smaller and thicker. Seal the shaped dough in plastic wrap, and refrigerate for 2 hours to overnight.

5. When ready to bake, preheat oven to 400°F.

6. Remove the dough from the refrigerator and plastic wrap, and cut the disc shape into 8 even wedges. Place the wedges on a baking sheet lined with parchment paper. Lightly brush heavy cream on top of each scone, and sprinkle each with a layer of turbinado sugar.

7. Bake the scones for approximately 22 minutes.

8. In a small bowl, whisk together all ingredients for the honey lemon drizzle.

9. Drizzle the honey lemon mixture over each scone prior to serving.

TIP: This is a classic scone recipe that can be used to make all kinds of scones, from savory to sweet. Don't be afraid to experiment with flavors.

PEACE, LOVE, AND GRANOLA

MAKES APPROXIMATELY 2 POUNDS OF GRANOLA

8 cups rolled oats

½ cup sunflower seeds

½ cup chia seeds

½ cup hemp seeds

2 tablespoons sesame seeds

1 cup chopped almonds

1 cup chopped pecans

1 cup chopped walnuts

2 cups raisins and/or sweetened dried cranberries

1½ teaspoons salt (optional)

½ cup brown sugar

¼ cup maple syrup

¾ cup honey

½ cup coconut oil or sesame oil

1 tablespoon ground cinnamon

1 teaspoon freshly grated nutmeg

1 tablespoon vanilla extract

2 egg whites

1. Preheat oven to 325°F. Line 2 large baking pans with parchment paper or foil.

2. In a large bowl, combine the oats, sunflower seeds, chia seeds, hemp seeds, sesame seeds, almonds, pecans, walnuts, and raisins.

3. In a separate bowl, stir together the salt, brown sugar, maple syrup, honey, coconut oil, cinnamon, nutmeg, and vanilla, and then add this wet mixture into the dry oats mixture and combine well.

4. In another bowl, beat the egg whites until frothy, and then add them to the granola.

5. Pour the granola onto the lined baking pans, and spread out evenly.

6. Bake until crispy and toasted, about 30 to 40 minutes, rotating the pans around halfway through for even baking.

7. Remove the pans from the oven, and let the granola cool in the pans.

8. Store the granola in an airtight container.

DEBRIANNA'S

"IF I COULD TURN BACK TIME" TOMATO TARTE

MAKES 2 TARTES. SERVES 4 PER TARTE.

2 gluten-free
piecrusts, prepared*

2 tablespoons Dijon mustard

2 cups Gouda, Gruyère, and
Asiago mix, cheeses grated

6 medium tomatoes
(3 per tarte), sliced about
¼ inch thick

1 (15-ounce) can artichoke
hearts (not marinated), strained
and sliced

½ to 1 cup pesto
(¼ to ½ cup per tarte)**

2 tablespoons chopped
olives (optional; Niçoise
are traditional)

Salt, to taste

Freshly ground black
pepper, to taste

* I use a gluten-free piecrust available in my grocery store's frozen foods section. I let it thaw for about 15 minutes and then parbake it for 10 minutes in a 400°F oven. If you want to make your own non-GF piecrust, check out Chef Olly's piecrust on page 265.

** If you don't have pesto, use 2 tablespoons olive oil and 2 garlic cloves, minced. Use enough to gently toss the tomatoes and artichoke hearts to coat them.

1. Preheat oven to 400°F.

2. Paint the bottom and sides of the piecrusts with a thin layer of Dijon mustard, using about 1 tablespoon per crust. Then cover the mustard with the grated cheese mix.

3. Gently mix the sliced tomatoes and artichoke hearts with the pesto, to coat, and then place on the piecrust, over the cheese mix.

4. Sprinkle with chopped olives.

5. Bake for about 35 minutes or until the crust is golden and the cheese is bubbling.

TIP: I love to serve this tarte with a side of grilled romaine. The tarte also works well with shrimp for an alternate option. Toss 16 raw and cleaned shrimp (8 per tarte) with 2 tablespoons olive oil and 1 tablespoon minced garlic. Add 8 shrimp to the top of each tarte after it has baked for 25 minutes, and then let them bake 10 more minutes. Voilà.

COMFORT ZONE BE DAMNED SHAKE IT UP SHAKSHUKA

Ⓥ   SERVES 2 TO 4

⅓ cup olive oil

1 teaspoon harissa

2 teaspoons tomato paste

3 medium or 4 small bell peppers, chopped into small cubes (I used green, yellow, red, and orange)

4 garlic cloves, finely chopped

1 teaspoon freshly ground cumin

1 tablespoon honey

1 to 2 tablespoons sea salt, to taste, and more for finishing

1 to 2 tablespoons freshly ground black pepper, to taste, reserving a pinch for assembly

4 cups crushed ripe tomatoes

4 eggs

⅓ cup crumbled feta for finishing

4 teaspoons finely chopped fresh parsley for finishing

1 tablespoon whole-milk yogurt for finishing

FUL

1 teaspoon cumin seeds

6 garlic cloves, finely chopped

2 teaspoons sea salt, and more to taste

Zest and juice of 1 lemon

2 (15.5-ounce) cans fava beans or butter beans, rinsed*

1 (15.5-ounce) can chickpeas

½ cup olive oil, and more for finishing

4 lemon slices

2 teaspoons chopped fresh parsley

Kalamata olives (optional) for serving

Pita bread, warmed, for serving

1. In a 12-inch cast-iron pan, combine the olive oil, harissa, and tomato paste, and warm over low-medium heat, allowing the mixture to swirl.

2. Add the peppers, garlic, cumin, honey, sea salt, and pepper, and sauté over medium heat until the peppers are translucent, about 12 minutes.

3. Add the crushed tomatoes, and bring to a simmer. Cook about 12 minutes more to thicken. The sauce should be bubbling.

4. Make 4 holes in the sauce, and insert the eggs gently, taking care not to break the yolks. Cover the eggs with sauce to cook the whites through; the yolks will remain more poached. Simmer the eggs like this for about 10 minutes. If you want the egg yolks cooked through too, cover the pan for the last 3 minutes. (I prefer mine runny.)

5. Remove the pan from the heat, and set it aside for a few minutes. Then begin assembling the individual servings, which is best done in standard-size pasta bowls. Start by scooping out 1 or 2 eggs with the tomato sauce, and then add some extra sauce and a portion of ful on the side. Finish off each dish with the feta, parsley, yogurt, and a pinch of sea salt.

TIP: This delicious dish can be enjoyed for breakfast, lunch, or dinner. Here are the instructions for cooking fresh young fava beans: There is approximately 1 cup of peeled favas per 1 pound of beans you buy at the store or farmers market. You must first break open the pods and remove the beans from their protective skins. Next, bring a pot of salted water to boil, and then blanche the beans for about 2 minutes. Have a bowl of ice water at the ready, and after blanching, drain the beans immediately and put them in the bowl of ice water to shock them. Remove the protective skins, and they are ready to eat or, in this case, to mash up to make the ful.

* If you use fresh beans for this, which is always best, follow the instructions in the tip for cooking fresh fava beans. I used canned and this dish was still great, but fresh beans are a delight beyond compare.

HOW TO MAKE THE FUL

1. In a large enough mortar and pestle, grind the cumin seeds to make a powder, and then add the garlic, sea salt, and lemon zest and juice. Macerate together. If you don't have a big enough mortar and pestle, you can use a smaller cast-iron pan and mash everything with a wooden spoon after you grind the cumin.

2. Add the fava beans, chickpeas, and olive oil to the garlic mixture, and combine in a cast-iron pan. Add the lemon slices, and cook for 10 minutes over low heat. As the pan heats up, start smashing the beans to your liking with a wooden spoon and add a bit more sea salt, to taste, as well as 1 teaspoon parsley.

3. Before serving, add an additional olive oil drizzle and more parsley on top along with a few kalamata olives. Plate with a side of warmed pita bread fresh out of the oven.

I did everything I'd dreamed about doing in Egypt, but as much as exploring its ancient sites and cities blew my mind, I think it was a food experience that changed my life the most on that odyssey. The experience occurred in Cairo when I ate ful mudammas for the first time. It was in a small, nondescript café around the corner from the Cosmopolitan Hotel. I would have missed the café if the line had not been going out the door during dinner. I think I ordered some kind of chicken dish the first night, but the ful mudammas side dish that accompanied it was the stunning standout. Ful mudammas is an ancient, pre-Ottoman and pre-Islamic national dish of Egypt. Traditionally a breakfast food (though people eat it at all other meals too), it consists of slowly simmered, freshly cooked fava beans seasoned with a squeeze of lemon juice, olive oil, garlic, and select spices. When I say this is an ancient dish, it's because archaeologists have found remnants of ful mudammas in twelfth-dynasty Pharaonic tombs!

Like baguettes for the French, ful mudammas is a daily staple of most Egyptian diets, so the price of beans is regulated by the government in order to ensure that they are affordable to even the poorest citizens. The first night I experienced this dish, it was clearly made with fresh favas; it looked like a creamy, earthy stew with the addition of chile and cayenne pepper and was served with pieces of freshly baked pita bread and topped with pickled beets, parsley, onions, tomatoes, and cumin. Compared to the favas we can get in the United States, these seemed like a rare heirloom varietal that I had never seen nor eaten before. I was told by the restaurant's chef that he prepared it a day in advance because the beans need to be soaked and cooked overnight. I smoked an apple-flavored hookah pipe or two afterward and ended up going to this restaurant six nights in a row for dinner. My kids always roast me about how when I really like something, it stays with me for life.

Lisa's Nana on a camel in Cairo.

MIC DROP TRUFFLE OMELET. THE END.

SERVES 2

8 medium cremini mushrooms, sliced

2 tablespoons olive oil

1 tablespoon unsalted butter

2 garlic cloves, chopped

2 dashes sea salt

2 dashes freshly ground black pepper

4 large eggs, well whisked

2 tablespoons heavy cream or half-and-half

½ teaspoon smoked paprika

⅛ teaspoon green Hatch chile powder

1 teaspoon chopped fresh parsley

1 teaspoon chopped fresh sage

1 teaspoon chopped fresh basil or fresh thyme

⅓ cup soft goat cheese

1. In a nonstick pan (I use a ceramic pan, not a metal coated one), sauté the mushrooms with the olive oil, butter, garlic, 1 dash sea salt, and 1 dash pepper.

2. When the mushrooms are cooked three-quarters of the way, remove and set aside in a bowl. Keep the olive oil, butter, and garlic residue in the pan.

3. Whisk together the eggs, heavy cream, remaining salt and pepper, paprika, chile powder, and half of each herb. Set aside the other half of each herb to sprinkle on top of the omelet.

4. Over medium heat, pour the egg mixture into the frying pan. Circle it around to get the mixture to start evaporating and cooking in layers. Wait until the mixture is almost dry, and then lower the heat to avoid burning the omelet.

5. Add the sautéed mushrooms to one side of the omelet, and distribute the goat cheese in nickel-size pieces over the mushrooms.

6. When the omelet is ready to flip, use spatulas to flip the egg side over the mushroom side.

7. Cook the other side, and then turn the heat off and carefully slide the omelet onto a plate.

When I was in France staying with my friend Géraldine Robert and her family one weekend off from school, we would frequently cook, and Géraldine loved to show me the French way of doing things. And so it became her mission in life to introduce me to French culture. Sometimes I would laugh, because there was this earnest sense of pity in her voice when she would say to her mother, Fabrice, "*Maman*, look. Can you believe this? The poor girl can't make even an omelet properly." Her mother would reply, "Well, then of course you must teach her." And she did. And the simplest thing never tasted so delicious. A little melted butter in the pan; a thin, crêpe-like egg and cream mixture with fresh herbs from their potager outside; a pinch of *sel de mer* (sea salt); and what I deemed a tiny smidgen of Gruyère. It was delicious, and I have been making them the same way ever since.

One weekend several months later, during the Easter holidays (which is a three-day holiday in mostly Catholic France), Géraldine invited me to her grandmother's house outside Lyon where a lovely celebration feast would be enjoyed by the entire Robert *famille*. I'd had about five years of elementary-school French-language study and about two years of American prep school French, and I thought I knew my way around a complex verb conjugation. This was bolstered by my pseudo progress in the last six months at an all-French-speaking girls' school in Lausanne, Switzerland. Anyway, I figured going to the countryside wouldn't be too hard and that they would be a little more forgiving there—*n'est-ce pas?* At best, people would ask upon hearing my accent if I was from southern France. Or even worse, "You must be from Canada?" which would inevitably be followed by the classic Frenchie eye roll.

Fortunately for me, while it can be extremely intimidating to be around native French speakers who are witty, smart, and all about the idioms, the Robert family was the nicest famille ever, so they cut me some slack at Grandma's. Right off the bat, Gérard, Géraldine's dad, complimented my improving French, which elated me for about five seconds. So there I was, hanging out at a beautiful French country house with the most heavenly scents emanating from *la cuisine*. Fabrice wanted me to feel at home and would even give me a little mother's hug now and then. She knew I was incredibly homesick my first semester abroad at school in Switzerland. And yet I was terribly nervous. I don't know why. I guess I was petrified of making a mistake. So I lingered around and felt pretty shy around this rather large group of super-loving French people who treated me like a daughter. Fabrice kept telling me that Géraldine would be there any moment. When Géraldine waltzed through the door, I felt like I could breathe again. She was the most gorgeous girl, eighteen to my newly minted sixteen, and I just thought she was the coolest chick ever. She rode a motorcycle! She had effortless style! She read literature and loved cinema! And she was an astounding mimic, constantly making me laugh. She then ushered me outside with about eight of their relatives, and I took part in a delightful *Pâques* (Easter) contest in the backyard, proceeding to roll raw eggs down a hill—and I won! They all kept toasting me and saying, "*C'est incroyable! La fille américaine a gagné!*" (This is incredible! The American girl won!) I was really getting into the festivities at this point and starting to let my guard down.

We eventually sat down to the delicious meal. I thought I should ask to help *Grand-mère*. Perhaps I had a few too many glasses of wine beforehand, or perhaps my brain synapses scrambled the words for the different farm animals like a fluffy omelet—I'll never know. What I graciously intended to ask (in French) was "Grand-mère, may I help you in the kitchen with the leg of lamb (*gigot d'agneau*)?" For some reason, what came out instead of *gigot* or even *jambon* (ham) was *cochon*, which translated to an unintentional but very derogatory "Pig, can I help you in the kitchen?" The entire party stopped for one full second and then burst into uproarious laughter. I knew instantly what had transpired, and I turned purple. I started to stutter; I couldn't get any words out. I wanted desperately to save face and apologize; however, the French words for "I'm sorry" escaped me. My mind went completely blank. Grand-mère thought I was nuts. Forget the egg-rolling contest win—those newly earned foreigner points were long gone. I burst into tears and ran for the nearest bathroom, shut the door, and bawled my eyes out. I would not leave the bathroom. Finally, I became so hungry I peeked out the door into the main part of the house. Most of the relatives were outside at the dinner table. I tiptoed into the kitchen, and Fabrice covered me with kisses, telling me everything would be okay. I apologized to Grand-mère (with the correct *vocabulaire* this time) and she hugged me too. That's when I lost it all over again.

Eventually after this certifiably *américaine* weep fest, I came to the conclusion that I must face the music. So I went outside. Everyone was apologetic and doing the Frenchie shrug, "It happens." There was some slight melodic laughter again—but this time around I was laughing with them about my own ridiculousness.

When I was in my thirties, Géraldine lived in Montreal with her second husband, Bruno. She confessed to me on a trip to New York that this *on s'est bien amusé* (continually amusing) Easter story held a special place in their family lore for years. "That crazy *américaine*! Remember her? She called Grand-mère a *cochon*!"

Géraldine and Lisa in Paris.

DEBRIANNA'S

PURE PLEASURE APPLE DUMPLINGS

SERVES 4

SAUCE

½ cup fresh apple cider

1 teaspoon grated fresh ginger or ½ teaspoon dry ginger

1 tablespoon maple syrup

1 tablespoon freshly squeezed lemon juice

DUMPLINGS

6 tablespoons (¾ stick) unsalted butter, softened

3 tablespoons brown sugar

1 teaspoon ground cinnamon

¼ teaspoon ground cardamom

½ teaspoon freshly grated nutmeg

⅓ cup chopped walnuts

2 tablespoons raisins

4 large Granny Smith apples, cored, and peeled if desired

1 (11-ounce) package piecrust (I use Trader Joe's because it's flat)

1 egg, beaten

1 tablespoon unsalted butter to grease the pan

1. Preheat oven to 400°F.

2. Combine the ingredients for the sauce, and simmer for 15 minutes.

3. Mix the butter, brown sugar, and spices until well blended, and then add the walnuts and raisins. Divide the butter mixture into each apple center.

4. Divide the piecrust into quarters. Roll each quarter of the crust into a circle large enough to wrap an apple.

5. Place each apple in the center of a crust quarter, wrap with the crust, and twist closed to fold over. Brush egg all over.

6. Grease a small baking dish with butter, and place the wrapped apples on it evenly spaced apart. Pour the sauce over the apples, and bake until the apples are soft and the pastry is golden, about 30 to 40 minutes.

Thaw Out Your Frozen Soul
Fresh Spinach Spanakopita

MAKES APPROXIMATELY 12 SERVINGS

½ cup (1 stick) salted butter, melted

½ cup ordinary olive oil for basting

½ cup high-quality olive oil (I used a Croatian olive oil) for filling

1 large onion, peeled and finely chopped

1 shallot, finely chopped

1 bunch green onions (including bulbs and green tips), finely chopped

18 ounces baby spinach leaves, kept whole, or 2 bunches spinach, roughly chopped

2 garlic cloves, finely chopped

1 bunch fresh flat-leaf parsley (including stems), finely chopped

3 tablespoons chopped fresh dill

1 teaspoon chopped fresh peppermint

2 teaspoons sea salt, or to taste

Freshly ground black pepper, to taste

¼ teaspoon freshly grated nutmeg

4 large eggs, beaten

10 ounces crumbled Greek feta

8 ounces ricotta or cottage cheese

1 box (24 sheets) phyllo dough

Toasted sesame seeds for finishing (optional)

1. Preheat oven to 350°F.

2. Combine the butter with the ordinary olive oil in a small bowl, and then brush a thin layer of it into a baking pan of approximately 15 x 10 x 2½ inches. (I used a glass Pyrex standard rectangular pan.) Set the rest aside for basting the phyllo dough.

3. In a large stockpot set over medium heat, sauté the high-quality olive oil, onion, shallot, and green onion until translucent. Lower the heat, and add the spinach, garlic, parsley, dill, and peppermint. Then add sea salt, pepper, and nutmeg. Turn over with a wooden spoon until the spinach cools down and the liquid evaporates, stirring often. Remove the mixture from the heat and set aside to cool.

4. Beat the eggs in a large bowl, and then add the cheeses. Mix together and set aside.

5. Place the entire stack of phyllo dough sheets* onto a cutting board or other flat surface. Wet and then ring out a dish towel and cover the stack of sheets with the towel to keep them moist and prevent them from drying out.

6. Pull 1 phyllo dough sheet at a time out from under the towel; brush 1 side with the butter and olive oil mixture, and then place it buttered side down into the rectangular pan. Repeat until there are 9 layers.

7. Add the cooled spinach mixture to the cheese and egg mixture, and combine well. This is the filling.

8. Pour a thick layer of filling across the phyllo dough stack, evening it with a spatula.

9. Continue buttering the phyllo dough sheets and adding them to the pan, buttered side down. When you get to the last layer, tuck in the edges, butter the top well, and then create a large diamond-shaped slit across the top. Do not cut down to the spinach layer; only cut through the top 6 or so layers, so steam can escape and the dough gets fluffy.

10. Bake the spanakopita for 1 hour. It should be golden brown when removed from the oven.

11. After removing the spanakopita, let it sit for a few minutes, and then serve immediately as a side dish or a main course. Traditionally, it is cut into triangles or diamond shapes. If you like, you can sprinkle toasted sesame seeds on each serving.

QUICK OLIVE OIL TUTORIAL

I use two kinds of olive oil in this recipe: a higher-grade oil (like Croatian, extra-virgin, cold-pressed, or controlled appellation), and a lower-grade oil (like those produced by domestic, less expensive brands) for mixing with the butter and basting the dough. Olive oil is like wine in that there is an entire spectrum of quality, and it is determined by a range of factors, such as where the olives were grown, the type of olives used, how they were pressed, and what they were aged in. I encourage you to try purchasing a higher-quality olive oil than you normally use and see what happens—perhaps you will discover a more complex flavor when you make your filling. My Great-Aunt Georgia actually wrote in the margin of this recipe, "Use the good stuff" for the filling. She was right!

TIP: This is a very rustic dish, so don't worry about imperfections with the phyllo. It is very forgiving and bakes aesthetically. If you refrigerate leftovers after it cools, just heat them up in the oven prior to a second serving. They will get crispy and buttery again.

* Unless you want to make homemade phyllo dough with a broomstick handle like my Great-Aunt Georgia and Nana did, you can buy organic phyllo dough in the freezer section of most upscale markets. I buy mine at Whole Foods, and the package contains 18 sheets in the standard cookie-sheet-size rectangular shape. Take the box of phyllo out of the freezer 10 hours before you intend to make it, so whether that's overnight or early in the morning, do the math to determine the right time to remove it. For example, if I take mine out of the freezer at 8:30 in the morning, I put it in the fridge to thaw for 8 hours. Then I remove it from the fridge around 4:30 p.m. and set it on the counter (still in the package) for 2 more hours (until 6:30 p.m.), bringing the dough sheets to room temperature. Then it's ready to take out of the package and handle.

HOLLIE'S HOMEGROWN'S

(V) (GF)

FIG AND LAVENDER JAM

MAKES 36 OUNCES

9 cups ripe fresh Adriatic figs, stems removed (use halves for a chunky jam or quarters for a smooth jam)

¾ cup HH Lavender Herb Infused Honey or plain honey with 1 teaspoon chopped lavender buds

½ cup sugar

1 cup red wine (I suggest a cabernet sauvignon or merlot)

1 teaspoon HH Orange & Marigold Seasoning Salt or sea salt mixed with 1 teaspoon orange zest

½ cup balsamic vinegar

1. Place the cut figs in a large stainless-steel pot, and then stir in all other ingredients. Cover the pot, and let the ingredients sit at room temperature for 2 hours.

2. Remove the cover from the pot, and bring to a boil over high heat for 5 minutes.

3. Reduce heat to medium high and continue to cook, stirring constantly with a wooden spoon as the mixture starts to thicken, for about 10 more minutes. When the jam starts to pull from the sides of the pot, remove from heat. Avoid the jam sticking to the bottom or burning.

4. Ladle or spoon the jam into clean canning jars, leaving half an inch of space between the top of the jam and the rims of the jars. Wipe the rims of the jars with a clean dishcloth or paper towel, and then tighten the lids.

5. Allow the jars to cool to room temperature, and then refrigerate immediately. The jam will last in the refrigerator for up to 2 months.

TIP: If you want to make the jam shelf stable (so it doesn't have to be refrigerated), follow the canning instructions from the jar company. Make sure to label the jars with the date you made the jam, or put the date on a decorative label tied to a ribbon if the jam is a gift.

Lisa's sister Hollie Lucas-Alcalay.

EVERYDAY 4-EGG QUICHE

SERVES 6

Piecrust

4 eggs

½ cup heavy cream

1 cup milk

Salt, to taste

Freshly ground black pepper, to taste

¾ cup crumbled goat cheese

A few handfuls shredded cheese of choice (Hal recommends a Mexican cheese blend or Colby Jack), and more for finishing a layer on the quiche

Avocado or kalamata olives, sliced

1. Preheat oven to 350°F.

2. Once the oven has finished preheating, prebake the piecrust for 10 minutes or until lightly browned.

3. While the crust is baking, mix the eggs, heavy cream, milk, and salt and pepper, to taste, together in a large mixing bowl. Use a frothing whisk while beating the eggs to dissolve the egg yolks into a more even texture. Add the goat cheese and shredded cheese.

4. Pour the egg mixture into the prebaked piecrust. Garnish with avocado or kalamata olive slices.

5. Bake the quiche at 350°F for 30 minutes. Halfway through, add a layer of shredded cheese to the top of the quiche. Keep an eye on it while it bakes. Should air pockets or bubbles appear, pop them to ensure an even bake.

6. Once the quiche is fully cooked, allow it to cool for 15 minutes before serving.

Soups, Salads, & Sandwiches

From the Hearty Black Bean and Kale Soup with Parmesan Crisps

Ⓥ

SERVES 4 TO 6

BLACK BEAN AND KALE SOUP

5 tablespoons olive oil, and more for finishing

½ yellow onion, peeled and chopped

2 carrots, peeled and sliced into thin rounds

1 large russet potato, peeled and cubed

1 shallot, minced

3 garlic cloves, minced

1 tablespoon chopped fresh thyme

1 bay leaf, crushed

½ teaspoon ground cayenne pepper

Sea salt, to taste

Freshly ground black pepper, to taste

4 cups chicken broth or vegetable broth

½ cup farro

2 (15.5-ounce) cans black beans or fagioli beans

½ cup chopped fresh parsley

½ cup chopped scallions

¼ cup chopped fresh chervil

1 bunch lacinato kale, stems removed and chopped

Freshly squeezed lemon juice and zest for finishing

Freshly grated Parmesan for finishing

PARMESAN CRISPS

5 tablespoons unsalted butter, softened

¼ teaspoon sea salt

¼ teaspoon paprika

1 garlic clove, minced

2 tablespoons freshly grated Parmesan

Several slices of your favorite bread

TO MAKE THE BLACK BEAN AND KALE SOUP

1. Add olive oil, onion, carrots, potato, shallot, garlic, thyme, bay leaf, cayenne, sea salt, and pepper to a slow cooker, and cook for about 7 minutes.

2. Add 2 cups water and remaining ingredients except kale and garnishes and bring to a boil. Cover and reduce heat to simmer for 1 hour.

3. Turn off the heat, add the kale, and cover for 10 minutes.

4. Plate in soup bowls, and garnish each serving with a dash of sea salt, a crisscross of olive oil, 1 squeeze lemon juice, a bit of lemon zest, and some Parmesan.

TIP: This soup will be even more flavorful the next day. Meat eaters may enjoy it with 12 ounces andouille sausage, sliced ¼ inch thick, sautéed, and added to the soup before the onion.

TO MAKE THE PARMESAN CRISPS

1. Preheat oven to 350°F.

2. Mix butter, sea salt, paprika, garlic, and Parmesan, and spread mixture on bread slices.

3. Bake bread until golden brown, about 7 minutes, and then serve.

"Feeling Good Like I Should" Butternut Squash Soup with Poblano Crema

SERVES 6 TO 8

SOUP

1 medium butternut squash

Olive oil for coating squash and poblanos

Sea salt, to taste

8 large poblano peppers (reserve 1 for finishing)

½ medium yellow onion, peeled

3 cups chicken broth or vegetable broth

1 cup heavy cream

3 tablespoons unsalted butter or olive oil

½ teaspoon freshly ground black pepper

¼ cup marsala or sherry

2 garlic cloves, minced

1 teaspoon freshly ground cumin

1 teaspoon smoked paprika

1 teaspoon Chimayo red chile powder

1 teaspoon green Hatch chile powder

¼ cup plus 1 tablespoon chopped fresh parsley (reserve 1 tablespoon for finishing)

1 tablespoon raw honey

1 teaspoon roast chicken-based paste or vegetable-based paste

CREMA

¾ cup sour cream

Juice of 1 lime

2 tablespoons heavy cream

1 tablespoon chopped fresh parsley

2 small poblano peppers, seeded and chopped

2 teaspoons chopped chives

Sea salt, to taste

Freshly ground black pepper, to taste

1 garlic clove, minced

1. Preheat oven to 400°F.

2. Cut the squash in half lengthwise, and spoon out and discard the seeds. Place it skin side down on a baking sheet lined with parchment paper and brush with olive oil; then sprinkle sea salt on top.

3. Brush 7 poblanos with olive oil, and then lightly sprinkle sea salt on top.

4. Place the squash and poblanos in the oven. Roast the squash until it is golden brown with soft flesh, about 1 hour. The poblanos will roast much faster. It should only take about 10 minutes before their skin is bubbling and lightly charred, indicating they're ready to be removed.

5. Remove the poblanos, and place them in a glass bowl. Cover with plastic wrap and allow them to sweat for at least 5 to 10 minutes; then remove their skin and seeds, and devein.

6. Pulse all crema ingredients together in a food processor until smooth. Store the crema in the refrigerator until ready to serve the soup.

7. When the squash has finished roasting, remove it from the oven and let it cool until you can spoon out the insides for the soup.

8. In a stockpot, sauté and sweat the onion over medium heat. Add 2 cups of the chicken broth, setting the other cup of broth and the heavy cream aside, and then add the other soup ingredients while stirring.

9. Add the insides of the roasted squash and poblanos to the stockpot. Lower heat to simmer for 15 minutes.

10. Add the remaining 1 cup chicken broth and the heavy cream to the soup. Stir; then use an immersion blender to purée the soup.

11. Once you have a nice purée, keep stirring and raise the heat back to medium, being mindful not to burn the soup. It should be warm for plating and serving.

12. When you plate the soup, drizzle or spoon the crema over it, and finish each bowl with the reserved parsley and strips of the remaining poblano.

TIP: Leftover roasted chicken can be added to the soup to make a hearty main course.

THROW AWAY YOUR XANAX TRIBAL SUSTENANCE HOMEMADE MATZO BALL SOUP

MAKES 8 TO 10 SERVINGS

BROTH

8 to 10 pounds whole roasted chicken (the bulk of meat removed from your homemade roasted chicken enjoyed the night before or from a store-bought roasted chicken)

10 carrots, peeled and halved

7 celery stalks with the leaves kept on, roughly chopped

2 large onions with the skin kept on, quartered

Several handfuls whole fresh parsley

16 cranks freshly ground black pepper

2 large dashes coarse sea salt

2 bay leaves

1 teaspoon ground coriander

3 tablespoons roasted chicken-based paste or bouillon cubes

4 garlic cloves

4 fresh thyme sprigs

½ lemon, cut in half

1 teaspoon ground turmeric

½ cup dry sherry

1 teaspoon Chimayo red chile powder

Fresh dill sprigs for finishing

MATZO BALLS

1 cup matzo meal

1 teaspoon baking powder

½ teaspoon salt

1 garlic clove, finely minced

¼ teaspoon finely minced shallot

Several cranks freshly ground black pepper

1 tablespoon finely chopped fresh parsley

1 tablespoon finely minced fresh dill

½ teaspoon Chimayo red chile powder

¼ cup seltzer

3 large eggs

1 teaspoon roasted chicken-based paste or bouillon cube

3 tablespoons schmaltz*

MAKE THE BROTH

1. Place the chicken carcass in a 12-quart stockpot, and cover with filtered water. Add all other broth ingredients, except dill sprigs, and cook over high heat until just before a boil is reached. Then give a quick stir, cover, and reduce heat to just above a simmer; let simmer for at least 3 to 4 hours. Time it so that it will be ready 1 hour before dinnertime.

2. Make the matzo balls (see below).

3. After the soup has finished simmering, place a giant strainer over a large bowl or stockpot. Using potholders, remove the soup from the heat and strain everything out of the broth except the liquid. (I also allow the broth to stream through another finer-meshed sieve, a chinois, to remove any fine particles.)

4. Fish out the carrots, slice them thinly, and set them aside.

5. Compose bowls of soup with equal amounts of broth, matzo balls, reserved sliced carrots, dill sprigs, and leftover chicken shards.

MAKE THE MATZO BALLS

1. In a medium bowl, combine the matzo meal, baking powder, salt, garlic, shallot, pepper, parsley, dill, chile powder, and seltzer. Mix together and then set aside.

2. In another bowl, whisk together the eggs, chicken-based paste, and schmaltz.

3. Combine the wet mixture with the dry, but do not overmix. Cover and refrigerate for a minimum of 1 hour.

4. Remove the refrigerated matzo, and roll it into balls about the size of a quarter until you have about 25 balls.**

5. Set water to boil, and drop matzo balls into boiling water. Cook, covered, for about 30 minutes.

6. When the matzo balls are all floating and have about doubled in size, fish them out and place them on paper towels to cool.

This is an epic soup, maybe even a miracle broth. The recipe is tried and true, distilled from bubbies I have known and loved and aunts of dear friends and family members, with a Lisa twist. I know I make a good soup, because my stepdad, Stan, always thanks me for the tribal sustenance.

TIP: The longer you simmer the soup in step 1, the more the flavor will intensify.

TIP: You can also cook the matzo balls in the soup broth, but I like to cook them separately so the broth doesn't get cloudy or have loose pieces of matzo in it.

* For the schmaltz, if you don't have time to render up some chicken fat from the skins, you can use grape-seed oil or olive oil. I rendered the fat before I roasted the chicken for dinner and set it aside, no need to refrigerate. You could also buy rendered fat at a specialty grocery store.

** I make about 25 medium balls that float. Sometimes they sink, and that's okay too. Of course, you can make them whatever size you wish.

LISA'S

EASIER THAN JULIA CHILD'S CAESAR SALAD EUPHORIA

SERVES 2 FOR A MAIN COURSE OR 4 FOR AN APPETIZER

DRESSING

2 large garlic cloves

¾ cup olive oil

1 teaspoon sea salt,
or more to taste

2 eggs

Zest and juice of 1 large lemon

3 anchovy fillets

½ cup freshly grated Parmesan

Freshly ground black
pepper, to taste

½ teaspoon dry
mustard powder

LETTUCE

2 heads romaine lettuce

CROUTONS

¼ cup olive oil

3 tablespoons salted butter

½ teaspoon sea salt, or
more to taste

Freshly ground black
pepper, to taste

½ teaspoon smoked paprika

3 garlic cloves, minced

4 slices sourdough bread, cubed

¼ cup freshly grated Parmesan

TO MAKE THE DRESSING

1. In a food processor or blender, combine all ingredients for the dressing. Pulse until emulsified, and then taste for salt level, as anchovies vary in salty flavor. Add more salt if needed.

2. Pour the dressing into a mason jar with a lid and refrigerate.

TO PREPARE THE LETTUCE

1. Slice the lettuce into large quarters, and rinse with water.

2. Spin the lettuce with a salad spinner to remove any water still on the lettuce from the rinse, and then wrap it in a dry dish towel and refrigerate it in a salad bowl.

TO MAKE THE CROUTONS

1. Preheat oven to 350°F.

2. Combine the olive oil, butter, sea salt, pepper, paprika, and garlic in a cast-iron pan, and set over medium heat. Add the bread cubes, and coat the bread in the other ingredients to make croutons. Then add the Parmesan and stir.

3. Pour the croutons onto a baking sheet lined with parchment paper, and brown in the oven until crispy, about 5 minutes. Flip them halfway through to brown both sides.

TO MAKE THE SALAD

1. Take the salad bowl from the fridge, and remove the dish towel. Add the warm croutons to the lettuce.

2. Shake the dressing well, and pour some, to taste, over the lettuce and croutons. Toss to coat evenly. Serve immediately.

TIP: You can add grilled lemon chicken. It is a classic combination and creates the perfect light dinner. It is my favorite salad and always will be.

HOLLIE'S HOMEGROWN'S

CUCUMBER HERB GAZPACHO

SERVES 6

3 English cucumbers, peeled and coarsely chopped

2 small celery stalks with leaves, chopped

3 scallions (white and green parts), coarsely chopped

1 tablespoon roughly chopped fresh parsley, and more, finely chopped, for finishing

1 tablespoon roughly chopped fresh mint

1 tablespoon roughly chopped fresh dill, and more, finely chopped, for finishing

1 tablespoon roughly chopped fresh lemon thyme (if you can't find lemon thyme, mix 1 tablespoon fresh thyme and 1 teaspoon lemon zest)

1 teaspoon HH Lemon & Marigold Seasoning Salt or sea salt

1 large garlic clove, minced

2 tablespoons HH Herbs de Moraga Olive Oil or other high-quality olive oil

1 tablespoon freshly squeezed lemon juice

1 teaspoon lemon zest

1 tablespoon HH Rose Petal Vinegar or white wine vinegar

½ cup plain yogurt (use Greek if available for a thicker consistency)

1. In a blender or food processor, combine all ingredients except those for finishing and the yogurt. Process until smooth.

2. Add the yogurt and process to blend, about 1 to 2 minutes.

3. Transfer to a nonreactive container (a ceramic or glass jar), cover, and refrigerate for at least 1 hour before serving.

4. Finish with finely chopped parsley and dill before serving.

TIP: Gazpacho is traditionally made with tomatoes, but this cucumber version is particularly refreshing. It makes for a wonderful first course that goes well with grilled salmon, chicken, or portobello mushrooms, or squash and zucchini.

TORTELLINI SOUP

SERVES 4

8 ounces chicken sausage

6 cups chicken broth, homemade or low-sodium canned

2 cups sliced carrots, peeled

½ teaspoon dried thyme

2 cups thawed frozen peas or fresh peas (shelled)

19 ounces fresh cheese tortellini (premade fresh pasta)

2 teaspoons freshly squeezed lemon juice

Salt, to taste

Freshly ground black pepper, to taste

Freshly grated Parmesan for finishing

Crusty bread for serving

1. In a large pot, brown the chicken sausage for 5 to 7 minutes, breaking it down into small pieces as it browns.

2. Add the broth, carrots, thyme, and 2 cups water, and bring to a boil. Add the peas and tortellini and cook, uncovered, for about 5 minutes, until the tortellini starts to float. Stir in the lemon juice, and season with salt and pepper to taste.

3. Serve topped with Parmesan and accompanied by a side of crusty bread.

LISA'S

FEELING LIKE A KID AGAIN AMBROSIA SALAD CIRCA '74, CAN YOU DIG IT?

MAKES ENOUGH FOR 4 PEOPLE, OR 2 PEOPLE WHO
GAINED SIGNIFICANT WEIGHT DURING THE PANDEMIC
AND MUTUALLY AGREE THAT AN UNBELIEVABLY TASTY
FRUIT SALAD FOR DINNER IS DECIDEDLY AN OPTION.

1 cup bite-size cubes pineapple

1½ cups bite-size cubes kiwi

1 cup blueberries

1 cup bite-size cubes nectarines

1 large orange or 2 medium
oranges, cut into quarter slices

1 cup sliced red seedless grapes

1 cup shredded
unsweetened coconut*

1 teaspoon lime zest

1 teaspoon orange zest

1½ cups honey vanilla whole-
milk Greek yogurt

3 tablespoons honey, room
temperature

1 teaspoon vanilla extract

* I remember Franny letting
me crack a coconut open with
a hammer. That was fun for a
ten-year-old!

1. In a large bowl, delicately mix the fruit with the yogurt, honey, and vanilla.

2. Either serve immediately or cover, seal with plastic wrap, and chill in the fridge for 1 hour or overnight before serving.

TIP: As an adult who doesn't eat a lot of sugar these days, I love and appreciate this recipe. It has the right balance of flavors, so you can really taste the fruit. You could have this dish for breakfast with granola, bring it to a summer party, or gift it as a surprise treat for a friend. It's also delicious with a cup of cubed fresh Honeycrisp apples and/or cubed fresh mango.

Franny, Nana, and nine-year-old Lisa in 1977.

That Time We Ate Our Feelings 37

LISA'S

BLESS US OH GREEN GODDESS EVEN WHEN THE WORLD MAKES NO SENSE

(GF)

MAKES APPROXIMATELY 3 CUPS

½ cup olive oil

½ avocado

3 tablespoons roughly chopped fresh tarragon

2 tablespoons roughly chopped fresh chervil

1 small shallot, roughly chopped

1 garlic clove, roughly chopped

3 tablespoons tarragon vinegar or champagne vinegar

Juice of ½ lemon

½ cup mayonnaise
(I used store-bought mayo, but great if made from scratch)

¼ cup sour cream

⅛ cup chopped chives or green parts of scallions

⅛ cup chopped Italian fresh flat-leaf parsley

1 tablespoon anchovy paste or 3 anchovy fillets

2 dashes sea salt

Dash freshly ground black pepper

1. Place all ingredients in a food processor.

2. Pulse to reach a creamy consistency with all the herbs incorporated and the mixture emulsified.

TIP: Green Goddess Dressing lasts for a week when refrigerated in an airtight container. It's great on salads (with butter lettuce, romaine, or baby kale—it's too thick for spring mixes) or raw vegetables, or when used as a condiment for sandwiches or burgers or in place of tartar sauce with fish.

My Nana had a cousin named Mary
who lived in New Orleans. She was
100 percent Croatian and had a
southern accent, but her last name
was Corleone, as she had married
a Sicilian. Mary looked just like my
grandmother, but twenty years
younger. It wasn't until my sister
Hollie and I were planning our drive
back east to college in the fall that
we thought, *Hey, let's go early and
visit Mary we've heard about forever.*
Well, this lady was so much fun—
so much, in fact, that I can barely
remember our time with her. Hollie says, "I had
a nineteen-year-old college sophomore's liver at that time, and
she drank us under the table." It was a four-day party even though
this woman had to have been in her late fifties or early sixties.

Lisa, cousin Mary, and Hollie in New Orleans circa 1987.

We arrived in August and it was hotter than hell and a literal
swamp outside, as Mary lived on the water. She welcomed us
with open arms, and from that moment on, we were on the go.
She took us everywhere. She wanted to show us every amazing
thing NOLA had to offer. We had to sample the best jambalaya,
the best crawfish étouffée, the best gumbo. She made us beignets
for breakfast and had homemade pralines in a tin. Let's just say
it was a bit of a bacchanalian whirlwind tour. And just when we
thought we could get a little rest and go to bed early on the second
night, she said, "Oh you girls, don't be silly. We're goin' to a jazz
club tonight, so get ready to stay out until two." On a normal night
she was just getting started at eleven.

On the way home from a club later that night, we were stopped
at a stoplight when I remember Mary—who'd had her fair share
of drinks that night and must have thought I looked worried or
something—turning to me and saying, "Don't you worry, honey.
I know it's late, but I got my pearl-handled pistol right here in the
glove compartment." I looked at Hollie in the backseat, silently
asking, *Did she just say she had a pistol?* Well, sure enough, I opened
up the glove compartment and there it was. Mary immediately
grabbed it and started waving it around like Annie Oakley at a
gunfighting competition.

I cried, "Mary, please put that away!" And she said, "Alright, darlin'" and threw it back in the glove compartment. I immediately closed it. We made it home not long after that. You can be damn sure that thing was loaded.

There's something about Mary. She loved New Orleans. Hurricanes destroyed her house twice, and each time she built it back. My grandmother loved her, and they got along like two peas in a pod. They would talk for hours on the phone about food and recipes! They also reminisced over memories of their wonderful parents, who were also the closest of friends. My mom said that when she was little, whenever you went over to Mary's parents' house there would always be something appetizing cooking on the stove.

Mary's father, Barba Bortolo, had been a chef at the Roosevelt Hotel in New Orleans in the 1930s and 1940s. (As an aside, Bortolo's wife, Tete Antonia, was an incredible cook in her own right and owned her own diner in New Orleans.) After many years of brutal restaurant work, Barba and Tete decided to move their family to Petaluma, California, and they became chicken farmers in the 1950s—just like in the movie *Peggy Sue Got Married*, which was also filmed in Petaluma. At the same time, my Nana and her mom and dad (Tony and Maria Rakela) and the rest of the family had established their restaurant, Tony's Seafood, in Tomales Bay, not too far away from them in Petaluma. They had an idyllic life together during that postwar time in northern California. They had achieved the American Dream—all of them being immigrants and having worked to the bone the majority of their lives.

At some point, Bortolo's chickens got a disease and they all died, so he decided to be a chef again and got a job at the Palace Hotel in San Francisco, where the Green Goddess salad dressing had famously been invented by chef Philip Roemer in 1923 to honor George Arliss, who was staying in the hotel while he starred in a play called *The Green Goddess*. And there you go.

Lisa's Nana with her Aunt Antonia and Uncle Bortolo in the '40s.

LONGING FOR FINE DINING CLASSIC WEDGE SALAD WITH HOMEMADE BLUE CHEESE DRESSING

(GF)

SERVES 2

DRESSING

½ cup buttermilk

½ cup sour cream

½ cup mayonnaise

½ teaspoon sea salt

½ teaspoon freshly ground black pepper

1 garlic clove, chopped

½ teaspoon Chimayo red chile powder

3 tablespoons organic apple cider vinegar

2 ounces Gorgonzola

1 small shallot, chopped

1 teaspoon chopped fresh parsley

1 teaspoon chopped fresh chives

SALAD

1 head iceberg lettuce

6 bacon slices

1 large shallot, thinly sliced

20 grape tomatoes, halved

2 green onions, finely chopped

1 tablespoon chopped fresh parsley

Crumbled Gorgonzola, to taste

Freshly ground black pepper, to taste

PREPARE THE DRESSING

1. Pulse all dressing ingredients together in a food processor until the dressing becomes creamy.

PREPARE THE SALAD

1. Slice the iceberg lettuce into quarters, and then set aside, covered, in the fridge.

2. Fry the bacon, and then set on paper towels to drain. Using the bacon grease, fry the shallot slices, and then set aside with the bacon.

3. Remove the lettuce from the refrigerator and plate. Drizzle the dressing generously over the wedges, and add the tomatoes. Chop and add the bacon, and then add the green onions, parsley, Gorgonzola, and a few cracks of black pepper to each plate.

TIP: This salad is delectable and versatile, and you can use the dressing as a dip for any type of crudités or even dip your pizza in it.

Lisa and Morse.

I am fifty-four and I have a boyfriend. But he is more than that. It is said that angels live among us. Case in point: the one and only Morse Bicknell, who presents as a mere mortal on planet Earth but is actually more akin to the Bruno Ganz character in the Wim Wenders classic film *Wings of Desire*. It is a story about an angel named Damiel and his subsequent fall to Earth as he yearns to experience the confines and authenticity of human existence. Sometimes in the middle of the night when I roll over and watch Morse sleeping, his strong, muscled arms resemble resting flight wings folded tightly by his side. I have asked him repeatedly in all seriousness if he was ever an angel, and he always denies it with a hint of a smile—exactly how a humble, fallen angel would answer!

Even more proof that supports my angel theory is the fact that in addition to being an accomplished film and theater actor, Morse has other talents: the ability to speak French, German, Spanish, Arabic, Japanese, and Russian fluently, as well as masterfully play electric and acoustic guitar, bass guitar, piano, drums, clarinet, and harmonica with great aplomb. He is that rare creature who possesses an irresistible combination of intellectual sophistication and a bona fide innocence. And these virtues are, at times, coupled with such poignant school-of-hard-knocks survival stories that I am inevitably brought to tears every time he tells them, reminded that we are the same in a way: two souls who led parallel lives in different universes and both had to completely start over around the same point in midlife. We have both made a lot of mistakes, missteps, and unfortunate choices in the past. However, we now have wisdom and a shared challenge: to honor what we have left and make it the best it can be.

When Morse and I first started dating, he seemed too good to be true. I wondered why he had such a genuine, unconditional support for me from the get-go. I didn't know how to react to that. The period immediately after a divorce is beyond challenging. I told him I wouldn't be ready for any kind of relationship for a long time, as I had a lot to unravel and heal, not to mention find the person I had lost within myself. He said, "I'll wait." Most men would have just ghosted me. I was perplexed by his honesty about wanting to be my friend. He replied with complete sincerity, "Well, I am a different kind of man." Perhaps I was jaded. Perhaps I have been burned one too many times, as I am constantly surprised by his consistent acts of loyalty and devotion toward me and our life together—legitimate characteristics of a true gentleman who is also not afraid to tell the truth or admit he was wrong and who never hides his vulnerability but is instead emboldened by it. He knows who he is. I have never met a more kind and giving person, coupled with his clever sense of humor and irony. If he's not a celestial being that has chosen to give up immortality for life on Earth, then he's certainly the best human I've ever met.

Morse moved in with me and the kids right before COVID hit. One might think that having two teenagers at home during a pandemic would tear a couple apart, but instead it bonded us. We have played more board games than one could possibly imagine, experienced countless dinners together, dog walks, mountain hikes, and deep belly laughs—priceless hours that I will cherish when looking back on this time. Images like that of Morse sitting on the couch right now in total bliss with our dogs, Monty and Edgar, or my children, Seamus and Ronan, cracking up with us as we watch yet another classic episode of *The Office* will stay with me. How did I get so lucky to have another chance at happiness?

Morse once told me about his experience on his high school racewalking team. He excelled at this sport and placed second in nationals for his age group. You have to believe in yourself to accomplish these kinds of goals at fourteen. You have to be patient. You have to work hard and make sacrifices, and yet you can also find time for joy in life. He said that after a while he decided that every time he won a race, he would treat himself to real blue cheese dressing on his salad. Because he liked it and it made him happy. I adore this man who taught me the true meaning of love, and so I make this salad for him.

DEBRIANNA'S

Blissfully Healthy Carrot Salad Sandwich (It May Turn You into a Vegetarian)

SERVES 2, WITH LEFTOVER SALAD

4 carrots, peeled and grated

½ cup raisins

3 tablespoons mayonnaise

¼ cup finely chopped pecans (optional)

1 tablespoon hemp hearts or sunflower seeds (optional)

Sharp cheddar, sliced, to taste

Sprouts or microgreens, to taste

4 slices whole wheat bread for 2 sandwiches

1. Mix the carrots, raisins, mayonnaise, pecans, and hemp hearts together.

2. Build the sandwiches with the carrots mixture, cheese slices, sprouts, and bread.

Carrots seemed to be a thing in my family long before they were part of the go-to vegetarian culture. My paternal grandmother juiced carrots in the Norwalk Juicer that sat on her counter and completely ruled the space, like a giant dump truck—or maybe a queen. No one else I knew had one. She would push the carrots, one by one, through the tunnel, and out would run the orange nectar from the hard root vegetable. It was a glorious orange stream that would fill a small juice glass. Sweet, nutritious love.

My grandmother and I would often lie on her bed together, sipping carrot juice and listening to Dr. Linus Pauling, his voice of authority crackling through the transistor radio, expounding on the health benefits of natural food. Drawers in her kitchen were full of vitamins, whole wheat breads filled the freezer, and only real butter and good clean food were allowed. She was the first person I ever heard say, "Saccharine will kill you—eat only real food, and moderate your intake." Much of who I am in relation to food stems from her deep influence on me.

Years later, when I was a young adult, one of my first restaurant jobs was at a health food restaurant called MacAndrew's. The owners, Dr. and Mrs. Greene, went all over New England rounding up the best recipes and foods they could find and put the restaurant near Wesleyan University in a downstairs basement they redesigned with wood walls and framed handmade quilts from the 1800s. It was cozy and very popular, with lines up the stairs and out into the parking lot, full of folks from all over who came to sample the Vermont cheeses and fresh fruit platters with creamed butter, fresh local honey, and the house-made honey sprouted wheat berry bread we baked and sliced fresh daily, into 1-inch-thick slices for the platters and sandwiches.

I felt at home there, serving nutritious, delicious soups and salads, and even our infamous Häagen-Dazs sundaes with real Vermont maple syrup and fresh whipped cream topped with our house-made granola. We catered to folks who craved the taste of real food, not food made from packages and mixes. One of my favorite sandwiches we offered was the carrot salad sandwich, composed of shredded carrots wrapped in mayonnaise, their sweetness permeating through, raisins, sharp Vermont cheddar sliced thick, and alfalfa sprouts tucked into the thick-cut sprouted wheat berry bread. If my Gram had eaten there, she would have beamed at the choices on the menu and would likely have stuck herself right onto that amazing carrot sandwich.

Grandma Florence and baby Debrianna.

I Want My Mommy Cream of Mushroom Soup with Rosemary Crackers

SERVES 4

CREAM OF MUSHROOM SOUP

4 tablespoons unsalted butter

2 tablespoons olive oil

1 shallot, minced

3 garlic cloves, minced

¾ pound mushrooms, sliced (I used cremini and button mushrooms)

1 teaspoon chopped fresh thyme, and more for finishing

1 teaspoon chopped fresh parsley, and more for finishing

½ cup marsala

5 tablespoons all-purpose flour

3 cups chicken broth or vegetable broth

Sea salt, to taste

Freshly ground black pepper, to taste

2 teaspoons chicken bouillon or vegetable bouillon

¾ cup heavy cream

Truffle oil for finishing (optional)

ROSEMARY CRACKERS

½ cup all-purpose flour, and more for surface dusting

1 teaspoon sea salt, and more for finishing

1 teaspoon honey or granulated sugar

1 tablespoon finely chopped fresh rosemary

1½ tablespoons olive oil

Grated Parmesan for finishing

TO MAKE THE CREAM OF MUSHROOM SOUP

1. In a stockpot set over medium heat, combine and sauté the butter, olive oil, shallot, garlic, and mushrooms. When the mushrooms have cooked down a bit, reduce the heat to a simmer and add the herbs, marsala, flour, broth, sea salt, pepper, bouillon, and heavy cream. The flour should be added by sprinkling it in 1 tablespoon at a time while stirring.

2. Cover the soup, and allow it to cook at a simmer for 15 to 20 minutes.

3. Prior to serving, garnish with chopped thyme, parsley, and a drizzle of truffle oil.

TIP: You can also add a few slices of browned chicken apple or Italian sausage at the bottom of the bowl with each serving.

TO MAKE THE ROSEMARY CRACKERS

1. Preheat oven to 500°F.

2. In a medium bowl, combine the flour, sea salt, honey, rosemary, olive oil, and ½ cup water, and mix until a very sticky dough ball is formed.

3. Knead the dough on a surface lined with parchment paper and then floured, and roll out to about ⅛ inch thick.

4. Cut the dough into squares using a sharp knife, and then place them on a clean baking sheet lined with parchment paper. Brush lightly with water, and sprinkle sea salt on some and Parmesan on others. Bake until golden brown, about 10 minutes.

5. Remove the baked dough and serve the crackers with the soup.

TIP: Get creative and make a cheesy version of them or a version with black pepper and parsley, or let your imagination run wild with your favorite flavor combinations.

It's All So Freaking Awesome BLT with Creamy Parmesan Mousse

SERVES 2, WITH LEFTOVER MOUSSE

PARMESAN MOUSSE

2 cups heavy cream

1 large shallot, finely chopped

1 tablespoon olive oil

2 ounces dry white wine

1½ teaspoons chopped fresh thyme

Freshly ground black pepper, to taste

1¼ cups finely grated Asiago or Parmigiano-Reggiano

¼ teaspoon kosher salt (optional)

SANDWICH COMPONENTS

3 Italian sausage links

2 lettuce leaves

1 heirloom tomato, sliced

4 bread slices (I used a thick sourdough)

TO MAKE THE PARMESAN MOUSSE

1. In a large saucepan set over high heat, bring the heavy cream to just below a boil, and then reduce the heat to low. Simmer, stirring often, until reduced by ½ cup, about 20 minutes.

2. Meanwhile, sauté the shallot in the olive oil until it's translucent, and then turn the stove off and add the white wine. Turn the stove back on, and simmer over low heat until the wine is absorbed.

3. During the last 3 minutes of cooking the heavy cream, slowly add the sautéed shallot (it may bubble up), thyme, and pepper. Then whisk in the cheese and salt (taste it, as the cheese you use may be salty enough) until completely melted and smooth.

4. Transfer the mixture to a heatproof bowl and refrigerate until cooled and thickened, about 1 hour.

TO MAKE THE FREAKING AWESOME BLT

1. Remove the casing from the sausages, and shape them into 2 patties.

2. Grill or cook the sausages on the stove.

3. Build sandwiches with the grilled sausage (served hot), lettuce, tomato, bread, and Parmesan mousse, which should be used instead of traditional mayonnaise.

Years ago, my sister Lisa gave me a copy of *Angela's Ashes*, the Pulitzer Prize–winning memoir by Frank McCourt. It is a moving story set in the Irish depression amid the outbreak of both typhoid fever and scarlet fever, as told through the eyes of the young Frank, who manages to rise above the tragedy and find his way to America. It is a heart-wrenching and sometimes humorous story of triumph. In many ways, it reminds me of where we were during the height of the pandemic—with external forces of nature pushing and pulling on us as we tried to navigate the environment we created for ourselves.

On many uncertain days, I often turn to the comfort foods of my childhood. They seem to both ground me and open my heart to a past that, much like McCourt's, is studded with heartbreak and triumph.

My family technically immigrated to the US from France, but that was because they were displaced to France from Italy, due to World War II. Their cooking is a magical combination of French and Italian flavors, centered on peasant food. They cooked what they had and what they could get, limited only by their creativity.

Debrianna's sister Lisa, age thirty-eight.

As I peruse my freezer, stocked with meat that comes to my door via a subscription service we have with Moink, a company that delivers meat from family farms, I am overwhelmed with gratitude and aware of how lucky I am to have this luxury. When I started with them, it was pre-pandemic. The meat now comes delivered to my home monthly, and it is something I can feel good about, a truly welcome feeling—and it makes a mean lemon chicken (see Debrianna's Guaranteed Glee: Caramelized Lemon Chicken with Artichokes and Pasta, page 162)! Rummaging through the freezer, beyond the frozen chicken breast and cauliflower pizza crust, I see the ground pork that Moink sent us when they helped a farmer who had extra pork, and my mind sparks. My BLT is the ultimate comfort sandwich, and I will share it in the tiny box on my computer that Lisa also inhabits, as a way to spread joy to our Corona Kitchen family.

DEBRIANNA'S

Ultimate Coping Mechanism: Inside-Out Burgers

GF

MAKES ABOUT 5 BURGERS

1 large sweet onion,
peeled and thinly sliced

1 tablespoon bacon fat, duck
fat, or olive oil for sautéing

2 tablespoons spicy
barbecue sauce

1 pound Italian pork sausage

1 pound 85 percent lean
ground beef

1 teaspoon salt

1 teaspoon herbes de Provence

½ teaspoon freshly ground
black pepper

½ cup goat cheese and
¼ cup grated Asiago and
cheddar, mixed

Brioche or gluten-free
hamburger buns

1. Sauté the onion in the bacon fat until browned. Add the barbecue sauce and let cool.

2. Mix the pork sausage, ground beef, and spices together well, and then shape into ten ¼-inch-thick patties.

3. Place a dollop of the cheese mixture in the center of half the patties, leaving a border. Top each with an onion slice and about 1 teaspoon of the onion-barbecue sauce. Cover with the remaining patties, pinching the ends tightly together, so the onion slices and cheese stay in the center.

4. Grill the patties until they're cooked through, about 3 to 4 minutes per side.

5. Serve each patty on a brioche bun or your favorite gluten-free alternative.

The manager at Harry's, "home of the Big Roast Beef Sandwich," seemed to have a crush on me. I wasn't really sure at first if it was confidence in me or a crush, but there was definite interest, and we started dating. We were both young college students. He was tall with short, sandy brown hair and funny—the smart kind of funny that made me think he may have some real depth—and he was my shift boss. Plus, he had an Austin-Healey sports car. And he tried to get me to read Ayn Rand's *Atlas Shrugged*.

There were all kinds of rules at the restaurant that I found unpleasant and awkward. For example, the phone greeting. There was no internet or cell phones back then, only phones with cords, and we had to answer the phone with this spew: "Hi! This is Harry's—home of the Big Roast Beef Sandwich! I'm Debrianna. How may I help you?" We also had to wear uniforms: brown pants and button-down shirts perhaps inspired by that beef theme. They had orange trim and were kind of militant, despite the color. And then there was the fact that things I would never do with food in my home seemed to be common practices at the restaurant—like the way the beef patties were cooked and left to sit under the heat lamp for so many minutes, or the way the frozen fries had to be handled in a certain manner to reach the proper crisp. There was also a rule for the "correct" amount of ice per cup. And there was the way we had to pretend that what we called "roast beef" was actual roast beef. These should have been clues that this was not the job for me, but alas, there was Bobby and his Austin-Healey.

I was on my shift when Bobby asked me to get more roast beef out of the walk-in freezer. I walked into the giant stainless-steel room that was the freezer and looked around. Shelves of frozen everything were in there. I looked at all the shelves and did not see roast beef. I walked back out to tell him we were also out of it in the freezer, that there was none left, hoping he would not get in trouble, but he looked at me like I was crazy and said, "Yes, there is."

"Okay." I shrugged and went back to see where I must have overlooked it.

Fries, patties, bags of stuff. No rumps of roast anywhere. Damn. "No, Bobby," I went back and told him, "there isn't any roast beef."

"Yes!" he yelled, frustration raising his voice a little too loud, trying to cover his relationship with me. "There are at least twenty of them." He pulled me with him into the walk-in.

"Here." He pointed to frozen, whitish bags. "This is the roast beef. So next time I ask you, get it. Got it?"

He grabbed a white bag and left. I walked over to the nineteen other bags on the shelf and looked carefully at what looked nothing like a rump of roast, then turned and followed him. He seemed irritated. "This has to soak for two hours before we can use it! Christ, I hope we don't run out before that."

"It has to do *what*?"

"It has to soak. So that it can congeal. Then we can cook it. Geez."

I hated *Atlas Shrugged*. And it was *not* roast beef.

DEBRIANNA'S

HEAVEN ON EARTH FRIED CHICKEN SANDWICH

SERVES 4

BUTTERMILK MARINADE

1 cup buttermilk or
whole-milk yogurt

1 egg

½ teaspoon smoked paprika

3 garlic cloves, finely minced

1 teaspoon onion powder

3 teaspoons kosher salt

2 teaspoons freshly ground
black pepper, and more to taste

Four (8-ounce) boneless,
skinless chicken breasts

POTATOES

4 russet potatoes

3 garlic cloves, smashed

1 tablespoon chopped
fresh thyme

1 tablespoon chopped
fresh parsley

¼ cup olive oil

2 teaspoons salt, or to taste

1 cup grated
Parmesan or Asiago

GARLIC HOT PEPPER SAUCE

½ cup mayonnaise

1 garlic clove, minced

1 teaspoon hot pepper sauce

DREDGE

2 cups all-purpose flour

2 tablespoons cornstarch

1 teaspoon kosher salt

Freshly ground black
pepper, to taste

Peanut or vegetable oil for frying

ASSEMBLY

4 brioche buns or other buns
of choice

Lettuce slices for serving

Pickles for serving

Tomato slices for serving

1. In a medium bowl, combine the buttermilk, egg, paprika, garlic, onion powder, salt, and pepper.

2. Place the chicken breasts between sheets of plastic wrap, and pound to an even thickness. Add the chicken to the buttermilk mixture, and let sit until ready to fry.

3. Switch to making the potatoes, and cut them lengthwise into ¼-inch slices; then toss them with the garlic, herbs, olive oil, and salt.

4. Spread the potato slices on a baking sheet, leaving space between the slices. Bake 30 minutes, and then toss with half the cheese and flip the slices over. Bake another 10 minutes, and then toss with the remaining cheese and continue baking.

5. While the potatoes are baking, make the garlic hot pepper sauce by mixing the mayonnaise with the garlic and the hot pepper sauce, and then set the sauce aside.

6. In a separate bowl, prepare the dredge by whisking the flour, cornstarch, salt, and a couple twists of pepper.

7. Add peanut oil to a deep skillet and set over medium heat to reach 350°F.

8. Remove the chicken from the buttermilk, dredge it in the flour mixture, and then add it to the hot peanut oil. Fry until crispy, about 6 to 8 minutes depending on the thickness of the chicken, turning every 1 or 2 minutes. You should be able to cook 2 chicken breasts at a time.

9. Remove the chicken and pat dry with a paper towel.

10. Add the chicken to the buns with lettuce, pickles, tomato slices, and a layer of the garlic hot pepper sauce. Serve with the potatoes.

Breads, Biscuits, & Other Handmade Carbs

LISA'S

Nana Said Her Zucchini Bread Will Fix All Your Problems

Ⓥ

MAKES 1 STANDARD LOAF

6 tablespoons (¾ stick) unsalted butter, room temperature, and more for buttering the pan

1 cup brown sugar

2 eggs

1 medium zucchini, grated

¼ cup applesauce

¼ cup sour cream

Zest of 1 lemon

½ teaspoon vanilla extract

½ teaspoon freshly grated nutmeg

1 teaspoon ground cinnamon

2 cups all-purpose flour

1 tablespoon ground flaxseeds

1½ teaspoons baking powder

1 teaspoon sea salt

½ teaspoon baking soda

1 cup raisins

½ cup pine nuts

1. Preheat oven to 350°F.

2. Combine all ingredients in a large mixing bowl.

3. Butter and flour a loaf pan, and pour mixture in. Bake for 65 minutes.

My Nana meant the world to me. This zucchini bread was something she baked en masse and gave as a gift at Christmas, housewarmings, baby showers, and luncheons with her girlfriends. At any given time if you went to her back porch and opened up her extra freezer, there would be at least ten loaves in perfect military order wrapped in plastic wrap and *then* foil with the date in masking tape on the top. Her penmanship was characteristically her own, with her lovely 1930s handwriting and classic phonetic spellings in English (her second language to Croatian). If she were alive today, I think she would be thrilled by this cookbook. Nana, I'm sending a big hug and kiss to you in heaven, with all the super Virgo love I can muster.

At age eighteen, Nana was filled with hopes and dreams in her newfound America, having hailed from a tiny island in the Adriatic Sea in the 1930s. Strong, beautiful, compassionate, loyal, and somewhat shy, she came out of her shell, eventually making great friends and working until her fingers bled. I can only imagine the big-band swing dances and classic movies she and her friends frequented in San Francisco. She met my grandfather during wartime at such a dance. He, too, was of Croatian descent but was born in the US and learned how to speak her language so they could be together. They wrote a multitude of letters to one another before she would go out with him. There were other suitors and a possible fiancé, but she always knew Dida was the one. And he remained the only one for her until the day she died, just shy of her ninety-ninth birthday. They were a real team in the truest sense of the word. And she outlived him by twenty-nine years. Everyone else from her generation was long gone by the time she died. She was the sole survivor for at least a decade past her peers.

I've never known another person who worked as hard and loved us as much as Nana did. Growing up, I didn't think there was anything she couldn't do. Her faith, generosity, and tenacity were second to none. She was always our family rock and had our backs. She encouraged us and protected us. She nurtured us, and boy, she fed us oh so well. I love you, dear Nana! *Hvala ti i bog vas blagoslovio!*

Nana and Dida on their wedding day in 1943.

DEBRIANNA'S

La Famiglia!
Snap Out of It Ravioli

SERVES 4 TO 6

DOUGH

2 cups all-purpose flour, and more if dough is too wet (optional) and for dusting work surfaces

6 large eggs (2 whole and 4 yolks only)

1 teaspoon kosher salt

1 tablespoon corn grits for baking sheet (to prevent sticking)

FILLING 1

8 ounces drained whole-milk ricotta

½ cup pesto (if you want to make fresh, check out Lisa's pesto recipe on page 103)

FILLING 2

3 links Italian hot sausage (cooked, drained of oil, and chopped small)

8 ounces drained whole-milk ricotta

¼ cup finely chopped fresh parsley

2 tablespoons fresh basil, finely chopped

1. On a large, clean work surface, pour the flour in a mound, and then make a well in the center about 4 inches wide. Pour the eggs, egg yolks, and salt into the well, and then use a fork to beat thoroughly. When combined, gradually incorporate the flour into the eggs to form a wet, sticky dough.

2. Using a bench knife, scrape excess dough from fork and fingers. Begin to fold additional flour into the dough with the bench knife, turning the dough until it feels firm and dry and can form a craggy-looking ball, about 2 to 5 minutes.

3. Press the heel of your hand into the ball of dough, pushing forward and down. Rotate the ball and repeat. Continue kneading until the dough develops a smooth, elastic texture. If the dough feels too wet, add flour in 1 teaspoon increments. If the dough feels too dry, add water slowly using a spray bottle. Wrap the ball of dough tightly in plastic wrap and allow it to rest on the countertop for 30 minutes while you prepare the surface.

4. Place a sheet of parchment paper on a tray or cutting board, and dust lightly with flour. Unwrap the rested dough and cut it into quarters. Set 1 quarter on a lightly floured work surface, and rewrap the remaining dough.

5. Use a rolling pin to flatten the quarter of dough into an oblong shape about ½ inch thick.

6. Set a pasta maker to the widest setting, and pass the dough 3 times through the machine.

7. Place the dough on a lightly floured work surface. Fold both ends in so that they meet at the center of the dough, and then fold the dough in half where the end points meet, trying not to incorporate too much air into the folds. Using a rolling pin, flatten the dough to ½ inch thick.

8. Pass the dough through the rollers 3 additional times. Narrow the setting by one notch and repeat. Then narrow by one additional notch and repeat. Continue passing the dough through the rollers,

reducing the thickness by one setting each time until it reaches the desired thickness. It will become very delicate, elastic to the touch, and slightly translucent. Cover with plastic wrap or a kitchen towel to prevent drying, and then repeat with remaining dough quarters.

9. Form the ravioli using a ravioli press or a knife and free-form.* Use water and a pastry brush to paint the edges, and press closed around the filling.

10. Lay the ravioli as they are made on a baking sheet sprinkled with corn grits, and cover with a towel. I will often put the tray in the freezer and, once frozen, pile the ravioli we are not using in the freezer bag.

11. If you want to eat the ravioli immediately, fill a large stockpot with water, salt it (until it tastes like seawater—about 1 tablespoon), and bring to a boil. Add the ravioli carefully, and when they float to the top, they're done! Same directions for frozen ravioli.

* I use my husband's grandmother's ravioli press, but forming by hand works too.

Bob Cesca.

Debrianna in Ravioli Land.

When my siblings and I were young, if we were sick or sometimes just unhappy, my mom would make pastina. It is a pasta that comes in the shape of teensy stars. She would float these magical stars in warm milk with some sugar and a bit of butter. That pale, creamy, slightly golden liquid held secrets. As soon as the spoon dipped in, the tiny stars would emerge like dreams floating on top of sweet milky clouds. Whatever was wrong melted away after the first taste and sent me to a place to bury sadness for a few moments, offering a place of connection. It was like a pasta with superpowers.

The kitchen connects souls when words fail us. My friend Bob Cesca is a master at words. He writes them in his column, speaks them in his podcast, and educates us with his vernacular, knowledge of history, and perspective. He partly shares my Italian heritage, so he understands the language of pasta. But Bob can't cook. So when we invited him onto Corona Kitchen, I cooked for him. Even through the internet, his face in one of the tiny boxes that make up our video-sharing world, I could see he knows that the pasta shapes matter, that the sauce is everything, and that what is tucked inside is the precious secret. Open the magic envelope, and the joy spills out. The first bite into a handmade ravioli takes you on a journey sparked with bursts of cream and spice and comfort, languidly rolled under and over pasta and tomatoes. Bob knows this feeling, the magic of homemade pasta, because he has lived it the way I have. Even though I am in Santa Fe and he is in Washington, DC, we share this appreciation over the ethers.

This is what has amazed me about those times—that we could be together and have these moments where we found our way to one another through the kitchen. It is a place where we share our stories and our creativity and find our way to "normal." It is a place of connection.

And these days, that happens a lot. Welcome to Ravioli Land.

If You Aren't Italian, You Are Now, Homemade Ricotta

MAKES 3 TO 4 CUPS

1 gallon whole milk (preferably with low pasteurization; ultra-pasteurized milk will not work)

1 cup heavy cream

2 teaspoons to 1 tablespoon high-quality sea salt, to taste

½ cup freshly squeezed lemon juice, or more depending on the acid level of the lemon*

* The acid level can be determined by watching the reaction. If you are not seeing the curd form, add a bit more lemon juice.

1. Line a colander with 3 to 4 layers of lightly dampened cheesecloth, and then set the colander in a large bowl or pot so it can drain. Attach an instant-read or candy thermometer to the inside of a 7- to 8-quart stainless-steel or enamel pot.

2. Pour the milk, heavy cream, and sea salt into the pot, and slowly warm the mixture over medium heat, stirring occasionally with a wooden or silicone spatula. Warm the mixture to 185°F, stopping the raising of the heat before it reaches a rolling boil. Let the mixture simmer for about 20 minutes, stirring occasionally.

3. Remove the mixture from the heat, and slowly pour the lemon juice over its surface. Once all the lemon juice has been added, let the mixture sit for a moment, and then stir very gently for 1 to 2 minutes to encourage curds to form.

4. Gently ladle the curds into the lined colander. Fold the ends of the cheesecloth over the curds to cover loosely. Drain until it reaches your desired consistency: 30 minutes for a soft ricotta and up to a few hours for a very firm, dry, dense ricotta. Refrigerate if draining for more than 2 hours.

5. Transfer the drained ricotta to an airtight container, reserving the whey for another purpose if desired. The ricotta should keep for up to 3 days in the fridge or up to 3 months in the freezer.

TIP: When making ricotta, you can use white vinegar instead of lemon juice, but I love the lemon flavor. Do not use Meyer lemons, as they do not have enough acid. If you want a creamier ricotta, replace 1 cup of the milk with 1 cup heavy cream. I use the leftover whey to cook pasta, to make smoothies, or to water the garden, but dilute it because of the salt.

For years, my mother never told us her actual birth date. Instead she implied that it was somewhere around January 27, 28, or 29, so she could ensure we always missed her birthday. No matter how we tried to plan for it, we were always wrong. This insanity is what I grew up with.

The "magic" of my mother's illness was that it was consistently inconsistent in its anger and pathology. The other constant was her unending creativity. When we were little kids, my mom used to bake outrageous cakes. My first birthday cake was cut into the shape of a rocking horse; it was a white cake with colorful gumdrops for spots. The cake shapes got more complex as the years and children went on. When we got older, we used to help her make the cakes for the younger siblings, creating shapes and special designs with candy and frosting long before the crazed era of spun sugar and modeling candy. Though Mom was ahead of her time, she eventually lost interest and stopped creating these sculptural wonders—and I lost interest too; by the time I was twelve, I wanted a cannoli for my birthday cake. The cannoli's crispy cookie shell was filled with soft, not-too-sweet ricotta and a few of the tiniest chocolate chips, and the white powdered sugar would melt across my lips, carrying me to a magical place inside myself where I thought elves must make these delights only for queens.

My Uncle Victor usually brought a cannoli to me from New York City, a place that to my mind seemed exotic and far away, where celebrities like Nancy Sinatra lived. In reality, the city was only two hours away from where we lived in Connecticut. By the time I was fifteen, I wanted to learn to make cannoli myself. I now shared that spirit of adventure in the kitchen, but thankfully not the crazy part of my mom. That year, Uncle Victor brought me a cannoli-making kit. It had a metal tube to create the tunnel for the filling. I made the fragile cookie dough that must be spooned out with the wet end of a teaspoon into a circle, fried lightly, and then carefully lifted out of the hot oil and wrapped around the metal tube to dry into that hollow, ready to receive the filling. It was a process that would take hours, but I was always filled with intent and focused on my goal. When I was in the kitchen cooking, no one bothered me. Usually it was a pretty safe space, a place to create and breathe, to think and share. It still is.

Today I make a different kind of cookie with a ricotta cream. I don't wrap them in the tube, and they are not fried but baked. I like to take two and stuff them like an Oreo. The crispy pistachio cookie lies atop fresh ricotta cream with tiny shavings of dark chocolate and a hint of orange zest. When I make them I always think of my Uncle Victor—who once gave me a scrap of paper with his number on it and said in his broken English, "You need me, you call me"— and say a little thank-you for all those birthday cannoli.

Zen Guide for Surviving with Green Chile Brioche

MAKES 1 LOAF

DRY INGREDIENTS

2 cups all-purpose flour, and more (optional) for step 4 and for dusting work surface

1 teaspoon sea salt

2 teaspoons sugar

1 teaspoon freshly ground black pepper

1 teaspoon red pepper flakes

1 teaspoon Chimayo red chile powder

WET INGREDIENTS

1 teaspoon active dry yeast

½ teaspoon honey

⅓ cup whole milk, tepid (warmed on the stove), and more (optional) for step 4

3 large eggs

¼ cup Hatch green chile

¾ cup (1½ sticks) sweet butter, softened, and more for buttering a bowl

1 egg mixed with 1 tablespoon half-and-half (for egg wash)

1. Mix the dry ingredients together in an electric standing mixer with a paddle.

2. In a medium glass bowl, use a wooden (not metal) spoon to gently stir the yeast with the honey and milk, and then let the mixture sit for 10 minutes, covered with a dish towel. The yeast should activate and create a foam.

3. Combine the yeast mixture with the eggs and chile, and transfer the mixture to the standing mixer with the dry ingredients. Beat at medium-low speed until a sticky dough is formed. Allow the dough to stand for 1 minute; then scrape down the sides of the mixer with a spatula. Beat on medium while adding the butter in 3 portions. Then scrape down again, and beat for another 30 seconds to form a smooth dough.

4. Change the mixer's paddle to a hook attachment, and knead the dough for 1 minute. Add either a dash of flour or a dash of milk if needed to obtain a shiny, silky dough that still sticks a little until incorporated.

5. Remove the dough from the mixer, roll it out on a floured surface, and then shape it into a smooth ball.

6. Butter a bowl, place the dough ball inside, and cover with plastic wrap for the first rise. The first rise should be 2 to 4 hours, depending on the room temperature or if you have a bread proofing setting for your oven. The dough should double in volume. Cover with a dish towel.

7. Preheat oven to 350°F.

8. Remove the dough from the bowl. I decided to use the Nanterre ball method for an attractive finish. For this, you divide the dough into 8 equal balls and then place them 2 x 2 in a greased bread tin. If you want, you could also braid the dough or simply fashion 1 large ball to fit the tin. Let rise (proof) again for 30 to 60 minutes.

9. Glaze the top of the dough with the egg wash and bake until golden brown, 30 to 35 minutes.

10. Allow the dough to cool in the pan for 5 to 10 minutes prior to serving.

I remember the night I made this bread during quarantine. All the sentient beings in my house were asleep, leaving the kind of still quiet where you can hear the clock ticking. Sigh. I love the late-evening silence. It smelled wonderful in the kitchen, and this brioche turned out beautifully. I thanked all the Corona Kitchen members for hanging in there with me, as I haven't had the time or inclination to make something that takes this kind of herculean effort in many years. Sometimes you forget what you are capable of. The night I made this bread I had a serious epiphany—realizing while talking with Debrianna earlier that day on the show that I had never even looked closely enough at my own oven's control panel to notice that there was a "bread proofing" button. It was an aha moment—a realization I'd been missing something that had been in front of me for so long.

Debrianna and Lisa celebrate the cookbook photo shoot.

Living in my house, working so hard to keep a roof over our heads the last seven years, still recovering from the aftermath of a painful and financially debilitating divorce, and not living in a way to make the effort on a regular basis to create this level of food where, yes, it takes long hours and time and full-blown chemistry, I forgot how much excitement, wonder, adrenalin, art, and fun there is to it. And I forgot how much I missed it. Doing the daily, multifaceted docuseries "experiment" of Corona Kitchen has changed me. I never again want to let cooking be a chore or something that I only do during holidays.

I want to remember to make cooking a regular thing for my loved ones so that we can really enjoy and savor glorious ingredients and take the time to appreciate the caring that goes into the food that we create. This whole diatribe is about being present, ultimately. Pre-pandemic, my life went by too fast in America. After making this brioche, I was so tired—but it was a good tired, like after-you-run-a-marathon tired. It was a labor of love, and I knew there would be some heavenly "yum" sounds the next day with the brioche and eggs enjoyed by my darlings. The process is worth it. They are worth it. I am worth it too. Thank you, Debrianna, for being my partner on this venture. It is so much more than a cooking show—pushing us both in positive directions that we must have needed. I am grateful for you, my dear soul-sister friend.

RED CHILE HONEY BUTTERMILK BISCUITS YOU CAN COUNT ON

MAKES ABOUT 10 BISCUITS,
DEPENDING ON THE SIZE OF GLASS USED TO CUT THEM

BISCUITS

2½ cups all-purpose flour, and more for surface dusting

2 tablespoons baking powder

1 teaspoon sea salt

½ cup (1 stick) unsalted butter, frozen and then grated

2 teaspoons honey, room temperature

1 cup and 2 tablespoons buttermilk (reserve ½ cup buttermilk for brushing biscuits before baking)

Butter (either salted or unsalted), melted, for coating the pan

HONEY BUTTER

1 tablespoon honey

2 tablespoons salted butter, melted

½ teaspoon Chimayo red chile powder (optional)

1. Preheat oven to 425°F.

2. Combine the flour, baking powder, and sea salt. If using a food processor, pulse a few times to mix. If combining by hand, use a whisk and make sure everything is evenly distributed.

3. Add the frozen butter, and pulse until the flour coated with butter resembles tiny peas. Then add the honey and buttermilk, and pulse about 25 additional times, until a raggedy dough is achieved. If using a big bowl, use a fork or pastry cutter to help reach this consistency. Work quickly if you are in a warm temperature, as the dough needs to stay as cold as possible so that the butter will create steam in the oven and give the biscuit height.

4. Spread the dough on a floured surface. Fold each side inward like an envelope and then roll it out using a rolling pin. (I use a silicone-and-metal rolling pin for pastry that helps keep the dough cold.) Repeat two more times. On the final roll, roll the dough out to about 1 inch thick.

5. Cut out the biscuits. I used a water glass that was about 2½ to 3 inches across the top. If using a glass, do not turn the glass when you press it down. Just press down and lift straight up.

6. Brush a 12-inch cast-iron pan with melted butter, and then arrange the biscuits in a circle in the pan. Brush the tops with the additional buttermilk. Bake until golden brown and cooked all the way through, about 20 minutes.

7. Prepare the honey butter by mixing its ingredients together.

8. After removing the biscuits from the oven, brush their tops immediately with the honey butter.

TIP: I have found that a cast-iron pan is the absolute best for baking biscuits. In other pans, they never turn out as good.

Freaking Good Times Potato Spelt Focaccia with Olives

MAKES 1 LOAF, BUT RECIPE EASILY DOUBLES TO MAKE 2

SPREAD

Gorgonzola, crumbled, to taste

8 ounces mascarpone

POTATO TOPPING

2 medium Yukon Gold potatoes, diced into ½-inch pieces

3 tablespoons ordinary olive oil

1 tablespoon kosher salt

2 teaspoons finely chopped fresh rosemary

1 teaspoon chopped fresh thyme

1 garlic clove, minced

FOCACCIA

½ teaspoon sugar

1½ teaspoons active dry yeast

¾ cup whole milk, warmed, or water

1½ cups spelt flour

1½ cups bread flour

½ teaspoon sea salt, and a sprinkle for before baking

2 tablespoons higher-quality olive oil, and more for drizzling over the dough

¾ cup mashed potatoes*

Flour for table prep

Ordinary olive oil for greasing and coating dough

⅓ cup chopped oil-cured olives

2 teaspoons fresh rosemary removed from the stem and roughly chopped

TO MAKE THE SPREAD

1. Mix the Gorgonzola into the mascarpone.

TO MAKE THE POTATO TOPPING

1. Preheat oven to 400°F.

2. In a large bowl, toss together the diced potatoes, olive oil, salt, rosemary, thyme, and garlic. Line a baking sheet with foil, and spread the coated potatoes over the foil.

3. Bake the potatoes for 10 minutes, flip, and bake for another 10 minutes. They should become tender and lightly browned. Remove from oven and set aside.

TO MAKE THE FOCACCIA

1. Add the sugar and yeast to the warm milk, and stir with a wooden spoon. Let sit to proof for 5 minutes or until foamy.

2. In a large bowl, stir together the spelt and bread flours and the sea salt. Add the higher-quality olive oil, mashed potatoes, and yeast mixture. Stir the mixture, adding water if needed to combine.

3. Lightly flour a work surface, and knead the dough on it by hand until smooth, about 5 to 6 minutes.

4. Lightly grease a bowl, place the dough inside, and cover with plastic wrap. Let sit in a warm spot until doubled in size, about 1½ hours.

5. Line a 9 x 9-inch baking pan with parchment paper, and lightly grease it. With oiled hands, punch down the dough, and then spread it into the pan. Flip it so the olive oil is on both sides. If the dough doesn't reach the edges of the pan, let it rest 5 minutes and then pull again.

6. Allow the dough to rise a second time in a warm spot. Cover with plastic wrap, and let sit in a warm spot until doubled in size, about 1 hour.

7. Preheat oven to 400°F. Fry the top of the dough evenly, and then sprinkle the top of the dough with sea salt and give it a drizzle of olive oil.

8. Press your fingertips across the top of the dough to create dimples. Scatter the potatoes and olives over the top of the dough. Sprinkle the rosemary over the top and drizzle liberally with the higher-quality olive oil.

9. Bake the focaccia for 20 minutes, and then turn the pan around and bake it for another 15 to 20 minutes or until a thermometer inserted into the center registers 190°F.

10. Remove the focaccia from the oven and allow it to cool to just barely warm. Cut it into squares, and serve it warm with the Gorgonzola and mascarpone spread.

TIP: Any herb and olive oil spread will work in place of the Gorgonzola and mascarpone.

* I like to cook the mashed potatoes in chicken or vegetable stock.

ATTITUDE ADJUSTMENT SIMPLE BOULE

MAKES 1 LOAF

1 teaspoon honey

2¼ teaspoons active dry yeast*

1¼ cups water or whole milk, warmed

1½ teaspoons sea salt

2 cups all-purpose flour, and more for coating dough and bowl

½ cup whole wheat flour

1 tablespoon ground flaxseeds

* This is the equivalent of 1 package of Red Star Active Dry Yeast.

1. Set the oven on a standard bread-proof setting, or find a nice, warm (pet-free) place in your home to let this dough rise.

2. Combine the honey, yeast, and warm water in a large mixing bowl. Use a wooden spoon to stir gently, and then let the mixture sit for 5 to 10 minutes to allow the yeast to activate. The yeast will produce bubbles when it activates.

3. Add the sea salt and flours gradually. Mix lightly with a spatula, or use your hands to incorporate fully.

4. Flour all sides of the dough and bowl, and then cover with a dish towel. Let the dough rise until it doubles in size, approximately 1 hour.

5. Roll the dough out onto a floured work surface. Do not punch it, as tempting as that may be. You want to keep its air bubbles intact.

6. Lightly flour across the top of the dough, and start to shape it into a ball using the pull method: Take each corner and gently press into the middle. Repeat this a few times, and then flip the ball over and gently shape the dough into a round loaf. Generously flour the bowl again, as well as the top, sides, and bottom of the dough, and place the dough in the bowl.

7. Cover the dough with a dish towel, and let it rise for another 30 minutes. While it's rising the second time, preheat oven to 460°F and either place a Dutch oven inside to heat up or choose an alternative method to bake the bread. (I used a 12-inch cast-iron skillet to bake the bread and an 8-inch skillet to hold the water for the steam during the bake.) If you use 2 skillets, place the larger skillet on the higher rack and the smaller one on the rack beneath it.

8. When the dough has risen for the second time, skip to step 9 if using a Dutch oven. If using 2 skillets, remove the top cast-iron skillet, place it on the stovetop, and roll the dough into the cast-iron with the seam side—the side that was on the bottom of the bowl—facing up. Then quickly put the skillet back on the top rack of the oven, drop 8 to 10 ice cubes into the lower cast-iron pan, and close

the oven. The steam is really important to the success of the bake, so you don't want to lose any of it. Bake for 35 minutes.

9. If you are using the traditional Dutch oven method, remove the Dutch oven using potholders. Roll the dough in it, cover it, and return the Dutch oven to the oven. About 20 minutes into the bake, open the oven, and uncover the bread to allow the top to brown. Then bake, uncovered, for 15 more minutes.

TIP: This endeavor takes about 3 hours, whereas most artisanal rustic loaves can take up to 16. Trust me, folks, that you can't mess this up even if you don't have a Dutch oven, and it's so worth it! Also, I wasn't sure about using cast-iron skillets, but they worked very well.

My sisters, Hollie and Heidi, and I used to spend the summers with Nana and Dida in one of the hottest places in the US: Harquahala Valley, Arizona. In August it can reach 120°F in the shade! We tried to fry an egg on the sidewalk once—and it worked. Our grandparents' ranch was in the middle of nowhere, but we thought it was heaven. Nana taught us how to make bread when I was about seven, Hollie was four, and Heidi was just barely one. I remember Nana taking out the flour, salt, and water and then the magic ingredient that would make the bread rise. She explained how the yeast needed to be activated to start the gluten, and this happened through kneading the dough. I missed my friends from home a little bit that day, and she said sometimes when she missed her parents, who had long ago left this world, kneading the bread for an hour or so helped her feel better.

Nana liked to be alone with her thoughts. It must have been so hard to leave the only country she knew, and her friends and family for another place halfway across the world. She was always busy with something interesting: a task to master or a new hobby to learn. She was fearless and determined. I kneaded the dough that first time until my arms ached—but I didn't even notice. Because I got lost in her stories while I worked. And that simple crusted bread was so good, I wanted to make it again and again. So, as was often the case with my grandmother, she capitalized on that enthusiasm and bought more yeast down at the tiny little market in town called Smitty's. I swear I baked a loaf a day for two weeks!

Lisa communes with her nana's spirit in the dough.

The following summer I became fascinated with cakes. I made a new cake every few days and continued to give them away. Nana introduced me to German chocolate cake that summer, and we had to go into Phoenix to buy the shredded coconut, as they didn't have it at Smitty's. At night we would play gin rummy or cribbage. Instead of TV, our nightly entertainment was the thrilling sounds of crickets and croaking frogs and the nearby irrigation ditches' sound of rushing water in the desert twilight. We also liked to go hunting for rocks for the garden, and Dida taught me how to drive a truck while sitting on a stack of phonebooks. He never once raised his voice. We played in the plastic kiddie pool that Nana would put ice cubes in because it was so unbearably hot outside. We watched paper boxes dance in the wind down the dirt road like it was a ballet performance. And then toward the end of August, the monsoon season would begin, and the first rain would fall on the land. The petrichor scent of that rain mixing with soil is the best smell on Earth. If I ever have to drive on I–10 West, I wish for it to rain so I can roll down my windows and take in that glorious perfume of sage, cactus, and paloverde trees.

When my parents came back from their trips to pick us up, my sisters and I did not want to leave our grandparents and go back home. Nana and I had a pact. She promised to contact me after she left this world. I think she does in dreams and when I cook. Corona Kitchen inspired me to want to bake bread again. This is classic Nana influence at work from the other side.

Potato, Ricotta, and Onion Impeachzza

SERVES 4

1 tablespoon unsalted butter, melted

2½ tablespoons olive oil

2 medium onions, peeled and thinly sliced

2 garlic cloves, minced

1 teaspoon sugar

Enough chicken or vegetable stock to cover potatoes

3 small to medium potatoes, sliced ⅛ inch thick

1 tablespoon chopped fresh rosemary

2 teaspoons chopped fresh thyme

Salt, to taste

2 tablespoons chopped fresh basil

Ricotta (use Debrianna's If You Aren't Italian, You Are Now, Homemade Ricotta, page 64, or a 16-ounce container of part-skim or whole-milk ricotta)

1 pizza dough (use Debrianna's recipe, page 144, or store-bought fresh pizza dough)

3 cups shredded cheese (we love a combo of Asiago and Pecorino Toscano)

Crushed red pepper flakes for finishing (optional)

1. Add the butter and 1 tablespoon olive oil to a skillet; then add the onions and garlic, and cook until translucent. Sprinkle the sugar on the onions, and cook over medium heat until caramelized. Set aside.

2. In a medium saucepan, bring the stock to a boil. Add the potatoes and cook until tender, about 5 to 7 minutes. Drain, and then add back the potatoes and let sit over low heat to dry.

3. Toss the potatoes with the remaining olive oil and the rosemary, thyme, and salt.

4. In a separate bowl, add the basil to the ricotta.*

5. Preheat oven to 425°F. Roll out the pizza dough, and place it onto a pizza stone or pizza pan. Top with a spread of the ricotta and the onions, shredded cheese, and sliced potatoes. Bake until crispy, about 10 to 15 minutes.

6. Garnish with the red pepper flakes prior to serving.

* If the ricotta is stiff, you can add a bit of cream or half-and-half to loosen to a spreadable consistency.

All my life I have been obsessed with the idea of having a home. It kept me in relationships far past their expiration date.

"Let's get married."

"Really?" I ask as my twenty-nine-year-old heart skips a beat or two.

"Yes. I want to get you a ring. My new patient is a jeweler. I can get a big stone from him," he says, bragging a bit. "We can go pick something out."

I grab his face and kiss him. I have waited for this moment for two long years.

"But, honey, I don't want a ring," I say, looking deeply into the light green of his eyes.

"I want land."

Needless to say, *that* didn't go well in the end, but when we broke up, we both made a profit on the land we bought on Rabbit Road.

A few years later, I tried to buy the fourplex I was living in with my longtime friend Susan, who lived next door, but in those days, we needed 20 percent down. With my being "female," my dad just could not understand why I would want to own property and be a landlord. Why didn't I just get married, he queried. So I convinced the guy I was living with to buy a house. I would be half owner—just between us, not on paper. Instead of making financial contributions to the down payment, I paid half the mortgage and I was the labor. I poured myself into that house, ripping out the carpet and laying Saltillo tile, pouring concrete like a pro, painting walls and ceilings, gardening the yard like Martha Stewart, and making the handmade custom curtains, which in the end were all I was left with. Oh, and to be fair, he gave me a check for one thousand dollars. His parting words were to tell me I would never own my own home, that I would never be able to qualify on my own.

After our split, I was still looking for my home. I considered building a yurt. Maybe I could get a plot of land and all my theater friends would help me if I promised to cook for them. You can always bribe actors with good food. I obsessed over yurt magazines, and my eyes were constantly on the lookout for plots of land. My best friend, Jane, thought I was nuts and had a better plan.

Jane and I had just opened a mortgage business, because we feared we were "aging out" of acting. She, unlike me, saw houses as financial investments. I wanted a house that was a home. *My* home. When the time was right, she held my hand as I leapt and bought my first house.

My housewarming party was a "bring your own flagstone" party. I cooked for anyone who brought one, and that's how I got my patio done. I needed a toolshed, so I watched videos, bought my first jigsaw at Lowe's, and built a lean-to on the side of my house to hold my jigsaw and two screwdrivers. But it still was not a home, just me and my roommate in a space.

A year later, on a trip to Philadelphia, I met the man who would become my husband. I invited him to visit me, and when he did, I took him to every favorite place I had so he'd fall in love with me *and* New Mexico. I baked homemade chocolate babka and made candied bacon for our little excursions. He proposed marriage to me with a mouthful of popcorn while we were at the movies watching *Lemony Snicket*.

We are uniquely matched. People thought we were nuts to be adding on a dining room while planning our wedding, but we looked at it as one big party. For our wedding, we had a "bring a lasagna" contest and a photo booth for all our guests to enjoy. I had been looking for a house my whole life, but he was the one who helped me see the home that was in me all along. I can't imagine my home without him. During lockdown, being able to be in my home with a husband I adore was a great blessing.

And he loves my cooking. Which is a good thing, because that is my offering. When he was at art school in Italy, he became enamored with many things, one of which was white pizza. I love tomato sauce on mine, but this version, his favorite, truly is scrumptious.

Debrianna and her husband, David, on their wedding day in 2006.

DEBRIANNA'S

HANDMADE'S TALE POTATO RICOTTA GNOCCHI

SERVES 4 TO 6

4 russet potatoes, quartered

Enough water or chicken or vegetable stock to submerge the potatoes

1 heaping teaspoon salt, and more for salting cooking water

2 cups all-purpose flour, and more if dough is sticky (optional) and for table prep

1 teaspoon freshly ground white pepper

1 tablespoon freshly chopped basil

1 egg

1 cup ricotta

Salted butter, for finishing (optional)

Freshly ground black pepper for finishing (optional)

Sea salt for finishing (optional)

Parmesan, grated, for finishing (optional)

Tomato sauce for finishing (optional)

1. Place the potatoes in a pot, and cover with water or stock. Add salt if using water. Cook until just fork tender, and then strain. Reserve about ¼ cup water or broth in case you need it for the dough later. Return the potatoes to the hot pot and allow excess water to evaporate.

2. Remove the potatoes, and let cool on a tea towel to absorb any excess moisture.

3. Peel the potatoes, and then grate them into a large bowl or use a ricer.

4. Gently toss the flour, salt, white pepper, and basil in the bowl. Make a well in the center, and add the egg and ricotta to it. Whisk together and then add the potatoes, working out to the edges and making a crumbly mix.

5. Use your hands to form a smooth dough. If the dough is sticky, you may need to add a bit more flour or some of the reserved cooking liquid. Be careful not to overflour or overwork the dough, or it will become too tough.

6. Turn out the dough onto a lightly floured work surface and form it into a loaf shape about 1 inch thick. Cut the loaf shape into slices about ¾ inch thick; then roll each slice into a rope about 1 inch thick, and cut them into pieces for the gnocchi. Use a gnocchi board or the tines of a fork to make ridges.

7. Lay the gnocchi pieces on a baking sheet lined with parchment paper. Either cook within 30 to 40 minutes, or store in airtight freezer bags in the freezer for 2 to 3 hours.

8. To cook the gnocchi, boil it in salted water until the pillows rise to the surface. Strain and then toss with finishing ingredients of choice.

TIP: You can use leftover mashed potatoes, but the quality of the potatoes matters. If they are runny and gummy, the gnocchi won't turn out well. Light and fluffy mashed potatoes work best. If using leftover mashed potatoes, add the flour slowly so as to avoid adding too much. You want a dough that is pliable and not sticky or overworked.

Standing beside the apartment-size white stove, the burners covered with a pot nearly her size bubbling full of tomatoes, my Gramma stirs the sauce in a circle with a large wooden spoon. The pot is not the one she uses to smash the laundry she still washes in the kitchen sink but one that is darkened from years of tomatoes and stews.

Stuffed in her full apron with straps that cross her back, her feet in oxfords and her perfectly wound gray bun at the nape of her neck, my Gramma hums, wipes her hands on a cloth, and then turns to the gray Formica dining table in the living room of her cramped apartment. On the ground floor of a house, we sit on the aluminum chairs with the black vinyl cushions, as we do every Saturday, and look out at the yellow clapboard house across the driveway with the long porch, welcoming fall.

On Saturdays, we prepare for Sunday dinner. First, the pot of sauce. Gramma opens cans of tomatoes with the can opener attached to the wall. They lay in wait, while the aroma of frying sausages and garlic rises from the bottom of the pot. The tomatoes splatter noisily as they join the brown bits gathered at the bottom, simmering, waiting for the end of the day.

Then, the pasta making begins. Puffs of flour emerge from sacks that sit comfortably on the end of the long table; nearby, the small TV on a stand flickers cartoons for me. Gramma's strong hands scoop mounds onto the table—a small one for me and a larger one for her. Side by side, we add the egg and water. She takes her fork and swiftly mixes them together until, like magic, a dough takes shape. My small hands fumble over the egg, and she gently pulls the wet mixture back together, telling me in her broken Italian-English to be patient.

Leaves rustle by the lace hanging in the open window, the palm leaves wrapped over the curtain rod, left over from Easter. Aunt Mary waves from the long porch holding her steaming cup of Chock full o'Nuts, and Gram nods, her hands splotched with bits of dough. She looks down and says, "*Momento.*"

Her heels clacking on the gray-and-white linoleum squares, she pulls the handle of the fridge open and returns with a small white-and-yellow-flowered Pyrex bowl. Inside are leftover mashed potatoes. There will be gnocchi for tomorrow.

If only we could let go of the way it was before the virus, staying home would be so different now. We have lost the connection to ourselves in relation to food. It takes time to prepare, time to create. We had zero free time before the virus, obsessed with staying busy. It used to be that staying home wasn't a punishment; it was how it was. Those languid Saturdays at my grandmother's hip, a time gone by, a time to remember, when life was slower and making food was our communication. Sundays full of family and hours of eating love on a plate. Plate after plate. During the dark days of the pandemic, I shared love in the form of a small container of mashed potatoes and clouds of flour.

LISA'S

Ⓥ

NEVER FEAR THE CLASSIC HERB AND CHEESE SOUFFLÉ

SERVES 6 WITH A 6-CUP SOUFFLÉ DISH
OR 7 WITH 7 INDIVIDUALLY SIZED RAMEKINS

3 tablespoons unsalted butter, and more for dish prep

5 tablespoons all-purpose flour, and more for dish prep

2 cups whole milk

½ teaspoon freshly grated nutmeg

½ teaspoon sea salt

4 cranks freshly ground black pepper

1½ cups freshly grated Comté*

½ teaspoon smoked paprika

1 teaspoon finely chopped fresh thyme

3 egg yolks, slightly beaten

4 egg whites

½ teaspoon cream of tartar

* Or use Gruyère or Swiss, which are traditional, or goat or cheddar—whatever you prefer!

1. Preheat oven to 360°F. Place an oven rack on the bottom rung of the oven.

2. Butter a standard-size soufflé dish well, and place it in the refrigerator to set the butter.

3. In a saucepan set over medium-low heat, whisk the butter, flour, milk, nutmeg, sea salt, and pepper together to make a béchamel sauce. Keep whisking until the sauce thickens enough to coat a wooden spoon; then remove the saucepan from the heat.

4. After the sauce has slightly cooled, gradually add 1 cup Comté and the paprika, thyme, and egg yolks. Keep whisking until the mixture is very smooth, and then set it aside.

5. In a large standing mixer or with a hand mixer, beat the egg whites and cream of tartar on high until stiff peaks form, as with a meringue.

6. Remove the soufflé dish from the refrigerator, and butter again. Then dust with flour and set aside.

7. Pour a portion of the béchamel and cheese mixture into a large mixing bowl, and then fold in a portion of the egg whites with a spatula, slowly and carefully combining. Keep adding more of each until fully incorporated. Do not overmix; the soufflé should be fluffy and airy.

8. Pour the mixture into the soufflé dish, and smooth the top. Gently sprinkle the remaining Comté on top, coating evenly.

9. Bake the mixture until the top of the soufflé is golden brown and it has risen, 35 to 40 minutes. Do not open the oven door while baking, as that will cause the soufflé to collapse. Instead use the oven light to see the dough.

TIP: Soufflés are a grand presentational moment and hold for only about 3 minutes before they begin to deflate. Once you get the hang of it, they are easy to make. You can adapt them by adding fresh spinach or any kind of veggies or fresh herbs and different kinds of cheeses or ham.

Do you ever wonder about the many workings of fate? Have you discovered an object that speaks to you? Have you heard a voice as clear as a bell inside your head, saying something like "This large glass mixing bowl is really important to your life path. You don't have the first clue as to the reason right now, but it is. Trust me"?

I didn't know destiny would arrive with an everyday object. This happened to me about nine years ago, at a time when I had completely lost my sense of self. I was drowning from working as a full-time executive producer for a TV network while simultaneously raising two small children as well as compartmentalizing an Oscar-worthy role as a people-pleasing wife. There was so little of me left in my day-to-day that I think the universe felt bad I was so clueless and threw me a life preserver.

I found this bowl on a lunch-break spur-of-the-moment visit to a fancy kitchen store, and I am not kidding—when I held it in my hands, it actually spoke to me. It said, "Girl, you better buy me or you are doomed." And I really liked the bowl too. It was no frills, just beautiful, heavy, and stable—a well-made culinary necessity. It was expensive, but there was a lifetime guarantee. And I liked it so much more than the clanky-sounding, industrial stainless-steel bowls waiting at home that I abhorred, but I never once mentioned my displeasure in them.

I asked myself, "Why buy the bowl now? You don't need this." The inner voice replied, "Oh yes, you do. You know why. Because it's something you actually like, and it's something you would buy for yourself." And so I bought it. And promptly hid it in the closet of my old house for a few years before the divorce. I never cognitively acknowledged the promise of a better life in the future—that was a deeply buried thought; instead, I hid it because it didn't go with the sleek, modern style of my sand-and-gray-toned custom kitchen. It would not have been welcome there. I forgot all about it until I moved out. Flash-forward to many years later. Today, I probably use the bowl every day. Corona Kitchen viewers see it all the time. It's especially fun to fold egg whites in, like when I made this soufflé, and it sounds lovely when you whisk. It's a great glass bowl, and I can see right through it.

Screenshot from the early days of Corona Kitchen.

CHEESE FILLING

1½ cups cottage cheese

1 cup crumbled Bulgarian or Israeli feta*

1 teaspoon bread crumbs

1 egg yolk (reserve egg white in separate bowl)

* Bulgarian and Israeli feta are milder and less salty than Greek feta.

EGGPLANT FILLING

1 large eggplant

1 teaspoon olive oil (optional)

1 egg yolk

Pinch salt

PUFF PASTRY

Flour for table prep

2 sheets puff pastry

2 large egg whites

½ cup raw sesame seeds

YOU CAN'T EAT JUST ONE BULGARIAN BUREKA

MAKES ABOUT 18 BUREKAS, SERVING 4

The recipe for this absolutely delicious and savory filled puff pastry was passed down from generation to generation in the Alcalay family (and in many other Eastern European families). According to family lore, the Alcalays were Sephardic Jews originally from Spain who fled to Bulgaria during the Spanish Inquisition, taking all of their recipes and cultural heritage with them. Meanwhile, Sephardic Jews from Turkey during the Ottoman Empire were introduced to the popular "Asian dumpling." This evolved throughout the Balkans into a puff pastry (and sometimes phyllo dough) version, merging it with the local version of the dish, the empanada, and adapting it to make it kosher. *Börek* + empanada = bureka.

TO MAKE THE CHEESE FILLING

1. In a mixing bowl, combine all ingredients except the reserved egg white. Use a fork to mix until well blended. Make sure to break up any large chunks of feta.

2. Refrigerate mixture until ready to assemble the burekas.

TO MAKE THE EGGPLANT FILLING

1. Preheat oven to 400°F.

2. Place the eggplant on a baking sheet lined with foil, and then bake until soft in the middle, 20 to 30 minutes. (If using a convection oven, broil for 20 minutes.) Remove from oven, and let rest until cool enough to touch.

3. Make 2 parallel cuts lengthwise along the eggplant, and open it up (like an envelope pocket). Gently remove all seeds, and then remove the skin.

4. With a large knife, finely chop the eggplant until it has a mashed potato consistency. If the eggplant mash is very moist and watery, heat it in a sauté pan with 1 teaspoon olive oil for a few minutes until the water evaporates.

5. Allow to cool, and then add the egg yolk and mix together.

6. Refrigerate mixture until ready to assemble the burekas.

TO MAKE THE BUREKAS

1. Preheat oven to 350°F.

2. On a smooth, clean, lightly floured surface, unfold 1 puff pastry sheet. Use a rolling pin to roll the sheet to a 12 x 12-inch square. Cut the sheet into 3 rows of 9 equal-size squares, each about 4 x 4 inches. If you purchased the sheets already cut to 4 x 4, just remove the paper, and they are ready for the next step.

3. Place 2 teaspoons of one of the fillings (cheese or eggplant) in the center of each dough square. Fold the dough squares in half on the diagonal, making a triangle.

4. Using your thumb, press down firmly on the dough, and continue to press the outer, open edge of the triangle to seal. You can also crimp the edges with the tines of a fork to help seal. Make sure the edges are well sealed, so the filling doesn't spill out while baking.

5. Place the sealed burekas on a baking sheet lined with parchment paper, and repeat steps 2, 3, and 4 until the baking sheet is full. Leave 1 to 2 inches between burekas, so they don't stick together.

6. If planning to freeze the burekas, skip to instructions below. Otherwise, whisk together the egg whites and 2 teaspoons cool water in a small bowl. Use a pastry brush to brush a light layer of the egg wash on the surface of each bureka, and then sprinkle the burekas with sesame seeds.

7. Bake the burekas until light golden brown, about 15 to 20 minutes.

8. Serve warm or store in a sealed container or zip-top bag.

Vegetables, Side Dishes, & Super Starters

DEBRIANNA'S

BRING ON THE BLISS OAT RISOTTO

SERVES 4

5 dried shiitake mushrooms

4 to 5 cups chicken or roasted vegetable stock

4 tablespoons unsalted butter

1 leek, halved lengthwise and thinly sliced crosswise (discard the dark green top)

1 shallot, thinly sliced

1 cup chopped fennel

8 ounces cremini mushrooms, sliced

1 cup steel-cut oats

Freshly ground white pepper, to taste

1½ cups grated cheese (aged Gouda or Merlot BellaVitano or Pecorino Toscano is excellent)

Salt, to taste

1. In a small bowl, soak the shiitake mushrooms in warm water for 20 minutes or until soft. Reserve the soaking water and add to the stock; then thinly slice the mushrooms. Remove their stems if they are too hard.

2. In a large saucepan, melt 2 tablespoons butter. Add the leek, shallot, and fennel, and cook over medium heat, stirring occasionally, until softened and translucent, about 5 minutes. Add the cremini mushrooms, and cook until they release their water and become dry.

3. Add the remaining butter, and stir in the oats and sliced shiitake mushrooms. Cook for 1 minute.

4. Add 1 cup of the stock mixed with the mushroom water, and simmer over medium heat, stirring frequently, until the stock is nearly absorbed. Continue cooking the oats, adding 1 cup of stock at a time and cooking until the liquid is nearly absorbed between additions. The risotto is done when the oats are chewy to tender and form a thick sauce, after approximately 25 to 30 minutes.

5. Season with white pepper. Stir in 1 cup of the cheese, and then taste for salt level and add more salt if needed. Sprinkle with the remaining cheese and then serve.

TIP: If you have leftover roasted chicken, you can shred it and add it in step 5.

"C'mon, it's nearly closing time," my friend Susan whispers in the middle of my living room, as if someone in authority might hear us. "Okay," I say, skeptical of the prospects. "Let's get there right at eight so we have the best choice. Last time I got beautiful rainbow chard."

Somehow Susan struck up a friendship with the produce manager at our local natural foods market. He told her at the end of the evening shift the amount of produce they tossed was appalling. And that was the beginning of our pseudo dumpster diving, before anyone called it that.

We arrive at the back door to the market. It's dark outside, and our anticipation is growing.

"I hope we can get some of those giant artichokes. They were too expensive, so I didn't buy them yesterday," I tell Susan in the hushed tones that I have adopted from her.

We are hopping slightly up and down, shifting our weight from foot to foot in the fall chill, waiting for the produce manager to appear.

The door bursts open. "Here ya go, ladies," he says in a muffled voice from behind the huge mound of cardboard crates he is carrying. We run to try and help him. We have struck gold! Cardboard boxes overflowing with day-old carrots and cauliflower, onions, and almost wilted greens. We carry what we can in huge crates to Susan's car and then come back for more, giggling like schoolgirls at the bounty.

"Okay, ladies. See you next week!"

We thank him profusely, astounded by our good fortune. We did this for the entire fall until our luck ran out and the manager was given the mandate that he had to throw all the produce in the dumpster and pour bleach on the (still usable) vegetables so no one would take them and "get sick." It was disappointing—but that time of bounty was a joy.

Susan and I made soups, stews, and casseroles, feeding our neighbors and friends. We stocked our freezers and cupboards with canned green beans and roasted tomatoes. I taught her the tricks I knew to make soup stock from the ends of vegetables and leftover roasted chicken bones. We used every bit of the throwaways.

Our only freezers were the ones at the top third of the refrigerator, and it was then that I swore I would someday own a separate one. Now that I do, my freezer has become somewhat infamous, not only on Corona Kitchen but to everyone I know—it is a place where mysteries are made and solved.

In my home today, we have a big refrigerator, a small refrigerator, and a freezer. I love the way they hum. For me it is a reassuring sound. The freezer is my imagination box, and having one makes me feel wealthy. As I peruse my freezer, stocked with everything from Moink meats to unusual flours and grains to vegetables from the summer garden, I look for inspiration. My eyes land on the steel-cut oats. I recall teaching Susan how to use oats for more than just breakfast. I love to use oats in place of rice, and we made a superb oat risotto with our haul of asparagus. In the spirit of those times of bounty, when joy was found in unexpected places, here is that magic.

LISA'S

BROKEN HEART HEALING SAVORY CRANBERRY CHUTNEY

MAKES ENOUGH TO FILL A QUART-SIZE MASON JAR
(ENOUGH FOR DINNER FOR 4 PLUS LEFTOVERS)

2 cups organic apple
cider vinegar

Two (12-ounce) bags organic
cranberries

1½ cups brown sugar

2 garlic cloves

1 shallot, minced

2 teaspoons ground cinnamon

1 teaspoon freshly
grated nutmeg

Zest and juice of
1 medium orange

Zest and juice of 1 Meyer lemon

2 teaspoons Angostura bitters

1 teaspoon Worcestershire sauce

2 tablespoons honey

2 tablespoons red chile
powder or ½ jalapeño,
seeded and minced

2 apples, peeled and diced into
½-inch cubes

2 tablespoons cognac, brandy,
or orange liqueur

2 tablespoons cornstarch

2 cipollini onions, peeled

2 tablespoons unsalted butter
(for caramelizing)

1 teaspoon sugar
(for caramelizing)

2 cups raisins, dried
cherries, or prunes

1½ cups pecans, walnuts,
or pine nuts, roasted

Juice of 1 lime

½ cup roasted pure green chile
roast (such as Hatch Green
Chile Roast)

1 teaspoon mustard powder

2 teaspoons sea salt

1. Pour the apple cider vinegar and cranberries into a saucepan, and bring to a boil. Cook for approximately 5 minutes or until you hear all the cranberries pop. Stir continuously to avoid burning the cranberries. Reduce heat to a simmer, and add the brown sugar. Cook another 5 minutes.

2. On the lowest heat, add the garlic, pressing each clove, and the shallot, spices, citrus zests and juices, bitters, Worcestershire sauce, honey, chile powder, apples, and cognac. Stir in the cornstarch until it is fully dissolved and the chutney thickens—another 5 minutes.

3. In a separate pan, caramelize the onions by sautéing them in 2 tablespoons butter and 1 teaspoon sugar over medium-low heat until they become translucent and slightly brown, about 10 minutes, and then add them to the chutney. Turn off the heat, and then add the raisins and nuts and stir.

4. Leave the pan on the stove to cool. After a couple of hours, transfer the chutney to a serving dish, and refrigerate until ready to serve. Or, better yet, make up to 5 days in advance and store in an airtight containers. The flavors are even more marvelous if you make it ahead of time.

TIP: This chutney is so good, you'll never eat cranberry sauce from a can again. You can eat it as is, digging in with a spoon; or mix it with regular mayo and put it on sandwiches; or even put it on cream cheese and crackers. I have made this chutney recipe for about thirty-five years, and it has the power to save a dry turkey or completely enhance a delicious one, and it has even helped a small bit to heal from the loss of a loved one.

My grandfather passed away on November 14, 1988. It was the first semester of my senior year at Bowdoin College. My sister Hollie, who went to American University in DC, and I flew home together, to go to his funeral in California, and it was one of the most emotionally draining times of my life. The pain of the loss is really inexplicable.

When I arrived back at school, I remained on campus for Thanksgiving and invited Hollie to stay with me, and we decided to cook together to somehow cope with the grief. After all of my roommates left for home for the holiday, we had the house to ourselves. It was a beautiful old house in Brunswick, Maine, with classic Federalist architecture and a tiny kitchen. So we bought a decent-size turkey and made Nana's famous stuffing, my chutney and sauerkraut, as well as all of the other family favorites. When we finally finished, I think we had enough food for ten people—and it was just the two of us. I packed up all the leftover food after Hollie left, and my roommates got to enjoy it when they returned.

I was so grateful to be with Hollie for Thanksgiving that year. There's a picture of us toasting Dida, who would have liked to have seen me graduate in person six months later. My uncle told me that the last thing Dida said before he died was "But wait, I can't die now. I have to go to Lisa's college graduation." I was the first grandchild to go to college, and it meant so much to him. Dida was an incredible human being—they don't make them like him anymore. He truly lived for his family, and when you were in his presence he made you feel like you could do anything. Joe Biden reminds me a lot of him. Initially, Biden wasn't my first choice for president, but now I'm thinking that somehow the universe knew what the United States needed at an unprecedentedly challenging time and gave it to us: a smart, caring, compassionate, decent, fair, empathetic, selfless, loving, hilarious, and sometimes cringeworthy grandpa. I know the absolute comfort of having someone like that in your life, because I had one too, a grandfather who was the best.

Flash-forward to many years later, and Hollie is pregnant with her first son, Jack. It is Thanksgiving, which has always been one of my favorite holidays. She and my brother-in-law Orion were living in LA at the time, and our family was going to meet at their house for the holiday. Hollie was about ready to give birth, but she still got up early and cooked all morning for the family. Sure enough, however, after we all showed up and while we were admiring how all the food was cooked and the table looked beautiful, Hollie's water broke. She and Orion jumped in the car and drove to the hospital for the birth, while the rest of us were in their house, just looking at each other and the food. I could tell we were all thinking the same thing: *Well, the food's just sitting here getting cold, and it's going to be a long wait until the baby is born, so we might as well eat it.* In typical Croatian fashion, we did not wait for them and had Thanksgiving without them! You snooze, you lose! We felt a *little* guilty, but we remedied that by toasting them many, many times, and plus, the food was absolutely delicious. We didn't want to waste it, right? The best part of it all was that I became an aunt for the first time with my nephew Jack. He was a delightful baby who has grown into an outstanding young man. And Hollie and Orion were so happy with the baby's safe arrival that they did not hold it against us that we ate their marvelous dinner, thank God.

Hollie and Lisa toasting Dida.

DEBRIANNA'S

How to Save Face *Patatas Bravas* with Two Aioli

SERVES 2 TO 4

2 large russet potatoes, cut into 1-inch chunks

2 tablespoons salt

1 tablespoon white vinegar

2 egg yolks

2 teaspoons freshly squeezed lemon juice

2 large garlic cloves, finely minced

½ cup safflower oil

½ cup and 2 tablespoons olive oil

½ teaspoon hot smoked paprika

1 teaspoon Dijon mustard

¼ cup chopped fresh parsley or scallions for finishing

1. Preheat oven to 450°F.

2. Place the potatoes in a pot, and cover with water. Add the salt and white vinegar, and cook until the potatoes are just tender. Watch them, because it won't take long, about 5 minutes. Strain well and set aside.

3. Combine the egg yolks, lemon juice, garlic, and 1 teaspoon water in a small food processor or by hand with a whisk. Add the safflower oil in a steady, very slow stream to thicken. Remove the mixture from the food processor, and add ½ cup olive oil in a steady stream as you whisk by hand—the olive oil can get bitter if added in the processor.

4. Separate the mixture into 2 bowls, and whisk the paprika into 1 and the mustard into the other. These are your sauces.

5. Toss the potatoes with the 2 tablespoons olive oil, and place on a baking sheet with space between the pieces. Bake 10 to 15 minutes, and then flip the potatoes to brown on both sides. Continue to bake until brown and toasty, another 10 to 15 minutes depending on the size of the potato chunks.

6. Serve the potatoes topped with parsley in a bowl, and serve the sauces in smaller bowls for dipping.

"Oh yeah! Deb's cooking!" My college roommates were thrilled.

"Yup. I am making my baby sister's favorite, chicken and dumplings, as soon as I get back from class."

Everyone in our dorm house was excited. The guys who lived next door to our beach house had taken a shine to both me and my roommate. Once a week, we'd all put money in a pot, and I would cook something for everyone. Coming from a poor family with many kids, I grew up cooking on a shoestring budget and was skilled at making a dollar stretch in the kitchen.

This once-a-week dinner get-together gave me and my roommate, also named Deb, a break from our usual weekly routine of grits, biscuits, and home fries. She, the southerner, was a biscuit lover, while I was a southern transplant who loved grits. We both adored home fries, or potatoes in any form.

"Look—it's Mr. Bill!" we squealed. We'd go nuts and make shapes out of the biscuit dough to add variety to our otherwise pauper budget.

"Oh my God, that smells amazing," hummed Duncan, the younger of our neighbor boys, inhaling the smell of the chicken in the pot while his golden retriever circled his legs. "I cannot wait. I'll be here by six, after practice."

I was excited to share this dinner with all of them, changing our regular fare of flour and water biscuits into tender dumplings— basically the same inexpensive ingredients but moved into a new sphere of sweetness under a tender chicken gravy.

I had gotten started a little late because of my class, and they'd wandered in soon after, cracking the lid, checking the pot. "Not 'til six—put the lid down!" I yelled from my room, hearing the metal clanging on the stove. "*Six!*"

I had bought the cheapest large chicken I could find at the local Piggly Wiggly, the only grocery store on the island of Wrightsville Beach. Most of America had not "discovered" the University of North Carolina Wilmington, and the town off the coast was still quaint and cheap, with white sandy beaches that stretched for miles. I was going to college on the beach, and I was getting to cook. I was in heaven. I felt the sting of running away from home and leaving all my sisters a little less with a pot of chicken in front of me and a house full of warmth and joy. On this occasion, I'd put the chicken in the pot as soon as I got home, remembering how my mom would simmer it for hours. I thought I had better set it to boil for it to be ready on time.

At the tender age of nineteen, I hadn't yet been told why the whole low-and-slow cooking thing for a chicken was important, but I definitely knew my way around flour. While the chicken was boiling away, I formed the dumpling mix using milk and real butter.

"It's five forty-five . . . " Bruce, the older neighbor boy, said with a whistle as he and his golden retriever wandered through the kitchen. He thwacked me on the butt with a dish towel.

"Yup. And that's not six," I said with a smirk, a flour cloud puffing around me. I couldn't help thinking I should have started earlier, since the chicken was still boiling. I dropped the sticky dumpling dough in balls one by one and then covered them with the stainless-steel lid.

When we sat down to eat, I revealed the platter of dumplings in a nice mound with carrots surrounding them and the chicken. The plate glistened in the center of the table. But as I stuck a fork into the chicken, it literally bounced out.

No one had ever told me about overboiling chickens. No one.

We all looked at one another as if we'd seen a ghost. I picked up the fork and tried to pierce the skin again—and *boink!* Again the fork bounced out, and this time it fell onto the floor beside the golden dog, who stared curiously at it. Everyone burst out laughing. I had no idea that the chicken needed to simmer, not boil. As we grabbed for the dumplings, all I could think was that I should have made potatoes and grits.

Thinking back to my college food adventures, I tell this story so that you don't make the same mistakes I did. Just make these *patatas bravas*. You'll thank me.

LISA'S

(GF)

IN A WORLD THAT CONSTANTLY DISAPPOINTS, THESE CRISPY CARAMELIZED BRUSSELS SPROUTS WITH PANCETTA AND WALNUTS NEVER WILL

SERVES 8

BALSAMIC HONEY GLAZE

1½ cups balsamic vinegar

⅓ cup honey

BRUSSELS SPROUTS

Salted butter for greasing the pan

50 small organic brussels sprouts, ends removed and sliced lengthwise, including leaves that fall

5 bacon strips, chopped into 1-inch pieces (I usually use pancetta)

3 garlic cloves, minced

1 small shallot, thinly sliced into matchsticks (julienned)

10 cranks freshly ground black pepper

Dash red pepper flakes

½ teaspoon Dijon mustard

1 teaspoon Worcestershire sauce

¼ cup olive oil

3 teaspoons sea salt, and more for finishing

1 cup halved walnuts (optional)

TIP: You can make a glaze with brown sugar in place of the honey—or you can make Debrianna's balsamic glaze on page 124.

TO MAKE THE BALSAMIC HONEY GLAZE

1. In a small saucepan set over medium-high heat, combine the balsamic vinegar and honey and bring to a boil, stirring constantly; then immediately lower the temperature and simmer until the liquid is reduced by at least half and the glaze coats the back of a spoon. This will take about 25 minutes.

2. Remove the glaze from the heat, and let cool. I ended up with about ¾ cup glaze, which is more than you need for this dish, but you can refrigerate it in a jar for future use.

TO MAKE THE BRUSSELS SPROUTS

1. Preheat oven to 425°F, and then grease a large roasting pan with salted butter.

2. In a large bowl, add all ingredients except the walnuts and a sprinkle of sea salt. Stir gently to incorporate.

3. Empty the contents of the bowl into the roasting pan and spread out the brussels sprouts, making sure their flat sides are down, as you want them to brown. Add the walnuts to the mix, and sprinkle with the reserved sea salt.

4. Roast the brussels sprouts in the oven for approximately 25 minutes. Halfway through, check to make sure the brussels sprouts are browning. Flip the mixture to make sure everything is roasted.

5. After the brussels sprouts are cooked and crispy, remove them from the oven. Drizzle some of the cooled balsamic honey glaze on them (a little goes a long way) while they're in the roasting pan. Use a spatula to mix, and then put them back in the oven for 2 or 3 minutes. Remove from the oven and serve as a side dish.

This is a story of my transgender son. He was born on September 11, 2002. One can look at it as a curse or a blessing that he came into the world on the one-year anniversary of a tragic day, and one can make a similar choice in how they view his entering the world in the body of one gender but with the heart and mind of another.

It was one of the best days of my life when my firstborn arrived. Complicated and questioning, whip smart and loyal to a fault, a witty humorist and trusted groundbreaker, avid reader and writer, solemn singer, visual artist, and path forger, he is also opinionated and political, an Earth warrior, and an animal lover. And he is so very brave with so much courage, more than most will ever possess, in his determination to be no one but himself. I love you with all my heart, R.A.S.

When Ronan was born, I blamed myself for not being able to give birth faster and have him take his first breaths on the tenth instead of the eleventh of September. But having brought him into the world on this day, I'll tell you a story that I have told him many times.

All I could think of while resting in the recovery room, alone with this beautiful, perfect baby in a bassinet next to me, was, my God, I'm going to have to explain 9/11 to this innocent creature someday. It was still so fresh in everyone's minds, and as a country we were all still reeling from it, only a year after it occurred. I closed my eyes, and his entire life flashed before me. How would being born on this day color his existence? Someday some kid is going to get to him at school before I can and tell him that his birthday rests on a day where not only the nation, but the world, mourns events of extreme tragedy and pain. It seemed so unfair, but as all things present themselves, we have a choice in the matter, and it's all in our perspective of how we want to see it. I didn't want to think about it—my little Virgo child was so new to planet Earth.

But then to my astonishment, I looked up at the hospital room's dry-erase board and saw that the schedule that had been on it the night before had been erased and replaced with a happy birthday message and a drawing of the Earth being held by loving hands.

Ronan stirred in his little swaddling blankets, so I picked him up and walked around a bit and then out into the hallway of Cedar Sinai Hospital in LA, where I found myself in front of the nursery where all the newborn babies were resting after their births in the last twenty-four hours. I noticed the nurses had been busy. There was a paper banner above the nursery that read "May these be the peace babies, born on this special day, and may they go out into the world and make it a better place." I burst into tears from the thoughtful and conscientious gesture of those loving neonatal nurses—complete strangers who reaffirmed my belief in human kindness. I stood there in awe, my baby restful and snuggling on my shoulder. He took a deep breath with his new lungs and sighed. I stood there for a while, rubbing his back, reading the banner over and over, and sending blessings out to all the other babies and their families with my mind, saying a silent prayer for the words on the banner to come true.

Having a child born on 9/11 definitely affected me. After I left the hospital, I decided to never again feel bad about it; instead, I let it fuel me in teaching Ronan and his younger brother about the world, being truthful and open to discussion and debate about why things happen the way they do and, most of all, about the importance of being an active and engaged member of society and working to better it. I'm proud to report these two outspoken Gen Z souls have a lot to say and that their intentions are marked by grace, wit, and concern for the well-being of all humans.

Lisa and her son, Ronan.

LISA'S

TIME TO LET IT GO THREE-MUSHROOM RISOTTO

(V) (GF)

SERVES 6 AS A MAIN COURSE OR 8 AS A SIDE DISH

1 medium onion or shallot, peeled and roughly chopped

3 celery stalks, roughly chopped

2 tablespoons higher-quality olive oil

2 cups arborio rice

1 bottle dry white wine (I used a combination of gewürztraminer and marsala)

Sea salt, to taste

Freshly ground black pepper, to taste

Juice of 1 lemon

½ cup (1 stick) unsalted butter

1 quart chicken or vegetable stock

3 handfuls finely sliced tender mushrooms (I used a combination of oyster, alba, and lion's mane—this dish is best with a variety of mushrooms. Use what you like!)

¼ cup roughly chopped fresh parsley, and more for finishing

¼ teaspoon (around 7 drops) white truffle oil, and more for finishing

¾ cup freshly grated black truffle cheese

¾ cup freshly grated Parmesan, and more for finishing

1. In a large skillet or stockpot, sauté the onion and celery with the olive oil over medium heat.

2. As soon as they are translucent, add the rice, wine, sea salt, and pepper, and lower the heat to low. Stir, and as you stir, wait for each liquid to absorb; then alternate adding in the lemon juice, butter, and stock in small amounts until all have been fully used and the risotto is creamy and cooked al dente (approximately 45 minutes—taste the rice; when it is cooked, it's ready).

3. Ten minutes before the rice is fully cooked, add the mushrooms and parsley. Turn off the heat once the rice is fully cooked.

4. Add the truffle oil and cheeses.

5. Garnish with Parmesan, parsley, and a drizzle of truffle oil prior to serving.

TIP: You will be stirring constantly the entire time the risotto is cooking, so prepare yourself for quite an arm workout.

I'm Gonna Be Somebody Someday Stuffed Heirloom Tomatoes with Cashews and Herbs

SERVES 2

4 heirloom organic tomatoes

1 teaspoon sea salt, and more for finishing

½ teaspoon freshly ground black pepper, and more for finishing

1 small onion, peeled and finely chopped

4 garlic cloves, finely chopped

¼ cup olive oil, and more for drizzling

½ teaspoon ground cayenne pepper

7 cremini mushrooms, sliced

1½ cups cooked basmati rice

½ cup vegetable or mushroom broth

1 packed cup roughly chopped baby kale, spinach, and Swiss chard blend

½ cup cherry tomatoes, quartered

½ cup almonds slivers, roasted

½ cup canned chickpeas

7 fresh basil leaves, torn, and more for finishing

1. Slice the tops off the heirloom tomatoes, and carve out the insides (like baby jack-o'-lanterns), setting aside the outsides and tops.

2. Season tomato insides with salt and pepper.

3. In a pot over medium heat, sauté the tomato insides with the onion, garlic, and olive oil. Add the cayenne and mushrooms, and continue sautéing for 2 minutes; then add the cooked rice and broth.

4. Turn the heat down to a simmer, cover, and cook until there is no more liquid, about 30 minutes. Then add the greens, cherry tomatoes, almonds, chickpeas, and basil. Incorporate and mix well.

5. Preheat oven to 400°F.

6. Fill in the hollowed-out heirloom tomatoes with the stuffing. Place the stuffed tomatoes on a baking dish, and put their tops back on. Drizzle with olive oil and bake for 30 minutes.

7. Finish with chopped basil, sea salt, and pepper prior to serving.

TIP: For a meat version, add ½ pound ground seasoned lamb or beef or chopped spicy Italian sausage, and increase the number of heirloom tomatoes to 8. You can also tweak this recipe by substituting a different grain for the rice, like quinoa or farro.

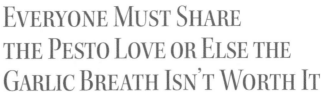

Everyone Must Share the Pesto Love or Else the Garlic Breath Isn't Worth It

SERVES 4

⅓ cup high-quality olive oil

2 garlic cloves, chopped

1 teaspoon sea salt

½ teaspoon ground cayenne pepper

½ teaspoon freshly ground black pepper

Zest of ½ lemon

½ cup pine nuts

½ cup freshly grated pecorino cheese

4 small bunches (4 loosely packed cups) fresh basil leaves

4 tablespoons unsalted butter

1 teaspoon Chimayo red chile powder

1. Combine all ingredients in a food processor or blender, or use a mortar and pestle (arm workout alert!). Pulse until the pesto takes shape and its texture starts to resemble coarse sand.

2. Stop and do a taste test to see if any additional flavor is needed, adding it if so, and then pulse 5 to 10 more times.

3. Serve immediately on pasta, polenta, bread, pizza, crackers—whatever sounds good—or freeze. My Nana always had pesto in her freezer from her overabundance of garden basil—utilizing those beloved reusable Cool Whip containers. And pesto lasts a long time! Once, while on a deep-dive freezer excavation at Nana's, I believe we found a Cool Whip container with a ten-year-old date on it, and you know what? We put that pesto on pasta and ate it all.

When I was a little girl, it became an accepted notion in our family that Nana would most likely live forever. Perhaps we thought that if you repeat something often enough you can will it into being. Amazingly, she lived to her ninety-ninth year. Imagine how much one can see and experience in a century. She was a night owl, and I definitely inherited this. I used to love to stay up late with her and have a nice, long storytelling session about the days before modern conveniences. For the last thirty-five years or so, her schedule included watching *Jeopardy!* before or while making dinner, then getting pulled into a movie or dramatic TV series, and she would be knitting an afghan the entire time—she didn't even have to look at her knitting needles. Multitasking wasn't ever part of her vocabulary; it was just what one did to maximize the number of things one could accomplish in a day. After the movie or show, she might have a little snack, like her favorite chocolate chip ice cream, and then she would get a second wind at, like, 11:00 p.m. and want to do a project or talk.

The documentarian in me was so curious about the past and would ask quite frequently what it was like when the world went from radio to television, or what it was like the first time she saw a man walk on the moon. She loved inventions and technology, and yet the advent of the internet and the concept of having us all on a video chat was something straight out of *Star Trek*. The thing she loved the most was the invention of polyester or any kind of wrinkle-free fabric. She had grown up with all-natural fabrics in the early part of the twentieth century, and ironing was, well, serious work and pretty much perpetual hard labor left to the women in the family. And you have to understand ironing was a love-hate for a Virgo such as Nana. She actually felt better when things were folded neatly and the cotton was clean and starched, but it was also a chore and took time away from going places or completing other, more important tasks of the day. I would observe her exhale as the laundry stacks were completed. I would see her relax at the assessment of a well-ironed dress shirt or conversely the small anguish that would erupt for a missed spot under a pleat of a skirt until it was remedied. And so it went. Iron the sheets, iron the shirts, the tablecloths, the napkins, the skirts, the pillowcases. As technologies advanced and nylon, rayon, and polyester came into the mainstream (and not just as a cheap substitution for silk), everything changed. That reassurance put an extra slice of happiness in her step when we would be shopping for a dress at a department store and the deciding factor in the purchase was "And you know, you wouldn't have to iron this one."

In her senior citizen years (which for her started when she was about twenty years past sixty-five), she shopped weekly with her friends at the discount stores and would buy countless black or navy synthetic blouses. I think they made her feel free. The other thing she really appreciated was the microwave to warm up leftovers. It gave her the biggest thrill every time she turned it on. She couldn't believe this box was able to heat up her lasagna in two minutes on the same plate she would eat from no less! It was a miracle of biblical proportions! My God, if she had known about frozen phyllo dough, she would have made strudel every weekend and bought an additional freezer to house boxes of it. It boggles the mind to think of the countless hours she spent rolling dough in her lifetime.

One of her other favorite things was Cool Whip—"Hey, did you know you can open this up and there is *zero* whipping involved?" When Nana passed away and the excavation of her kitchen cabinets began, we discovered she recycled everything you can imagine, never wasting a single reusable item. We must have found at least 150 cleaned and disinfected Cool Whip containers, stacked evenly and ready to use for leftovers. She also saved twisty ties, rubber bands, wrapping paper, ribbons, bows, and every plastic or paper bag she ever came in contact with, folded military style to maximize the space.

Nana would have been a great department head or director of operations for any branch of government or private sector company that required organizing information or tangible goods. The Depression-era frugality and zero-waste mentality never left her. She would not be the one to tell you we had to go without. There was always a solution, a way to make it work and save the situation. The woman was a marvel.

Nana, Great-Grandma Rakela, and Big Dida Tony getting ready to stomp grapes.

DEBRIANNA'S

You Need These Preserved Lemons, Like a Grateful Siciliana

MAKES A 1-QUART MASON JAR FULL OF PRESERVED LEMONS

Approximately 5 medium lemons (or however many can fit in your jar)

Kosher salt (enough to fill the entire jar)

Freshly squeezed lemon juice (optional, if more is needed to submerge lemons)

1. Quarter the lemons from the top to within ½ inch of the bottom, but do not cut all the way through. Sprinkle salt on the exposed flesh; then reshape to whole lemon shape.

2. Place 1 tablespoon salt in the bottom of a mason jar. Pack in the lemons and push them down, adding more salt, and keep layering. Press the lemons down to release their juices and to make room for the remaining lemons. If the juice released from the squashed fruit does not cover them, add only freshly squeezed lemon juice; do not use chemically produced lemon juice or water.

3. Leave ½ inch of open space above the juice, and then seal.

4. Let the lemons ripen in a warm place for 30 days, shaking the jar each day to distribute the salt and juice.

5. To use, rinse the lemons, as needed, under running water, removing and discarding the pulp if desired (I usually don't). There is no need to refrigerate after opening. Preserved lemons will keep for up to 1 year, and the pickling juice can be used 2 or 3 times over the course of a year.

TIP: According to the late food writer Michael Field, the best way to extract the maximum amount of juice from a lemon is to boil it in water for 2 or 3 minutes and allow it to cool before squeezing. Also, if you want to add spices to this, do so in step 3. I prefer leaving it pure, but 1 cinnamon stick, 2 star anises, and 5 whole cloves create a nice Middle Eastern flavor.

BUILD BRIDGES NOT WALLS GRILLED MEXICAN STREET FOOD CORN

(V) (GF)

SERVES 4

4 ears corn with husks

¼ cup mayonnaise

¼ cup full-fat sour cream or yogurt

¼ teaspoon chipotle powder

¼ teaspoon smoked paprika

1 teaspoon lime zest

Juice of ½ lime, and more for finishing

¼ cup crumbled feta

¼ cup freshly grated hard goat cheese or Parmesan

1 garlic clove

Chopped fresh parsley or cilantro for finishing

Freshly ground black pepper for finishing

Sea salt for finishing

1. Pull back the husks of corn, removing as much of the silk as possible but maintaining the husks. Soak the husks in a bowl of water with string you will use as ties for about 10 minutes.

2. While the husks and string are soaking, in a separate bowl mix the mayonnaise, sour cream, chipotle powder, smoked paprika, lime zest, and lime juice together.

3. Mix the cheeses in a separate flat bowl and set aside.

4. When ready to grill the corn, rub the corn ears with the garlic clove, pull up the husks, and use the wet string to tie the ends closed. Grill until the corn kernels start to brown.

5. Remove the husks, and paint the mayonnaise mixture on the corn; then roll the corn in the cheese mix to coat.

6. Finish with parsley, ground pepper, and sea salt, to taste, and a squeeze of lime juice prior to serving.

TIP: If you don't want to grill, you can blanche the corn for 3 to 4 minutes in boiling water and then " roast" it without the husks in a cast-iron pan on the stovetop.

My Uncle Gene was so much fun as a teenager. He was tall and slender with dark hair parted on the side and very neatly placed against his head. He always wore trousers with a belt and button-down shirt, sometimes a cardigan, making him look more like a smaller version of my grandpa than a teenager. He painted and played games with us and never seemed to mind that we were six and seven years old. He didn't seem to have any friends. I never heard him talk much about school, although the high school was just down the dirt lane that curled down the side of the stone house that my grandpa built in their small town in Connecticut. None of us kids knew then what special needs were. When we'd ask why Gene seemed different, my mom simply said Gene was a forceps baby. He was stuck and had to be pulled out. That's all she ever said. She never mentioned that they'd used harsh metal clamps. My grandmother never said anything at all about her youngest son. At seven, all I knew was that he was always there in the house, ready to play with us.

With pieces shaped like little castles and gray battleships, Stratego was my favorite game to play with Uncle Gene. It seemed like a pared-down version of chess. The goal was to capture the opposition's big ship and take the crown. You have to make a plan and try to execute it while being nimble, as the game changes with the opposition. I loved the planning and spontaneity of figuring out, on the spot and under pressure, how to adapt my response. It never occurred to me that my wins against my uncle could have been due to his condition. I just loved being with him.

My grandpa would often cook for us. Sometimes he'd make a fire in the fireplace and we'd roast hot dogs or marshmallows in the living room. The small but comfortable house filled with the scent of wood and sugar. Other times, we'd roast corn on the cob, putting the cobs on long metal skewers and then holding them carefully in the fire until the kernels became golden brown and then slathering them with butter and salt. Occasionally, Gramp would fry little fish he'd caught called smelts. They were crispy and salty and you would eat the whole fish, bones and all—and as with potato chips, you couldn't stop. My grandma would put out a big wooden bowl filled to the brim with the smelts, toasty brown and hot. We'd each get our own bowl and napkin and serve ourselves the crispy fishes as we gathered around the living room to watch Mitch Miller and The Gang on *Sing Along with Mitch* and follow the bouncing ball as we sang along. I can still sing any Mitch Miller song at the drop of a dime: "*That's where my money goes, to buy my baby clothes. I buy her everything to keep her in style, well, well, well . . .*"

Those nights and games of Stratego provided a life lesson that keeps on giving. With the pandemic, I felt that if I could think of it like a game of battleship, I could find fun in it—a challenge instead of distress. I have my Uncle Gene and my grandparents to thank for this. My Grilled Mexican Street Food Corn is an elevated version of our fireplace corn. C'mon, sing along with Mitch and follow the bouncing ball—"*She's worth her weight in gold, my lovely laaady. Say, boys, that's where my money goes, goes, goes . . .*"

Baby Debrianna, Uncle Gene,
Grandma Florence, and Grandpa Pep.

DEBRIANNA'S

NEVER HAVE YOU EVER FRIED GREEN TOMATOES

SERVES 2 TO 3

½ teaspoon freshly squeezed lemon juice

½ cup whole milk

½ cup all-purpose flour

½ cup cornmeal

1 teaspoon salt, and more to taste

½ teaspoon freshly ground black pepper

1 large egg, lightly beaten

3 medium green tomatoes, cut into ⅓-inch slices

Grape-seed oil or other high-temperature cooking oil

1. Combine the lemon juice and milk, and then set the mixture aside for 5 minutes.

2. In a shallow bowl or pan, combine ¼ cup all-purpose flour with the cornmeal, salt, and pepper.

3. Combine the egg with the lemon juice and milk.

4. Dredge the tomato slices in the remaining ¼ cup flour, dip them into the egg mixture, and then dredge them in the corn-meal mixture.

5. Pour the grape-seed oil to a depth of ¼ to ½ inch in a large cast-iron skillet, and heat to 375°F. Drop the tomatoes in batches into the hot oil, and cook 2 minutes on each side or until golden.

6. Place the hot tomatoes on paper towels on a rack and sprinkle them with salt.

LISA'S

GRANDMA PAPATONE'S SAUERKRAUT AND SPICY SAUSAGE CROATIAN STANDBY

SERVES 6 WITH LEFTOVERS

3 spareribs or short ribs on the bone

½ cup olive oil

2 large onions, peeled and chopped

2 (24-ounce) jars sauerkraut

4 garlic cloves, pressed

1 teaspoon freshly grated nutmeg

2 teaspoons sea salt

1 teaspoon freshly ground black pepper

1 tablespoon Chimayo red chile powder

2 bay leaves

½ teaspoon ground cayenne pepper

1 handful fresh parsley, chopped, or 3 teaspoons dried parsley

1 cup marsala, sherry, or dry white wine

2 cups chicken stock

6 spicy Italian pork sausages (or lamb, chicken, or beef)

1. In a large pot set over medium heat, lightly brown the spareribs in olive oil and then add the onions.

2. Empty the sauerkraut into a large strainer and rinse thoroughly, squeezing out excess water. Then add the sauerkraut to the sautéed meat and onions followed by the garlic. Stir well.

3. Add the nutmeg, sea salt, pepper, chile powder, bay leaves, and cayenne pepper, and then mix in the parsley, marsala, and chicken stock.

4. Cover and cook slowly on a low simmer for at least 2 hours. (In my family we put a turkey in and then let it simmer for 4 to 6 hours; the longer it cooks the better it tastes, but you may have to add more chicken stock if you leave it this long.) Stir every 15 minutes, and be careful not to let the sauerkraut burn. In the last 30 minutes, add the sausages. The spareribs will separate from the bone, and you can incorporate the meat into the sauce.

5. When cooked, cut the sausages into fourths and serve.

TIP: Kraut leftovers get better the longer they sit. Even after five days, incredible flavors. If it lasts that long.

My maternal great-grandmother, Mary Pleše Papatone, the mother of my grandfather Dida, is credited with creating this signature dish, which is one of the defining elements of our special holiday family dinners as Croatian Americans. Grandma Papatone had been raised on the mainland in the hills of Lika, and her cooking had a lot of Slovenian and Austrian influences. Her family would pickle their garden harvests to preserve food for the winter and make their own cheeses, and her recipes also included lots of delicious roasted lamb and beef dishes because her family owned cows. The way our people cooked back then reflected the particular region's topography and whether or not you could raise livestock. There were no grocery stores. You had a garden and a farm.

I would love one day to make a movie about the journey Grandma took to the US. Mary was part of an arranged marriage—a fifteen-year-old mail-order Croatian bride sent to a Croatian coal miner more than twice her age who had immigrated to the US. She landed first in Utah, at the turn of the century, and then moved on to the harsh realities of living in Montana at the time. She worked hard to survive in the mining communities and became a midwife. The day my grandfather came into the world, she gave birth to him in a barn, *by herself* at seventeen years old, on a cold, snowy December night, biting down on a rope. That, my friends, is the kind of DNA my siblings and I come from! When I had my first child, Nana reminded me of this story, saying, "Don't worry, you'll be okay. Think of what Grandma went through for Dida's birth for God's sake! If she did it under those circumstances, you can do this." She crossed herself at the thought of what Grandma went through.

For many too-difficult-to-get-into reasons, Mary had to leave her situation when my grandfather was very young. And so she went out to California to make her own way. Dida was raised by his Italian stepmother, Maria, and he had a loving family and many half brothers and sisters to have adventures with. Many of the townspeople told him his mother had died, but he never believed them. And since it was a small world back then, he had friends who visited California and returned with word that they had seen his mother! So he got her address and wrote to her. Then when he was on his way to California at age eighteen, as the first of our family to go to college, he vowed he would see his mother and reunite with her. He was determined, and he did reconnect with her. She had remarried, and he befriended her new husband. He found out he had more siblings. He loved them all dearly and forgave Mary for leaving him. She didn't want to see him initially because she felt so bad about abandoning him. I don't know how, but he understood why she left. He knew it was about her survival.

Dida and his mother formed a beautiful bond. He was an old soul, and he took care of her until the day she died. He loved our family fiercely and always supported us, always believed in us. He was capable of monumental forgiveness. He possessed compassion for others and was a true friend to many. And he was so funny, always doing impressions and making us laugh to break up any sorrow. He had experienced enough sorrow in his life, having lived through Montana winters as a boy and been raised by an alcoholic father who worked in the coal mine, not to mention surviving World War II and the Depression. It seemed to me that he went out of his way to appreciate any joy that came into his life, and he was truly blessed because he was so loved. I miss him every day. There is some solace knowing that our grandmother is now with him. Thinking about the two of them together again makes me happy. They were such special people.

Grandma Papatore.

DEBRIANNA'S

FOR THE RECORD, THE UNITED STATES WON THE CIVIL WAR CHEESY GRITS

MAKES ABOUT 4 CUPS

2 cups chicken or vegetable stock

2 cups whole milk

1 teaspoon kosher salt, or more to taste (optional)

Freshly ground black pepper, to taste

1 cup yellow polenta or coarsely ground cornmeal

2 tablespoons unsalted butter

¼ cup goat cheese or ½ cup freshly grated Asiago

1. In a thick-bottomed 2- or 3-quart pan set over high heat, combine the stock and milk and bring to a boil. Add the salt and pepper, and then slowly add the polenta to the boiling mix, whisking to prevent lumps.

2. Reduce the heat and let the mixture sit at a very low simmer, and then add the butter. Continue to whisk the polenta until it starts to thicken. Then cover the pan and let the polenta cook until soft and tender, about 25 minutes. Stir occasionally with a wooden spoon so that the polenta doesn't stick to the bottom of the pan.

3. Add the cheese and stir it into the polenta. Taste and add more salt if necessary.

Stephen visited for the week. He was the son of my mother's second husband, so technically he was only the stepbrother of Lisa, my middle sister, but we all loved him like our own. He spent a week with us every summer after Lisa was born. It always struck me as odd how alike Stephen and Lisa were despite sharing genes from only one parent. They both became doctors, and both were gone by their forty-second birthday—Stephen from AIDS and Lisa from breast cancer . . . but I digress.

Stephen was like a big brother I had once a year for a week and the occasional extra visit. We loved each other and would get into all kinds of mischief, telling stories late into the night, looking at the moon from our beds.

"Do you know how women get pregnant?" he once whispered into the night.

"No, do you?" I whispered back. I looked up to him even though he was only one year older than me, his nine years to my eight.

"Yes," he said confidently, and then nothing else.

"Well, are you going to tell me?" I asked and giggled anxiously, stifling it into the pillow.

"Are you sure you want to know?"

"Yes," I said, lying.

"Well," he said in an excited voice and turned toward me, the blankets ruffling under the moon's glow. "First, the man pulls the woman toward him." He stopped for dramatic effect.

"Yeah, and then what?" I asked, a little more intrigued.

"He kisses her a little, to soften her. Then he takes her leg and lays it over his."

"Yeah?"

"Then he takes a small knife out and makes a small slice in her leg and sticks his penis in it!"

"Oh no! Eww!" I yelled.

He rushed over to my bed and covered my mouth. "Shh!"

"Okay, okay. Eww!" I punched him softly, wondering if it was true. "How do you know that?"

"My friend Frankie told me. I thought you should know too."

"Yeah, well, then I am *never* getting pregnant. No one is cutting my leg," I said defiantly.

"Yeah, I don't want to cut anyone's leg either."

Eight years later, Stephen and I were teens looking at higher education. He was looking at medical schools, and I was hoping for college. His prospects were much more open than mine, as his mom had remarried favorably, to a doctor, after Ken, his alcoholic dad—and, well, his mom wasn't crazy. My mom, Marcelle, on the other hand, had already sabotaged my interview with Wharton, my dream school, claiming she was too sick to drive me there. So now I was secretly applying to colleges, my guidance counselor helping me without Marcelle's knowledge, but that's a different story for another time.

On one of Stephen's visits around this time, he suggested we make a Ouija board.

"Jesus, how are we going to do that?" I asked, looking at him with a smirk. I'd always wanted to play with one, but my mom thought they were creepy.

"C'mon, we can make one on the coffee table. Go get a black crayon and a teacup!"

The twins, my younger sisters, and I were always up for some kind of Stephen adventure. While they got the equipment, Stephen and I cleared the marble coffee table, lifting the heavy marble bust (a central feature of any good Italian family's home) off the center, and then removed the shiny brass ashtrays. No one smoked in our house, and if they did the ashtrays were cleaned and polished immediately, sometimes before the user was finished smoking.

When the twins came back, Stephen took the crayon and started writing the letters out *on the table* in two semicircles.

"Oh my God, Stephen. She'll kill us!" I yelled urgently. I'm the rule follower in the family.

"Don't worry, it will wipe off—it's marble," he said calmly, placing the cup at the bottom of the two circles with the handle facing the letters.

"Put your fingers on the edge of the cup, lightly," he said, facing me and looking into my eyes. "Ask a question."

The question I asked was, of course, about college. It answered: "North Carolina?" I was only applying to Northeast schools, my eyes still set on Wharton, but it ended up coming true two years later.

In Wilmington, North Carolina, at UNCW, I would learn about southern food and the time-honored New Year's Day tradition of collard greens and black-eyed peas, a tradition that I have kept for all these years, the most lasting part of my UNCW education. My Italian version of the dish has evolved over the years. I serve it on cheesy grits (Italian polenta). It's soft and welcoming. There is nothing better than cheesy grits to start off the year, with or without a Ouija board answering questions about what's to come.

LISA'S

Hold Your Family Close Ratatouille

SERVES 4

1 medium eggplant

1½ teaspoons sea salt, and more for lightly covering eggplant and finishing

1 medium onion or 2 small onions, peeled

3 medium heirloom tomatoes

1 orange bell pepper

2 medium zucchini squash

2 medium yellow squash

3 tablespoons high-quality olive oil

3 fresh thyme sprigs, and more for finishing

3 fresh oregano sprigs

½ cup fresh basil, and more for finishing

2 fresh sage sprigs

4 cranks freshly ground black pepper

1 tablespoon Chimayo red chile powder

4 garlic cloves, minced

Olive oil for coating pan

4 tablespoons unsalted butter

1 tablespoon marsala

¼ cup freshly grated Parmesan, and more for finishing

1. Prepare the eggplant by slicing it ¼ inch thick, lightly covering it with sea salt, and letting it rest on paper towels for 10 minutes to decrease bitterness and remove excess water. Then blot it dry and wipe it clean from salt.

2. Preheat oven to 400°F.

3. Prepare all vegetables to be of a similar size, slicing ¼ inch or thinner.

4. Spread the vegetables onto a baking sheet, and brush with olive oil. Then sprinkle with the herbs, 1½ teaspoons sea salt, pepper, chile powder, and garlic.

5. Use a brush to coat a 12-inch cast-iron pan with olive oil, and place the vegetables into a serpentine pattern to fill the pan, alternating for variety. Spread the butter on top, followed by the marsala and Parmesan. Then cover with foil, and bake for 1 hour. Remove the foil, and cook for an additional 15 minutes.

6. Finish with basil, thyme, a bit of Parmesan, and a dash of sea salt before serving.

TIP: We made garlic bread to accompany the ratatouille. Simply slice a baguette and coat each slice with a mixture of softened butter, garlic, sea salt, smoked paprika, and Parmesan, and bake until golden.

My Nana taught me almost everything I know about food. She lived to cook, and she and I were very close—probably closer than I am with my own mother. She grew up on a small Croatian island, in a place called Iz Veli, until she was sixteen years old. Fleeing the horrors of World War II in Europe, Nana came to the United States through Ellis Island. There is a plaque there with her name and those of her mother and brother. Her life story is the epitome of the American Dream. It took her father, my great-grandfather Tony Konatich, almost twelve years to save up enough money to send for his family in what was then the Kingdom of Yugoslavia.

Tony wrote to his daughter every week when they were separated. He was an illegal immigrant in the US and worked at least ten jobs at once to scrounge up the money they needed to pay for the family's passage over the Atlantic. It's strange to me now to remember how when I was growing up people always called Big Dida "an illegal alien," as if there was something wrong with him and he was not of this earth or human. The immigration debate remains a source of pain to reconcile in this country, but today it's clearly about not accepting people fleeing oppression because of the color of their skin. My great-grandfather was no different from the people crossing the border today. He was willing to work, become a citizen, whatever it took. He just wanted a better life.

After Tony's family finally arrived, he was eventually able to become a citizen, but before that he lived most of the time in fear of being deported, having jumped ship as a merchant marine for the Austro-Hungarians in Cuba and making his way from Mexico to California. He was a fisherman by trade and knew how to knit his own nets—and he was a fine cook, of course.

Eventually Tony opened his own restaurant in northern California, right on the water, about forty-five minutes north of San Francisco. Tony's Seafood was for decades, and still is, an institution in the Bay Area—a landmark place to eat the best, freshest seafood (and today it's even on Instagram!). He died when I was six, but I remember his laugh and his jubilance from eating good food—from overseeing the barbecued fresh oysters to preparing the ingredients and executing the exact cooking methods of the unmistakable dishes we all prepared for holidays. He spoke eight languages, including Greek. He and our Nana were cut from the same cloth. Both were tender, loving perfectionists and tough critics, but if you earned their respect in the kitchen, you were in their good graces forever. Boy, did they love to eat. Forget enlightenment—if you ever saw my Nana or her daughter Franny devour rock crab fresh from the Pacific, tossed with their own special vinaigrette, you were a witness to sheer delight.

Big Dida weaves a fishing net in the 1940s.

DEBRIANNA'S

SALT ROASTED POTATOES TO GET YOU THROUGH THE NIGHT

(VG) (GF)

SERVES 2 TO 4

2 cups kosher salt

8 small potatoes (I prefer Yukon Gold or multicolored potatoes), poked with a fork

1 teaspoon fennel seeds

¾ teaspoon crushed peppercorn

1 tablespoon roughly chopped fresh rosemary

1 tablespoon roughly chopped fresh thyme

1 tablespoon roughly chopped fresh parsley

2 garlic cloves, roughly chopped

2 tablespoons high-quality olive oil

1. Pour the salt into a 12-inch cast-iron pan, and set it over medium heat for 5 minutes or until warm.

2. Add all other ingredients except the olive oil, and half bury the potatoes. Then cover and let cook over medium-low heat until soft when pierced, about 40 minutes.

3. Remove and drizzle with olive oil.

TIP: These potatoes are crisp on the outside and creamy on the inside. I like to save the herbed salt and cook with it. You can also reserve it, break up the clumps, and reuse it for another round of potatoes.

There was a rug with three-inch gray shag that covered our small living room from end to end. The shag was so long that it was impossible to vacuum, so we raked it with an actual rake on Wednesdays and Saturdays. It looked beautiful and groomed like a lawn at least twice a week.

"Oh my God, I dropped it!" The same hollow cry rang out over the years that rug lay in our living room.

"My ring!"

"My barrette!"

"My earring!"

"Ahh, damn! I dropped the bobby pins!"

"Shit, a safety pin!"

As if swallowed by a gray fluffy Muppet in an imaginary belch, things of all mire disappeared into the gray, never to be seen again. We eventually stopped looking, hunched over in a mad crouch, pulling the shag hairs apart.

After the raking, it was a glorious sea of well-kept shag flowing in one direction, like calm water lapping the edges of a beach. But within hours, the Muppet from hell returned. Crossing it diagonally from the upstairs where our bedrooms were to get to the kitchen, our hands clasped a little tighter to whatever we were holding . . . in case . . . oh my God . . . whatever it was dropped into the beautiful gray abyss that was our living room.

We could go weeks, not hearing a cry about a drop, everyone at their best. The triple gray shag rug lying there in all its glory. Sometimes raked and quiet, sometimes in the fury before the raking. Like the tousled hair of a wild child, holding the center of our living room together, the red corduroy couches and typical Italian marble coffee table with the carved bust at the midline. Eventually we stopped moaning and stopped looking.

"Ouch. Oh my God!"

I stood in the middle of the gray swirl and lifted my foot to see a bobby pin jammed into it! A black bobby pin that had been in the shag for God knows how long. In fact, it had been hidden for so long that the plastic ends had worn off and the metal was jabbed into my foot, hanging there like a tooth from the kraken.

My sister Donna came running. "That's gross!"

"I know!" I screamed. "And it hurts! Help me!"

My sister looked at me with huge eyes and grabbed the bobby pin. A loud sucking sound released as she yanked it, leaving a gaping hole in my foot.

"Sorry, I just raked it yesterday," my sister said meekly, feeling bad and leaving me hobbling across the sea of shag, trying to catch the blood before it stained the wavy swamp creature.

"I know," I heaved out in quick breaths. "It's okay . . . not your fault . . . I hate this thing. I can't wait until we get a new rug—someday."

We learned to live with the beauty and flaws of that glorious rug until we got a new one—one on which we could see whatever was dropped and that brought our living room together. One that worked and did its job. I tell this story because it's a reminder that tough situations *will* end. The gray did. We can and do persevere. And in the meantime, salt roasted potatoes will help.

DIFFERENT IS GOOD GRILLED NECTARINE, GOAT CHEESE, AND PEAR PIZZA

SERVES 4

GLAZE

1 cup balsamic vinegar

2 tablespoons maple syrup

Hot sauce, to taste

PIZZA

4 slices prosciutto (or for a vegetarian version replace with ¾ cup chopped walnuts, toasted, and use a smoked salt for finishing)

1½ cups goat cheese, softened

½ cup crumbled blue cheese, ricotta, or feta

1 whole wheat pizza dough (see Debrianna's recipe on page 144)

1 tablespoon cornmeal for brushing

1 tablespoon olive oil for brushing

2 large nectarines, sliced

3 ripe figs, thinly sliced

½ cup loosely packed fresh basil, sliced chiffonade

1. Heat a pizza stone in a 450°F oven for 30 minutes.

2. In a small saucepan set over high heat, combine the glaze ingredients and bring to a boil. Once boiling, turn the heat down and simmer gently until reduced by half, 10 to 15 minutes. Set aside.

3. In a frying pan, warm the prosciutto until it just starts to curl; don't brown it. Turn the heat off, and then add the goat cheese to the warm pan. Stir until it becomes spreadable, and then add the blue cheese.

4. Slice the prosciutto into roughly ½-inch slices.

5. Pull the pizza dough into the desired shape and sprinkle with cornmeal. Place the dough on the hot pizza stone, and brush with oil. Spread the cheese mixture, and then add the fruit and prosciutto. Top with the basil.

6. Bake the pizza on the stone at 450°F for 15 minutes or until it is brown on the bottom. When done, drizzle with the glaze.

TIP: An alternative topping combination is nectarine, goat, and fig, which is also delicious. The leftover glaze makes a great salad dressing starter.

Hang In There, Kitty, It's Not the End of Summer Yet Bruschetta and Tapenade

SERVES 4

CROSTINI

2 smaller loaves fresh bread
(I used 2 types: a sourdough
boule and a standard bâtard),
cut into ½-inch slices

4 large garlic cloves

ROASTED GARLIC TAPENADE

1 garlic bulb

¼ cup higher-quality olive oil,
and more for finishing

2 cups kalamata olives, pitted

1 teaspoon anchovy paste

3 teaspoons capers

1 teaspoon sea salt

Juice of ½ lemon

4 cranks freshly ground
black pepper

2 tablespoons chopped
fresh parsley

BRUSCHETTA TOPPING

4 medium tomatoes,
roughly chopped

4 tablespoons extra-
virgin olive oil

2 garlic cloves, minced

1 teaspoon sea salt

21 small fresh basil leaves, torn

5 cranks freshly ground
black pepper

Balsamic vinegar for finishing

TO MAKE THE CROSTINI AND THE ROASTED GARLIC TAPENADE

1. Preheat oven to 400°F.

2. Bake the bread slices on an unlined baking sheet until golden brown, about 5 minutes. Remove and immediately rub each slice thoroughly with the raw garlic cloves. Usually it takes 4 cloves for 2 loaves of bread, as it disintegrates pretty fast. Set aside.

3. While the oven is still hot, slice off the tips (without removing the skin) of the garlic bulb, and then brush the tops of the cloves with olive oil. Wrap the garlic in foil and bake until soft, 10 to 16 minutes, and then remove the garlic from its skin and set it aside.

TO MAKE THE BRUSCHETTA TOPPING

1. Combine all bruschetta topping ingredients except balsamic vinegar in a bowl. Mix well and set aside.

TO MAKE THE ROASTED GARLIC TAPENADE TOPPING

1. Combine all remaining tapenade topping ingredients and the roasted garlic in a food processor.

2. Pulse until the parsley is combined, but not too finely. You should still be able to see a bit of the leaves.

TO ASSEMBLE THE BRUSCHETTA

1. Spread the tapenade on half the newly baked crostini, and on the other half spread the bruschetta mixture.

2. Drizzle olive oil on the tapenade, and balsamic vinegar on the bruschetta.

No Fail Herb Stuffing (Dressing) for Thanksgiving

SERVES 6 TO 8

3 tablespoons olive oil

4 tablespoons unsalted butter, and more for coating the dish

2 cups peeled and diced onions

1 cup peeled and diced carrots

1 cup diced celery

2 tablespoons HH Holiday Blend Seasoning Salt or 1 tablespoon dried sage, dried savory, and dried thyme mix and 1½ tablespoons sea salt

½ cup chopped fresh parsley

2 cups chicken broth

½ cup white wine (preferably chardonnay)

4 cups bread stuffing (plain, no herbs)

2 cups cornbread stuffing

Turkey gravy for finishing

HOLLIE'S STUFFING (DRESSING) ADDITIONS AND VARIATIONS

Add 1 of these ingredients while sautéing the onions, carrots, and celery:

1 cup chopped sausages

1 cup chopped button mushrooms

½ cup chopped sun-dried tomatoes

½ cup chopped cranberries, raisins, or dried apricots

Add 1 of these ingredients after adding the bread stuffing:

½ cup chopped pecans

½ cup chopped artichoke hearts

½ cup chopped corn

½ cup small cubes of tart Granny Smith apples

1. Preheat oven to 375°F.

2. In a large pot set over medium-high heat, heat the olive oil and butter. Add the onions, carrots, and celery, and stir, and then add 1 tablespoon HH Holiday Blend Seasoning Salt (or ½ tablespoon sea salt and dried herbs). Cook until well cooked through, about 10 to 15 minutes, and then add the parsley, stir, and cook an additional 5 minutes.

3. Add the broth and wine, and turn the heat to low to bring the mixture to a simmer.

4. Add the bread and cornbread stuffings and with a large spoon slowly mix to incorporate the stuffings, allowing them to absorb the liquid.

5. Add the remaining 1 tablespoon HH salt (or ½ tablespoon sea salt and dried herbs), and stir.

6. Coat a baking dish generously with butter. Add the stuffing mixture, and cover with foil. Bake covered for 35 minutes.

7. Remove the foil, and bake uncovered for an additional 20 minutes.

8. Remove the stuffing from the oven, and drizzle turkey gravy on top before serving.

Anytime Potato Latkes

MAKES 6 LARGE OR 12 SMALL LATKES

2 pounds (about 4 large) russet potatoes, grated

1½ teaspoons HH Holiday Blend Seasoning Salt or sea salt, and more to taste

2 large eggs

1 yellow onion, peeled and grated

¼ teaspoon freshly ground black pepper

1 tablespoon matzo meal or all-purpose flour

2 tablespoons peanut oil or coconut oil for frying

1½ cups sour cream for serving

1½ cups applesauce for serving

1. Place the grated potatoes in a large bowl, and add a pinch of salt and toss. Let sit for 5 to 10 minutes.

2. In a separate bowl, lightly beat the eggs.

3. Place the grated potatoes in the middle of a dish towel, and connect the four corners to make a pouch. Over the sink, twist the towel and let the liquid drain out of the potatoes (about ½ to 1 cup should release). Discard the liquid and place the potatoes back in their bowl.

4. Add the eggs, onion, remainder of the salt, and the pepper to the potatoes, and stir until coated and incorporated. Sprinkle the matzo meal in, and toss until combined and evenly coated.

5. Heat the peanut oil in a large skillet or on a flat-top grill set over medium-high heat.

6. Place a scoop of the potato mixture in the pan in a round clump and then flatten it using a spatula to ½ inch thick.

7. Lower the heat to medium, and continue to press down on the latke while it cooks, until golden brown on each side, about 2 to 3 minutes. Once golden brown, flip and cook the other side.

8. Transfer the latke to a paper-towel-lined wire rack to drain. Sprinkle with a tiny amount of salt, to taste.

9. Repeat steps 6 to 8 with the remaining batter.

10. Serve immediately with sour cream and applesauce or keep warm for 15 to 30 minutes on a baking sheet in a 200°F oven and then serve.

TOMATO, CUCUMBER, AND HERB ORZO SALAD

(VG)

SERVES 6 TO 8

2 cups orzo (or substitute with pasta, a bed of lettuce, or grilled or spiraled squash)

⅓ cup olive oil or HH Herbs de Moraga Olive Oil

2 tablespoons white wine vinegar or HH Rose Petal Vinegar

2 cucumbers, peeled and sliced into rounds

2 large tomatoes, sliced into small sections

1 teaspoon HH Lemon Basil Seasoning Salt or sea salt with 1 teaspoon lemon zest, and more to taste (optional)

Freshly ground black pepper, to taste

1 tablespoon finely chopped fresh mint

1 tablespoon finely chopped fresh basil

2 tablespoons finely chopped fresh parsley

Juice of ½ lemon

1. Cook the orzo according to the directions on the package. Drain and set aside to cool to room temperature.

2. In a large salad bowl, combine the olive oil and white wine vinegar. Add the cucumbers, tomatoes, salt, and pepper and toss. Add the herbs and toss more.

3. Add the cooled orzo and lemon juice, and gently toss to coat the pasta.

4. Taste and season with additional salt or pepper if necessary.

TIP: You can add a protein like sliced chicken breasts, grilled tofu, or thinly sliced flank steak for a heartier meal.

Vegetarian, Fish, & Eat Your Meat!

Main Courses

LISA'S

Everything's Going to Be Okay Vegetable Deluxe Potpies

Ⓥ

SERVES 6

SAVORY PIECRUST

2½ cups all-purpose flour

2 teaspoons whole flaxseeds

1 teaspoon salt

1 cup (2 sticks) unsalted butter, frozen and grated or cold and cut into small cubes

2 teaspoons chopped fresh thyme

1 tablespoon organic apple cider vinegar, cold

Flour for work surface

FILLING

1 cup peeled and chopped carrots

½ cup chopped celery

1 cup cubed Yukon Gold potatoes

½ cup peeled and chopped sweet onion

1 medium shallot, finely chopped

2 garlic cloves, chopped

3 tablespoons unsalted butter (I use a high-fat butter instead of regular butter—it lends a delicious, rich flavor)

2 cups vegetable broth

⅓ cup all-purpose flour

2 teaspoons cornstarch

2 tablespoons dry sherry or marsala

2 teaspoons sea salt, and more to taste

1 teaspoon freshly ground black pepper

1 teaspoon smoked paprika

1 cup chopped kale

¾ cup sliced medium button mushrooms

1½ cups petits pois

1 teaspoon chopped fresh thyme

1 teaspoon chopped fresh parsley

1 teaspoon chopped fresh rosemary

1 teaspoon chopped fresh sage

OTHER PIE INGREDIENTS

1 egg, for wash

1 cup sharp cheddar or English Cotswold

TO MAKE THE SAVORY PIECRUST

1. Incorporate all piecrust ingredients in a food processor, and then pulse and pour up to 1 cup ice water in by tablespoons until a dough ball forms.

2. Remove the dough, and spread it onto a floured surface. Knead it gently a few times, and form it into 2 round discs, 1 slightly larger than the other. Wrap each in plastic wrap and refrigerate. This is a double crust for 1 pie or 6 small ones.

TIP: Piecrust can be fickle. It's always best if you can make it in advance and then refrigerate it for at least 2 hours, preferably 4 or 5 hours. To this veggie version, you could add 1 cup roast chicken, pork, or beef.

TO MAKE THE FILLING

1. Boil the carrots, celery, and potatoes in water for 10 minutes. Strain and set aside.

2. Combine the onion, shallot, garlic, and butter in a large saucepan or cast-iron pan set over medium heat, and sauté until translucent.

3. Add the broth, flour, cornstarch, sherry, sea salt, pepper, and paprika, stirring constantly.

4. Whisk until the gravy thickens, and then lower the heat to a simmer. Add the kale, mushrooms, peas, and herbs. Stir everything together, and add a little more sea salt.

5. Turn off the heat and set aside.

TO MAKE THE PIES

1. Preheat oven to 425°F.

2. Whisk the egg well to make an egg wash.

3. Remove the dough from the fridge. Roll out the larger disc, and cut circles with a sharp knife about 2 inches larger than the bottom of the pan; pat them into small ceramic pie pans or don't cut the circles and pat the entire rolled-out disc into 1 large ceramic pie pan, covering the outer rim. Add the filling, top with the cheese, and then cover with the other dough disc in the same manner, rolled out, sealing the edges together around the pies with the egg wash in between the edges, crimped down.

4. Brush the remaining egg wash over the entire top of the potpies. Cut several slits in the top of each crust to release steam. Consider trying a fun design with any extra dough and a cookie cutter.

5. Bake for 35 minutes. Watch the potpies closely starting 20 minutes in—if you need to, cover them with foil to prevent the crusts from burning.

6. Remove the potpies, and let them cool for at least 15 minutes. Enjoy this ultimate comfort food. My brood always looks forward to these, gobbling them up like there's no tomorrow—right away, or you can also let them cool and then freeze to save.

There are times when the universe reveals what it's all about. And for the life of me, I am still gobsmacked every time it happens. Each time your small child opens their mouth to inform you that they are not of you. You may have given birth to them, but their mind and soul are their own. This revelation has led me to have two vegetarian children. It wasn't something I planned on. One day when Ronan was about three, he saw me preparing a chicken to roast in the oven and asked:

"What are you doing, Mommy?"

I replied, "Cooking dinner, my darling."

"But, Mommy, what is that?"

"It's a chicken, my love."

"It doesn't look like a chicken."

"Well, that's because it's not alive anymore."

I saw the wheels turn in his toddler brain to comprehend that this chicken had either given her life for our dinner or someone had taken it without the chicken's consent.

"I don't want to eat a chicken, Mommy."

"Why not? It's delicious. You've eaten chicken many times and loved it."

"I don't want to eat something that has once been alive and now is not. I can't do it."

"Okay. Can you eat the potatoes and carrots?"

"Yes. I can eat those."

And so my once meat-eating child became a vegetarian for ethical reasons as well as health reasons—on his own volition. What fierce animal rights advocates both children have become as young adults. Seamus, of course, following in Ronan's footsteps—100 percent on board with the nonconsumption of animals. Ronan came into this world with the maturity of a forty-five-year-old who'd seen it all. Seamus was already a PhD at age two, when he started reading and questioning street signs and billboard slogans from his car seat. I understood immediately there would be no room for negotiation with these two. It was as if their higher selves were informing me about who they were as beings over the past millennia, and this was not something they did—end of story. Over the last eighteen years, because of their convictions, I have learned how to cook things that I liked and knew from a vegetarian's perspective, and I have to say that this awareness has made me a better person. I have tried my best to respect their feelings over the years (from defending them at countless kiddie birthday parties to myriad family holiday gatherings where certain Croatian relatives gave me the what for) and put in the effort to make them tasty and innovative dishes without meat. And miraculously, they have also learned to accept those who eat differently from them. Who is the teacher and guide? You think it's you as a parent, but surprise! It is I who have probably learned the most life lessons from my Ro and Sea. God bless them. But I still love to eat a proper steak once in a while, and fortunately, they don't hold it against me.

DEBRIANNA'S

I Might Drink the Bourbon BBQ Sauce (with Low and Slow Ribs)

BBQ SAUCE

⅔ cup bourbon

1 small shallot, finely chopped

1½ cups low-sugar organic ketchup

¼ cup maple syrup

¼ cup freshly squeezed orange juice

¼ cup organic apple cider vinegar

¼ cup brown sugar

¼ cup brewed strong coffee

1 tablespoon soy sauce

1 teaspoon grated fresh ginger

1 garlic clove, minced

1 teaspoon hot pepper flakes or ½ teaspoon chipotle powder

2 tablespoons tomato paste

2 tablespoons Worcestershire sauce

2 teaspoons Dijon mustard

2 tablespoons molasses

RIBS

2 small racks baby back ribs, membranes removed

Dry rub or salt and pepper for coating

TO MAKE THE BBQ SAUCE

1. Pour the bourbon in a small saucepan, and set over medium heat. Add the shallot, and cook until reduced by about half.

2. Add the remaining ingredients, and simmer for at least 15 to 20 minutes.

TO PREPARE THE RIBS

1. Rub the ribs with your favorite dry rub or generously with salt and pepper.

2. Refrigerate the ribs for 1 hour to 1 day.

3. Preheat oven to 225°F.

4. Set the ribs in a pan so the racks are separated. They can be close but not on top of one another. Add about ¼ inch of water to the bottom of the pan.

5. Cover with foil, and bake for 2 hours. Drain most of the liquid and reserve.

6. Raise the oven temperature to 250°F, and bake the ribs for 2 more hours. By now the ribs should be very tender; if they're not, continue baking for another hour. While they are baking, either add the reserved juice to the BBQ sauce and simmer for 15 minutes to incorporate or save the juice for another use, such as on rice.

7. Remove the ribs, paint them with the BBQ sauce, and then cook them, uncovered, for another 15 minutes.

TIP: Serve the ribs with rice or Debrianna's Salt Roasted Potatoes to Get You Through the Night (see page 122).

DEBRIANNA'S

I'M NOT A SELLOUT STUFFED PORK CHOPS

 GF

SERVES 2

1 large shallot, thinly sliced

Olive oil or duck fat for sautéing

2 large cremini mushrooms, diced

Salt, to taste

1 garlic clove, chopped

½ cup frozen spinach, thawed with the water squeezed out

½ cup goat cheese

¼ cup grated Asiago

4 pork loin chops

Freshly ground black pepper, to taste

2 slices prosciutto

1. Sauté the shallot in olive oil until translucent. Add the mushrooms, and cook until they release their moisture. Salt lightly, to taste, and then add the garlic. Cook for 2 minutes, and then add the spinach and make sure any moisture is released. Remove from heat.

2. Add the goat cheese, stir until the cheese is spreadable, and then add the Asiago.

3. Pat the pork chops dry, and salt and pepper both sides. Lay 1 prosciutto slice on top of 1 pork chop with ½ of the prosciutto slice hanging over the edge. Layer the cheese mixture on the prosciutto; then fold and cover with the remaining ½ slice, and top with another pork chop. Try to cover the filling with the prosciutto. Butcher-tie the chops together. Do the same with the remaining 2 chops. If using bone-in, make a slit, like a pocket in the center of the chop, being careful not to cut all the way through. Stuff with prosciutto and cheese.

4. Grill each side of the pork chop for about 5 minutes. Then lower the heat and finish cooking until the internal temperature is 145°F, about 5 more minutes.

TIP: If you have leftover stuffing, use it in an omelet the next day. In this recipe, I had to "corona" the chops because all I had were boneless pork loin chops. Normally, I would prefer bone in.

I am not a sellout. That said, I have stayed too long in a relationship, way too long, simply to keep my home and as a result of being beaten down toward low self-esteem. Have I done it for personal financial gain? Nope.

It was the year *An Inconvenient Truth* came out, 2006.

"Want to go for a ride?" My coworker Mark poked his head in my office door, waving a set of new car keys. "I've got my new car outside."

"Sure. I'll come in a second. Working on this new loan application."

"Oh, wow. Is it a NINA?" he asked, referring to no-income, no-assets loans.

"No. I don't do those, Mark."

"Too bad. They pay way more," he said, sparkling his car keys at me. "See?"

"Mark, I don't do breather loans. I have to sleep at night."

"Too bad, they pay more—come see my new car!"

"Breather loan" is the term I gave to no-income, no-assets loans because to me they were like sticking a mirror under your nose to see if you're breathing—you are? Okay, here's the money. They made no good sense, and in good conscience I could not tell if the client could pay it back if no income or asset information was required. And that was what I thought my job was—to help people acquire a home or an investment property and be sure that I gave solid financial advice so they could maintain and grow their wealth.

Mark and many of the others in my office thought otherwise. Mark. And his new Hummer—a car I despised on so many levels. We had just invested in solar panels, and he's jacking around in a Hummer. Like in Al Gore's movie, I could see where our abuse of the planet was headed, how our unthoughtful behavior was going to become unsustainable. How can you build a housing market when people were getting loans without documentation of their legit income? It was insane. Like that Hummer.

"I don't know why you don't want to make money. See what you're missing?" I'd reluctantly followed him to his car, and now he looked over his shoulder at me bouncing around on the bench back seat, trying to act comfortable.

"Because I have to put my head on the pillow and sleep at night, Mark. I'm funny that way. Congrats on the new car. I've got to get back."

"How was it?" Felicia, my assistant, asked, her eyes wide.

"It was like riding around on a park bench, one that looks comfortable but isn't." Kinda like Mark, I thought. He was a hulky, well-built teddy bear of a man who was doing liar loans hand over fist, driving fancy cars, looking like a catch, but both Felicia and I knew he was in way over his head.

I never did those loans. The day the market crashed, as I knew it would, I pulled into the parking lot of my office in my all-electric truck. I parked next to the black thing known as "The Hummer." Someone had completely keyed the doors. I ran into the building to let Mark know and saw that he already knew. He looked near tears, slamming down the phone.

"Mark?"

"Those fuckers—they did it again. I just had it fixed," he yelled into the air as my eyes grazed his desk, a mess of credit cards.

"Are you okay?"

"Yeah, if I ever get my hands on those assholes, I'll break them," he muttered, trying now to ungracefully pile up the evidence of his overextension, credit cards mashing into his giant hands.

"I'm sorry that happened, Mark."

I walked into my office and closed the door, my head tilting back against it. The market was crashing. My clients were mostly safe. I didn't sell out. I didn't stuff my pockets and abuse the privilege I had with my clients. I could breathe.

CANYON LENDING
G R O U P

office
505 629 4433

fax
505 984 8664

Debrianna Mansini
canyonmortgage1@yahoo.com

502 west cordova road
santa fe, new mexico 87501

When You Miss Your Nana's Eggplant Parmigiana (and Your Nana)

SERVES 8

EGGPLANT

½ cup sea salt (or enough to sweat the eggplant)

3 pounds eggplant, peeled and sliced ½ inch thick

4 eggs, lightly beaten

3 cups seasoned bread crumbs

Canola oil, safflower oil, or other high-temperature oil for frying

2 tablespoons olive oil to coat the bottom of baking dish

MARINARA SAUCE

6 tablespoons high-quality olive oil

3 medium onions, peeled and chopped

3 garlic cloves, chopped

3 (28-ounce) cans San Marzano tomatoes or 6 large fresh tomatoes cooked and strained

1 (6-ounce) can tomato paste

1 cup Burgundy wine

1½ teaspoons instant coffee granules

12 fresh basil leaves, crushed

1 teaspoon marjoram

Sea salt, to taste

Freshly ground black pepper, to taste

FOR THE ASSEMBLY

1 to 2 pounds buffalo mozzarella,* sliced ¼ inch thick or grated

1 cup freshly grated Parmesan

Bread crumbs

* Nana called the mozzarella quantity "Enough fresh mozzarella to cover the pan." One to 2 pounds should be sufficient. It depends on how cheesy you like it.

TO MAKE THE EGGPLANT

1. Lightly sprinkle sea salt on both sides of the eggplant slices, and then stand them upright on paper towels for at least 30 minutes. Pat the eggplant dry after it has sweat. This process removes the bitterness from the eggplant.

2. Dip each slice of eggplant into the beaten eggs, and then dredge it into the bread crumbs, coating evenly.

3. Fry the eggplant in hot oil until golden brown and soft, about 2 to 3 minutes per side. Use enough oil to have a ½-inch depth of it in the pan, adding more oil to keep this depth as the eggplant fries if need be. Keep the temperature at 375°F. Once the eggplant slices are fried, drain them on paper towels, and then set them aside.

TO MAKE THE MARINARA SAUCE

1. In a 4-quart saucepan, heat the olive oil, and then add the onions and sauté until tender but not brown.

2. Add the garlic, tomatoes, tomato paste, and wine, and keep over high heat until boiling. Stir in the instant coffee, basil, marjoram, sea salt, and pepper, and simmer until thick, 1 to 1½ hours.

3. Taste to see if you need more salt. Set aside.

TO ASSEMBLE THE EGGPLANT PARMESAN

1. Preheat oven to 375°F.

2. Brush the bottom of a 13 x 9-inch baking dish with olive oil, and then spoon some of the marinara sauce to coat the bottom of the dish. Place single layers of eggplant slices on top of the sauce, and then spoon the sauce on top of the slices. Repeat this layering process until all the eggplant has been used, and then place slices of fresh mozzarella on top with grated Parmesan on top of that, finishing with a thin layer of bread crumbs.

3. Add cubes of butter to the corners and the middle, spreading evenly.

4. Cover with foil and bake for 45 minutes; then remove the foil, and bake or broil to brown the cheese for 5 minutes. Remove from the oven and serve.

WHEN YOU'RE READY TO PARTY, FRIED DOUGH PIZZA!

SERVES 4 TO 6

PIZZA DOUGH

1 tablespoon honey or
1 teaspoon sugar

1 tablespoon instant yeast

1 tablespoon olive oil,
and more for frying

1 teaspoon salt

1 cup bread flour

1 cup all-purpose flour (If you
need a bit more you can use
all-purpose. If you want to add
whole wheat or spelt, don't
substitute more than ½ cup.)

QUICK SAUCE

1 tablespoon olive oil

1 large garlic clove, minced

2 tablespoons tomato paste

½ cup red wine

1 (15-ounce) can tomatoes

1 tablespoon chopped
fresh basil

Crushed red pepper, to taste

Salt, to taste

TOPPING IDEAS

Shredded mozzarella

Pepperoni

Peppers

Sausage

Green chile

Mushrooms

Olives

TO MAKE THE PIZZA DOUGH

1. In large glass bowl, mix 1 cup warm water with the honey, yeast, olive oil, and salt, stirring with a wooden spoon. Gradually add some of the flours until a soft dough forms, and then slowly add the rest of the flours and mix until the dough forms a soft, smooth ball. It should not be too sticky or overly stiff.

2. Knead 3 to 5 minutes.

3. Cover the dough with a cloth, and let it rest for 10 minutes to 1 hour so the gluten relaxes.

4. Preheat oven to 350°F.

5. Fill a skillet about ½ to ¾ of an inch with olive oil.

6. Pull the dough into a 5- or 6-inch round, and gently place it in the oil. It will puff and bubble. Flip once golden, after 2 to 3 minutes, and allow the other side to bake to the same color.

7. Remove the dough from the oven, and add desired pizza toppings.

TO MAKE THE SAUCE

1. In a medium saucepan, heat the olive oil, and then add the garlic. Cook for a few minutes over medium-high heat, but don't brown.

2. Add the tomato paste carefully, and with a spoon smash it in the olive oil. Cook for 3 minutes, again taking care to avoid browning.

3. Add the red wine and mix until combined. Add 7½ ounces water and mix again. Add the tomatoes, basil, and red pepper. Add salt and let simmer until reduced to desired thickness, about 15 minutes.

TIP: You can even make this dough for dessert and top with cinnamon and sugar!

"Yay! Let's make fried dough pizza!"

I don't know how the idea for this came into being, but fried dough pizza was a favorite in my house growing up. The dough itself is basic bread dough, but that's where the basic part of it stops. Kind of like this wild ride we are on now, whose outcome presents so many possibilities.

My mom would pull on the soft bread dough, shaping it, and lay the pieces out on the dining room table, a row of oddly shaped and bubbled oblongs and rounds waiting for their turn in the hot oil. Toppings were lined up—some days it was sauce and cheese and whatever leftovers we had to add; other days, it was cinnamon, sugar, and butter melting over the hot, crispy exterior or powdered sugar and ground spices dusting the bubbled surface. This was the way my mom excited her brood of kids into forgetting we were poor. Marcelle transformed what little we had into joy. Maybe that is why COVID reminds me of what I have known all my life. Adversity is a secret opening. Look for the secret.

When Buzz Burbank, the radio voice of the news on both Bob Cesca's podcast and his own, said he'd love to come onto Corona Kitchen, we were thrilled! Because I've been a lifelong news junkie myself, this was a coup. But Buzz didn't want to cook; he just wanted to hang out with me and Lisa. Buzz is one of those who, during COVID, found more work, not less, in the rapid daily, sometimes hourly succession of news spewing that was also our life in that crazy time, so that was perfectly understandable.

As we chatted in our "preproduction" meeting (we say that laughingly—Lisa and I are the production team, the sound team, the camera crew, the gaffers, the production assistants, and the network), we asked if there was anything he wanted to learn, a new recipe maybe.

He said, "I love pizza! I would love to find new ways to make it."

Welp. This. Is. It. The pizza of my childhood.

The pizza of change and invention.

The pizza of old and new.

The pizza of the pandemic.

Debrianna and her twin sisters, Donna and Denice, with their cousins David and Lisa in the late '60s.

Michael J. Elston a.k.a. Buzz Burbank.

LISA'S

PAUL BOCUSE WANNABE RED SNAPPER WITH SCALLOPED POTATOES, TOMATO, AND KALAMATA OLIVE CONFIT TO IMPRESS YOUR FRIENDS AND FAMILY

(GF)

SERVES 4

FISH FILLET

4 fillets of a sturdy fish (ideally sea bass or halibut, but I have used tilapia and Dover sole too)

½ cup (1 stick) unsalted butter, clarified

1 large russet potato, thinly sliced with a mandolin to ⅛ inch thick

½ cup (1 stick) unsalted butter (use 3 tablespoons for sautéing each fish fillet)

Fresh parsley, chopped, for finishing

SAUCE

¾ cup olive oil

1 cup cherry tomatoes, sliced lengthwise

1 cup kalamata olives, pitted and sliced lengthwise

Zest of 1 lemon

Juice of 2 lemons

1 garlic clove, sliced paper-thin

¼ cup capers, drained

Sea salt, to taste

Freshly ground black pepper, to taste

1. Wash and towel dry the fish fillets, and then set them on a plate or platter and brush them with the clarified butter.

2. Dip each potato slice in the clarified butter, and then place them on the fish in a scalloped design resembling the scales of a fish. Brush the scalloped design on the fish 1 more time with the butter, cover with plastic wrap, and refrigerate for 1 hour.

3. Prepare the sauce by mixing all its ingredients in a skillet set over low heat, and let the flavors start to mingle together, stirring occasionally while you fry the fish in step 4.

4. Remove the fish from the refrigerator, and place it potato side down in a skillet with butter set over medium-high heat. Fry the fish until the potatoes start to brown. Press on the fish with a spatula to cook evenly, and very carefully flip once. Cook about 5 to 7 minutes on each side. If the fish still isn't fully cooked, you can cook in a 350°F oven for up to 8 additional minutes. A thicker fish, like halibut or sea bass, may benefit from this.

5. Plate the fish, and put 3 spoonfuls of sauce over each serving. Finish with parsley.

TIP: The potatoes should be crispy, and the delicious sauce can be used on pasta, chicken, an omelet, with cottage cheese, or even on toast.

"What if we take the train to Champagne this weekend?" Hollie, Heidi, and I were like, "Oh hell, *oui*!" So we said our goodbyes to Mom and Nana, and off we went by train to the *origine contrôlée* of the bubbly. Traveling with my dad, Louis, is always a good time, especially in wine regions of the world, because Dad is a legendary vintner (as well as a partner in Lucas & Lewellen Vineyards in Santa Ynez, California), and he knows pretty much everything about wine. After a two-hour train ride, we arrived in Épernay, ground zero of the Champagne region of France. I cannot even begin to explain the cloud our dad was walking on, as this was his Mecca.

We knew we were in for a good time when we were all set to visit the famous caves of champagne makers Moët & Chandon, Perrier-Jouët, and Louis Roederer. It was fascinating to see the caves, taste the champagnes, and learn their history. We also gleaned interesting tidbits such as what riddlers were, for example. Do you know what a riddler is? It's a wooden contraption where champagne bottles are placed and turned ever so slightly, bit by bit, until the champagne is carbonated naturally and is ready to be consumed. On the tour they explained a lot of the history of the famous caves, like how they hid people from the Nazis down there during WWII, all kinds of incredible lore.

When we emerged from the tour, Dad said, "Well, are you hungry? Because we're going to be having our dinner at the Royal Champagne Hotel's restaurant, which is a Michelin-star restaurant."

This restaurant is famous not only for its food but also for the view it provides of the stunning vineyards below it. When we walked up the stairs to where we would be seated, the view itself took our breath away. We were all then escorted to a grand circular table and enjoyed classic European table service, where there is a head waiter and junior waiters who serve diners all at the same time for every course. Hilariously—and ironically, for the best meal we all have ever experienced—barely any of us remember what they ate except for me! I remember I ordered the famous *poulet de Bresse*, the Bresse chicken. It had a delectable flavor and was cooked perfectly. Wait, because Hollie and I share the same brain—I'm wrong. Hollie does remember one thing: that she had some exceptional lobster ravioli and that, of course, we had the best champagne.

One of the things that we had learned on the tour was that the best champagne was one that was housed in a magnum. So we got a magnum of Perrier-Jouët Rosé that was simply heaven on earth.

But really one of the most memorable parts of the meal was when the six waiters came out at the same time with six silver-covered platters for our main courses, uncovered the dishes in sync, and placed them in front of us. It was a sight to behold, with a stunning amount of cutlery at each table setting. And we just laughed and laughed and laughed, and the food was so delicious, aromatic, and meticulously prepared that the word "extraordinary" doesn't even begin to describe it. I sadly don't remember what we had for dessert or what the other courses were, because we drank so much champagne, but I'm sure they were stupendous. No one else remembers anything either except that we all confirmed 100 percent we had a fabulous time. And everyone who attended that dinner swears to this day that it was the best meal they have ever had, so it must be true if we all feel that way, right?

On the way back to Paris, my stepmother, Jill, took photos of us all passed out on the banquettes, snoozing away. I'll never forget that trip. It was the best time I ever had with my dad. And did you know the great champagne maker Dom Pérignon was a monk?

Hollie, Heidi, Lisa's dad, Louis, and Lisa.

LISA'S

"I AM SPARTACUS!" ROMAN PASTA WITH ASPARAGUS, CRÈME FRAÎCHE, AND LEMON

Ⓥ

SERVES 4

16 ounces gemelli or fusilli pasta

Salted water for cooking pasta

30 young asparagus stalks

⅓ cup high-quality olive oil, and more for finishing

1 large shallot, minced

3 garlic cloves, minced

3 tablespoons unsalted butter

¼ cup white wine

Zest and juice of 2 large lemons

Red pepper flakes, to taste

Sea salt, to taste, and more for finishing

Freshly ground black pepper, to taste

1 teaspoon finely chopped fresh parsley, and more for finishing

½ cup grated Parmesan, Asiago, or pecorino, and more for finishing

⅔ cup crème fraîche

1. Cook the pasta in salted water (salt the water until it tastes like sea water) until al dente.

2. Prepare the asparagus by trimming the woody ends from the asparagus stalks where they snap and then cutting on the diagonal the rest of each stalk into thirds.

3. In a large skillet set over medium-low heat, sauté the olive oil, shallot, garlic, butter, and wine until translucent, about 3 minutes.

4. Add the asparagus to the sauce, and sauté everything for 3 minutes. Lower the heat to simmer.

5. Drain the pasta, and reserve ½ cup pasta water.

6. Add the lemon zest and juice, red pepper flakes, sea salt, pepper, parsley, reserved pasta water, cheese, and crème fraîche to the asparagus mixture, and combine well.

7. Add the pasta to the sauce in the skillet, and fold over.

8. Serve immediately with a drizzle of olive oil and finish with parsley, Parmesan, and sea salt.

TIP: You can add a 15-ounce can of cannellini beans (drained) and/or grilled lemon chicken to this. My kids describe this dish as "a ten out of ten."

LINGUINE *ALLE VONGOLE*, PUT THIS ON YOUR BUCKET LIST (A.K.A. LINGUINE AND WHITE CLAM SAUCE WITH HOMEMADE PRESERVED LEMONS)

SERVES 2 TO 3

⅓ cup high-quality olive oil

1 medium onion, peeled and chopped

6 garlic cloves, finely chopped

¾ teaspoon dried hot red pepper flakes

¼ teaspoon dried oregano

1 cup chopped artichoke hearts or cooked sausage, bacon, Swiss chard, or spinach (optional)

1 (10-ounce) can chopped clams with juice

16 fresh clams (8 littleneck clams per plate—if you want to add fresh, or you can skip)

⅓ cup dry white wine

¼ cup preserved lemons, blended to a paste or finely chopped (see Debrianna's recipe on page 106)

3 tablespoons unsalted butter, cold, cut into small pieces

½ pound linguine

Salt, to taste, and more for boiling water

⅓ cup chopped fresh flat-leaf parsley

White pepper, to taste

Grated Parmesan for finishing

1. Heat the olive oil in a 5- to 6-quart heavy pot over moderately high heat until hot but not smoking; then add the onion, stir, and sauté until golden, about 4 minutes.

2. Add the garlic, red pepper, and oregano and cook, stirring occasionally, until the garlic is golden, about 2 minutes. Add the artichoke hearts or optional ingredients.

3. Separate the clams from the clam juice, and then stir in the wine and clam juice, reserving the clams. Bring to a boil, uncovered, stirring occasionally until slightly reduced, about 3 minutes.

4. Add the preserved lemon paste and butter, whisking them into the sauce, and let simmer. If using fresh clams, add here and cover. When the clams are slightly open, they are done. Keep the heat on very low to keep it warm, covered. Discard any clams that don't open; do not eat them.

5. Meanwhile, cook the pasta in a 6- to 8-quart pot of lightly salted boiling water until al dente; then drain in a colander, reserving 1 cup pasta water.

6. Turn up the heat to medium, and mix the reserved pasta water with the reserved clams; then add the pasta.

7. Add the parsley and toss with sauce until well combined. Add salt if needed and white pepper. Top with Parmesan.

Like my comrade Lisa, I have cooking and serving in my DNA. My mom had eleven brothers and sisters. All of them at a minimum could cook, and several of them owned restaurants or worked in them. On holidays, that farm table was full of family and food. My favorite holiday other than Thanksgiving is the Feast of the Seven Fishes, a Catholic-based Christmas tradition birthed in the United States, not Italy. We were not religious. My mom refused to pass religion on to her girls, but she shared traditional foods. The feast is served on Christmas Eve, and when you are done, off you go to midnight mass. We generally skipped that part.

We were always told that the number of fish served is supposed to reflect a biblical event and had to be an odd number. If you ate an even number, it was bad luck. Doesn't seem too religion-based, but that was the story we were told. Seven fishes was a stretch for a poor family, and only once do I recall even making the top number of thirteen different fishes. The one thing we always had on Christmas Eve was red spaghetti and clams (Christ). Usually we had three fishes (Father, Son, and Holy Ghost).

That tradition has never left me. I have been serving the fishes for so many years in our small town that it has become a well-known event, and an invitation to my home to be served is coveted. It is the day my best friends, the "Christmas Jews," as they call themselves, arrive all the way from LA to partake.

It is a bounty of love that pours out of my soul and resides in each person as they partake of each carefully crafted dish, everyone passing plates and taking turns clearing and washing dishes, cheerfully serving one another little gifts from the sea. I think about this event all year, collecting recipes, pondering over which will be served in small plates, conjuring ways to accommodate special palates. I always end with spaghetti and clams, a nod to my childhood, the part of me that wants to serve, that wants to be seen on little plates of love—the part that loves tradition and the harking back to a time when I felt the love the best way my mom knew how to give it: through homemade food.

In this cookbook are two of my favorite Seven Fishes dishes: Hoki Poki Wasabi Fish (see page 165) and what is always my finale, Linguine *alle Vongole* (see page 152), which I now make with preserved lemons instead of the red sauce that I grew up with.

DEBRIANNA'S

Hot and Spicy Don't Harissa Me Chicken

SERVES 4

HARISSA

Makes 1½ cups

1 tablespoon cumin seeds

1 tablespoon caraway seeds

2 teaspoons coriander seeds

15 dried chiles de arbol

2 dried guajillo chiles

1 dried large ancho chile

6 garlic cloves

½ cup olive oil, and more
for storing

1 tablespoon finely minced
preserved lemon (see
Debrianna's recipe, page 106)

1½ tablespoons kosher salt

1½ teaspoons smoked paprika

1 tablespoon tomato paste

CHICKEN

1½ pounds bone-in, skin-on
chicken thighs

½ tablespoon kosher salt

Freshly ground black
pepper, to taste

3 tablespoons coconut oil

1 large red onion, peeled and
thinly sliced

3 garlic cloves, finely chopped

½ teaspoon ground cinnamon

½ teaspoon five-spice powder

1½ oranges, 1 sliced ¼ inch thick
and ½ left whole but juiced

1½ to 2 cups chicken stock

Zest of 1 orange

¼ cup roughly chopped fresh
parsley with leaves and tender
stems on for finishing

Flaky salt for finishing (optional)

TO PREPARE THE HARISSA

1. Toast the seeds in a dry skillet set over medium-high heat for 1
to 2 minutes, occasionally shaking the skillet. Remove and let cool.
Grind in a coffee grinder or with a mortar and pestle.

2. Add the chiles and toast. The ancho will puff up when done and
will likely take the longest. The time necessary to toast will vary but
should be around 3 minutes or less, so keep a watchful eye, shaking
the pan consistently over the heat. Remove the chiles, seeds, and
stems once toasted, and let cool.

3. Place the chiles, seeds, and stems in a pot of boiling water, and
simmer for 15 minutes. Turn off the heat, cover, and allow to sit for
30 minutes to rehydrate. Drain. Remove the stems. You can remove
the seeds too if you want. The more seeds you have, the spicier
the harissa.

4. Place all ingredients (the chiles, toasted spices, and remaining
harissa ingredients) in a food processor or blender until smooth.

5. Store the harissa covered with a layer of olive oil in a jar in the
fridge. It will keep for about 2 months.

TIP: Making your own harissa paste is well worth it. You can use any
combination of dried chiles. Enjoy on eggs, as a condiment for steak,
or in a multitude of other ways.

TO MAKE THE CHICKEN

1. Season the chicken thighs well with salt and pepper.

2. Pour the coconut oil into a skillet, and set over medium-high heat. Add the chicken thighs skin side down, and cook until browned, about 5 minutes per side. Transfer to a plate, and set aside.

3. Pour off all but 2 tablespoons of the fat from the pan, setting the juice aside, and reduce the heat to medium-low. Add the onion and cook, stirring, until translucent, about 2 to 3 minutes. Add the garlic and cook 30 seconds more, and then stir in 3 tablespoons of the harissa and the cinnamon and five-spice.

4. Place the orange slices in the bottom of the pan, and add the chicken back in on top of the orange slices along with the ½ orange. Pour in enough of the stock to come about halfway up the chicken. Add the orange zest, and bring to a simmer.

5. Partly cover, and allow the chicken to finish cooking through, about 15 minutes.

6. Toss the chicken in the sauce until coated.

7. Plate the chicken, and top with parsley and a sprinkle of the flaky salt. Serve with the braising liquid spooned over the chicken.

"He's so cheap that when he opens his wallet, the moths fly out."

That is what flew through my mind as I stared at my "new" Santa Fe apartment, grappling with the notion that if I had just married him, I woulda, shoulda, coulda received half of the value of the house I helped pay for. Instead, I walked away with my personal values intact, a thousand bucks, and the things I had created that made our house a home.

Yup, he was cheap. Buying anything that had made our house a home was . . . shall we say . . . challenging. Undaunted, I had my own sewing room in "our" house where I whipped up shower curtains, pillows, and bedspreads. I reupholstered our dining chairs with fabric that had old-fashioned jam and jelly jars in an antique pattern, with cornucopias of grapes and peaches on a tapestry of rich green and gold hues, reminding me of the old monastery tapestries in the Cloisters of New York City. I made drapes of royal purple corduroy and deep navy velvet that crushed the floor in soft piles on the Saltillo tiles that I laid.

The two spice cabinets in that house were filled to the brim with tiny mason jars holding secrets from the flea-market spice man. He had traveled all over the world and brought back treasures and treats from the Middle East and Europe—an apothecary of imagination. I concocted all kinds of things, because we rarely went anywhere special to eat, and sometimes I would create dishes for the secret dinner parties I would throw while he was away in New York. I would treat my close friends to a night of culinary delights.

And now my new life was staring me in the face over the boxes and crates piled to the ceiling. My friend Ruby was on her way to help me unpack. She had no idea that she was walking into a wallop of cardboard as far as the eye could see. I shoved open a path and started moving boxes by room, praying I'd find a space for at least some of my belongings and sort through the rest for "storage," when I heard raucous laughter.

"Oh my God. Girl, are you sure this is going to fit?" Ruby's voice floated over my anxiety and the cardboard and landed in my ear and through my heart like a butter knife.

"No, no, I'm not sure. Let's see what we can do. Can you start in the kitchen?" I left those boxes ready for her, thinking that task would need the least supervision. Anyone can fill drawers with utensils and cupboards with spices, right?

"Okay, you got it!" Ruby's cheer was infectious. She was just the right person to help me with this transition.

"He wanted the curtains," I mumbled.

"*What?*"

"Would you mind leaving all the curtains, since you made them specifically for this house?" he had asked sheepishly as I was tearing the bedding off the four-poster bed that I had helped build for a set and inherited from the theater.

"Are you nuts as well as cheap?" I'd shot back before I could edit my anger.

"That's what he wanted," I choked out over a belly of laughter. And that was how we began my unpacking. We went box by box until the spice cabinet.

"What is this for?" Ruby asked as she waved a golden powder at me over the box marked Spices. "That's turmeric," I explained. "I use it in Middle Eastern dishes."

"Why do you have so many jars of chiles?"

"Because they all have different flavor profiles. Some are smoked, and some are super spicy—ooh, don't sniff it! You'll sneeze!" I said too late as she opened the jar and stuck her nose in.

"Achoo!"

I tossed her the paper towels. "Sorry, I have no idea where the Kleenex is."

"And what's this?"

"Geez, Ruby, those are cinnamon sticks. It's where you get, ya know, cinnamon."

"Oh, it looks like bark from the wood in Larry's woodshop," she said and giggled. "Why do you have it like that instead of ground up? You're, like, some kind of witch!"

I never looked at my spice cabinet as a witch's brew of creativity, but now every time I open my cupboard and hunt for a cinnamon stick or plow through my jars of chiles, I smile to myself and think of Ruby.

This dish is for you, my dear friend.

SISTER LOVE CHICKEN ENCHILADAS WITH AUTHENTIC MEXICAN ROJO SAUCE

(GF)

SERVES 8, WITH 16 SMALL ENCHILADAS
AND ABOUT 12 OUNCES RED SAUCE

RED SAUCE

1 medium onion, peeled
and quartered

2 medium or large
tomatoes, halved

3 garlic cloves

12 dried ancho chiles

1 large cinnamon stick

2 tablespoons vegetable oil or
grape-seed oil

1 teaspoon dried
Mexican oregano

2 teaspoons HH Chile de Árbol
Seasoning Salt (for heat) or HH
Herbed Smoked Seasoning Salt
(for deep flavor) or sea salt

ENCHILADAS

3 or 4 tablespoons olive oil

1½ pounds boneless, skinless
chicken breasts

1½ tablespoons sea salt

6 cranks freshly ground
black pepper

2 teaspoons freshly
ground cumin

1 white onion, peeled and
finely chopped

2 garlic cloves, minced

5 whole green chiles, seeded and
coarsely chopped or canned

1 (28-ounce) can
stewed tomatoes

16 corn tortillas

¼ cup chopped green onions (white and green parts)

2 cups shredded cheddar and Monterey Jack mix

16 tablespoons sour cream (1 tablespoon per enchilada)
for finishing

TO MAKE THE RED SAUCE

1. Preheat a cast-iron or stainless steel frying pan (do not use nonstick) over high heat for 2 minutes. Do not use oil; the pan must be dry.

2. Place the onion, tomatoes (cut side down), garlic, and chiles in the pan. If they don't all fit, cook in batches. Toast the chiles, and lightly char the onion, tomatoes, and garlic for about 3 minutes. Using tongs, continually toss the chiles so they don't burn. Do not turn the onion and tomatoes; allow them to blacken on the edges.

3. Place all charred items in a large pot on the stovetop, and cover with water. Add the cinnamon stick and boil over high heat for 15 minutes to reconstitute the peppers and infuse flavors.

4. Remove the cinnamon stick, and then ladle the mixture into a blender. Fill only ⅔ full at a time (this should take at least 2 batches). Starting on low and gradually increasing the speed to high, blend for at least 3 minutes to fully incorporate. If large pieces of the chiles, onion, or tomatoes remain, continue to blend or use a strainer to remove the pieces.

5. Using the same pan in which you charred the onion, tomatoes, garlic, and chiles, add the vegetable oil and heat for 2 minutes over high heat. Add the blended red sauce, pouring slowly, as the high heat can make the sauce splatter. Add the Mexican oregano and salt, and stir for 1 minute only.

6. Turn off the heat, and immediately pour the sauce into a heatproof bowl. Use the sauce right away, or store it in mason jars. Allow the sauce to cool to room temperature with lids off prior to storing. When cool, put lids on, label the jars with the date the sauce was made, and refrigerate for up to 2 weeks.

TO MAKE THE ENCHILADAS

1. Preheat oven to 350°F.

2. Pour 3 tablespoons olive oil in a large skillet set over medium heat. Add the chicken, and season lightly with the salt and pepper. Allow to brown on all sides, and cook through. Sprinkle with cumin, and then remove from heat and allow to cool.

3. Add the onion to the pan, and cook until tender, 3 to 5 minutes. If the pan is really dry, add an additional tablespoon olive oil. Add the garlic, green chiles, and tomatoes and cook for 5 minutes over low heat.

4. Pull the cooled chicken breasts apart by hand or with a knife, and shred the chicken into thin strips. Add the shredded chicken to the pan, and gently stir for 3 minutes over medium heat.

5. Measure 1½ cups of the red sauce, and thinly coat the bottom of 2 baking or casserole pans (3-quart or 13 x 9 inches) with the sauce. Place the rest of the sauce in a large, shallow bowl, and dip each tortilla in the sauce to lightly coat; then place the tortillas on the baking pans.

6. Spoon ¼ cup chicken mixture into each tortilla, and then roll until the seam side is down and place in the pan. Continue until the entire baking pan is full.

7. Pour the remaining sauce evenly on top of the rolled tortillas, using a spoon to make sure they are coated with sauce.

8. Sprinkle the green onions over the sauce and then the cheese over the green onions and enchiladas. Bake until the cheese melts and lightly browns and bubbles, about 20 minutes.

9. Finish each enchilada with a dollop of sour cream prior to serving.

DEBRIANNA'S

GUARANTEED GLEE: CARAMELIZED LEMON CHICKEN WITH ARTICHOKES AND PASTA

SERVES 2

2 plump boneless, skinless chicken breasts

⅓ cup all-purpose flour

1 teaspoon smoked paprika

Salt, to taste

Freshly ground black pepper, to taste

4 lemons

¾ cup chicken stock

Pasta of choice for 2

4 tablespoons olive oil

4 tablespoons unsalted butter

Pinch sugar

2 garlic cloves, minced

1 teaspoon red chile flakes, or more to taste

1 cup (from a 12-ounce jar) chopped artichoke heart halves, grilled

½ cup chopped fresh parsley

Freshly grated Parmesan for finishing

1. Set a pot of water to boil for the pasta, but do not salt yet. While the water is heating up, slice the chicken breasts in half lengthwise, and pound them to an equal thickness.

2. Pour the flour into a shallow dish, and then add the paprika. Season both sides of the chicken with salt and pepper, and dredge in the flour and paprika mix.

3. Zest 2 lemons and squeeze the juice of 1 into ¾ cup of the stock. Cut the other 2 lemons in half; then thinly slice the halves and remove the seeds. Place the lemons in the boiling pasta water for 2 minutes, and then remove. A strainer can be helpful here. Pat dry and set aside.

4. Salt the water for the pasta, and then cook the pasta.

5. Heat a skillet, and add 2 tablespoons olive oil and 1 tablespoon butter. Sear each breast until golden, and then transfer to a plate.

6. Add the remaining olive oil and the dry lemon slices to the skillet. Add a pinch of salt and sugar, and cook until caramelized, about 3 to 5 minutes, adding the garlic halfway through. Add the red chile flakes and remaining butter, artichoke hearts, parsley, and chicken stock with lemon juice. Reduce heat and let simmer until the pasta is ready. Add the pasta once cooked, and then add the chicken.

7. Remove the pasta and chicken, and plate it. Serve with Parmesan.

LISA'S

CHEESE FONDUE. BECAUSE. CHEESE FONDUE.

SERVES 2

1 garlic clove

1 cup dry sherry or marsala

3 cups Emmentaler, grated

3 cups Gruyère, grated

2 cups Comté, grated

2 tablespoons freshly squeezed lemon juice

1 tablespoon cornstarch

1 teaspoon ground white pepper

Dash freshly grated nutmeg

1. Slice the garlic in half lengthwise, and then rub it around the inside of a fondue pot.

2. Turn the heat on, and add the sherry to the pot. When it begins to bubble, add the cheeses, 1 handful at a time, while continually whisking.

3. When the cheeses have partially melted, add the lemon juice, cornstarch, white pepper, and nutmeg.

4. When the cheeses are fully melted, remove the pot from the heat and set it on a fondue rack with a gel fuel–type fondue heating device beneath it to keep it warm.

TIP: We served the accompaniment on fondue spears: prosciutto, crisp apples, cornichons, and, of course, slices of fresh baguette. This is delicious with a chilled gewürztraminer or French Chablis.

What's better than delicious bread with melted cheese? Not much. It is pure bliss. I have been ruminating a lot about contentment lately—how many different types of it there are and what it means to have it in your life on a regular basis. For many years, my hard-driving television producing and writing career took precedence over what I considered the frivolity of "the talent." I had given up on my favorite passions in exchange for a serious life with serious responsibilities that would yield serious hard-earned achievements. I didn't dance, I didn't act, and I didn't sing. (Wait, I take that back—I *did* continue to perform seven days a week, but it was with my young children on the "stage" of their tiny bedrooms in LA, on a wool IKEA carpet with a rainbow motif, always to rave reviews.)

Your joy will always find a way out—like sunlight through the cracks in the darkness. I left performing when I was in my late twenties and didn't return to it until my late forties. The reason for the departure is another story, but one can imagine how getting back into professional performing after such a long absence would be life-changing. While I am still a serious writer and producer, I have carved out room for this other side of me that yearns for and needs to express as an actor, and now I see it is possible to do both. Each feeds the other in a positive way.

I truly love to make film and TV for a living. And these days no matter whom I am working with, there always seems to be some sort of magic involved. Like the sorcery involved in creating Corona Kitchen with Debrianna. And you know, what is life without cheese, really?

DANCE THE HOKI POKI WASABI FISH

SERVES 4

1 lime or lemon

1 cup wasabi mayonnaise

1 tablespoon minced garlic

1 tablespoon grated fresh ginger

White pepper, to taste

¼ teaspoon salt

Rice crumbs (GF) or panko

2 pounds white fish fillets (like cod or hoki), washed and pat dry

Butter for coating dish

1. Preheat oven to 400°F.

2. Zest the lime into the wasabi mayonnaise, and then squeeze the lime's juice into it and mix.

3. Add the mayo and all other ingredients except the rice crumbs, fish, and butter to a shallow pan. Place the rice crumbs in another shallow pan.

4. Coat the fish fillets in the mayo mixture and then in the rice crumbs.

5. Place the fish fillets in a buttered baking dish or nonstick pan, and bake 20 to 25 minutes.

GREAT-AUNT GEORGIA'S LIFE IS NOT THAT COMPLICATED MOUSSAKA

SERVES 6

Salt for reducing eggplant bitterness

2 medium eggplants, peeled and sliced

⅓ cup* olive oil, and more for greasing the pan

1½ pounds ground lamb

1 onion, peeled and finely chopped

½ cup chopped fresh parsley

2 medium tomatoes, chopped

½ cup dry red wine

Pinch ground cinnamon

Pinch sea salt

Pinch freshly ground black pepper

2 eggs

1 cup cottage cheese

½ cup bread crumbs

Dash freshly grated nutmeg

1 cup freshly grated Parmesan, and more for finishing

* I used my best judgment here, as Nana didn't write an amount!

> My Nana wrote next to the recipe in pencil, "This quick, easy, good."

1. Preheat oven to 350°F.

2. Salt and drain the eggplant to eliminate bitterness (see instructions in Lisa's eggplant parmesan, page 142), and then pat dry and sauté in olive oil. Once finished, allow to dry on paper towels to absorb excess oil.

3. In the same skillet, combine the lamb, onion, and parsley. Brown and stir to keep crumbly.

4. Drain the fat, and then add the tomatoes, wine, cinnamon, sea salt, and pepper. Simmer over low heat until the liquid evaporates, and then remove from heat.

5. In a medium bowl, beat the eggs, and then mix in the cottage cheese and whip for 1 minute.

6. Grease a 9 x 13-inch baking dish and dust lightly with bread crumbs. Place alternating layers of eggplant and meat sauce in the dish, layering each with some of the cottage cheese and egg mixture and a sprinkle of Parmesan and bread crumbs.

7. Bake for 30 minutes, and then remove and let cool for 15 minutes before serving. Finish with a sprinkle of Parmesan on each serving.

A little shout-out and thank-you to my Great-Aunt Georgia John Kitchupolos Papatone. I know you are up there with my Nana probably watching these *Corona Kitchen* live-stream shows and laughing at my mistakes and praying I don't embarrass myself too badly with your namesake recipes. I want you to know how much I appreciate everything you did when we were young. The time and effort you put into preparing your extremely work-intensive specialties with such artistry is nothing short of marvelous—from the brilliantly crafted, hand-embroidered tablecloths and linens you made to the wedding-china table settings and animated conversations that brought everyone such comfort and sometimes grief over the ones we had lost. I am so grateful I was allowed to be in on these cooking sessions. And you never forgot to bless the loved ones who were no longer with us. I remember you reciting special prayers in Greek over the food as we cooked. You were a beautiful soul and put so much love into these delicious meals.

I was proud and delighted to be a helper in the large-scale dessert operations of Thanksgiving, Christmas, and Easter with you. While baking with aplomb, effortlessly, Nana would share the stories of our homeland, and Aunt Georgia would share the stories of her homeland of Greece, and then they would both reminisce on their myriad travels with Dida and Georgia's husband, Uncle Gus (Dida's half-brother). Aunt Georgia always spoke passionately about where she wanted to go next, and I remember getting caught up in their desire for adventure. I couldn't wait to visit these places. She kept our cultural history alive within us in America. And while my memory of her vigilance and exactitude with the making of many recipes remains, I sure can feel the love raining down from her and all the other extraordinary women in our family who cooked and nurtured us from the heart as they made these fierce, all-consuming, labor-of-love dishes of our ancestors.

Uncle Gus, Aunt Georgia, Nana, and Dida.

I Wanna Be Curled Up on My Couch with the Cats Stuffed Meatloaf

SERVES 8

MEATLOAF

1 (1-pound) package frozen broccoli

2 tablespoons olive oil

3 garlic cloves, minced

2 teaspoons kosher salt

¾ cup half-and-half and water mixed in equal parts, and more half-and-half if needed for creaminess (optional)

1¾ cups bread crumbs

1 medium onion, peeled and chopped

Handful fresh parsley

1 pound ground beef

1 pound ground pork

2 teaspoons chopped fresh thyme

2 fresh sage leaves, chopped

1 teaspoon herbes de Provence

2 teaspoons freshly ground black pepper

1½ teaspoons ground fennel (optional)

3 large eggs

1 cup chopped green chile peppers

3 cups shredded cheese (I used an aged Gouda and Pecorino Toscano mix)

SAUCE

2 garlic cloves, chopped

2 tablespoons olive oil

2 tablespoons tomato paste

½ cup red wine

1 (16-ounce) can tomatoes

2 teaspoons honey

½ teaspoon chopped fresh thyme

½ teaspoon salt

1 teaspoon Worcestershire sauce or coconut amino acids

1. Defrost the broccoli and set it aside.

2. Preheat oven to 350°F.

3. Lightly toast the garlic in the olive oil, and then add the tomato paste and cook for a few minutes. Add the wine, tomatoes, honey, thyme, salt, Worcestershire sauce, and ½ cup water, and simmer until the sauce thickens, about 20 to 30 minutes.

4. Meanwhile, sauté the defrosted broccoli in olive oil, 1 garlic clove, and ½ teaspoon salt. Cook until the moisture is eliminated, about 6 minutes, and then remove it from the heat and let cool. You may need to chop it if the florets are large or it won't roll well.

5. Pour the half-and-half mixture over the bread crumbs.

6. In a blender, blend the onion and parsley until smooth. Add the mix to the bread crumbs, and let sit 5 minutes or until most of the liquid is absorbed. You might need to add more half-and-half to make it creamy.

7. Mix the ground meats, spices, remaining salt, and 2 cloves chopped garlic. Add the bread crumb mixture and eggs, and mix well.

8. Spread half the mixture on a sheet of parchment paper or plastic wrap cut into a rectangle about ½ inch thick and the width of your loaf pan. Spread the filling in layers with the broccoli, green chile peppers, and cheese, and then use the parchment paper to roll it like a jelly roll and put it in the loaf pan.

9. Cover the meatloaf with sauce, and bake until it pulls away from the sides of the pan or reaches an internal temperature of 160°F, about 40 minutes.

TIP: The wonderful thing about meatloaf is that it lends itself to your creativity or to what you have in your kitchen. I often make it with spinach and mushrooms. I usually add a layer of sliced prosciutto, but during COVID, I used ground pork instead of ground turkey and went from there. And it was delicious. I served it with baked butternut squash, but those salt-roasted potatoes (see page 122) would be amazing with this.

DEBRIANNA'S

Grateful for Vegan Scallops with Rice Noodles (You'll Never Miss the Scallops)

SERVES 2

MARINADE

1½ cups roasted vegetable broth

2 teaspoons light miso

1 teaspoon olive oil

MUSHROOMS

4 stems of king oyster mushrooms (also called trumpet mushrooms), cut into 1-inch pieces

1 cup roasted vegetable broth

¼ cup dry white wine

3 garlic cloves, minced

1 teaspoon soy sauce

½ teaspoon kelp flakes (optional)

1 tablespoon vegan butter

1 shallot, sliced

PASTA

Rice noodles for 2

1 cup vegetable broth

¼ cup white wine

1 teaspoon ground fennel seeds

2 tablespoons sliced sun-dried tomatoes, drained

¼ cup finely chopped fresh parsley

1 tablespoon red pepper flakes

1. Set the broth in a pot over high heat. Once hot, turn the heat off and add the miso and olive oil. Stir to combine.

2. Place the mushroom stems in the marinade, and refrigerate for 2 hours to overnight. (I like to store them in a 1-gallon plastic bag, pushing all the air out.) When ready to use, remove them from the refrigerator and drain completely.

3. Place the mushroom stems in a skillet set over medium-high heat. Add the broth, white wine, 1 teaspoon of the minced garlic, soy sauce, and kelp flakes and simmer until the mushrooms have completely absorbed the liquid, about 15 minutes. They will shrink as they cook.

4. Add the vegan butter, remaining garlic, and shallot, browning the stems on each side. Avoid burning the shallot or garlic. Remove the mushroom stems and reserve, keeping the garlic and shallot in the pan.

5. Prepare the rice noodles according to the directions on the package.

6. Add the broth, wine, and fennel seeds to the skillet with the shallot, and cook to reduce by half.

7. Add the tomatoes, parsley, and red pepper flakes to the skillet, and simmer for 2 to 3 minutes; then add the noodles. Allow the noodles to absorb most of the liquid.

8. Toss the mushroom stems, the "scallops," with the noodles prior to serving.

Lisa's

Don't Worry About It Cioppino (A Tony's Seafood Original)

GF

SERVES 4

Olive oil to coat the bottom of the pot

1 large onion, peeled and chopped

3 garlic cloves, chopped

1 (28-ounce) can diced tomatoes with juice or 3 large fresh tomatoes

2 tablespoons red wine vinegar

½ cup dry white wine

½ cup chopped fresh parsley

12 teaspoons freshly chopped basil

1 teaspoon sea salt

½ teaspoon freshly ground black pepper

1 bay leaf

5 drops hot sauce (optional)

Various fresh seafoods (I like a mix of 1 pound fresh red snapper, filleted and cut into large pieces; 15 littleneck clams; 8 whole crab legs, kept in their shells; and 1 pound shrimp, shells removed and deveined— but feel free to substitute with other shellfish and whole fish.)

French bread for serving (optional)

1. Heat the olive oil in a very large pot set over medium heat, and then add the onion and garlic and sauté until soft.

2. Pour in the tomatoes, red wine vinegar, and white wine, and bring to a boil. Add the parsley, basil, sea salt, pepper, hot sauce, and bay leaf. Reduce the heat to medium low, and simmer until the liquid is reduced almost completely, about 1 hour.

3. Add the seafood, cover, and cook until the seafood is properly cooked and the clams, if using, have opened. Discard any clams that haven't opened; do not eat them.

4. Spoon into bowls, and serve with crusty French bread.

Franny was born in San Francisco and grew up about forty-five minutes north of the city. Her family lived on the water, and when I say "on the water," I mean their house and Tony's Seafood, their restaurant, were built on posts over the waves of the Pacific Ocean on Highway 1. Every day my mother's grandpa Tony and my grandmother's brother, Felix, as well as my grandpa Steve (a.k.a. Dida), would take a boat called the *Naški* out in the wee early morning hours and fish. After a few hours they would bring their haul of fresh fish back in, cook the catch of the day, and open the restaurant to the public.

It was a pretty hectic scene safety-wise to raise two kids right on the ocean like that in 1946, with my grandma working full-time in the kitchen cooking all the meals for the restaurant. She's lucky that she had her mother, Maria Rakela, to take care of my mom and Uncle Steve. But kids will be kids, and they were a curious bunch. One time Franny cut herself pretty severely on coral, and the blood ran down her leg into the tide pools, but my grandfather fortunately happened to be right there and ran to get a big towel to stop the bleeding and then sped them off to the emergency room, which was an hour away. She could have bled to death. Dida's hair tuned white that day.

Franny and Nana living by the sea.

Nana taught Franny to swim by putting a rope around her two-year-old self, lowering her off the dock, and saying, "Okay, now, Francie, swim. Swim!" Yikes. Picture my mom as a little one being total shark-bait hors d'oeuvres. A lot of people don't realize that this area of northern California is called the "red triangle" for a reason—basically it's a breeding ground for great white sharks. No joke, my great-grandfather Tony was on the cover of the *San Francisco Chronicle* in the late 1940s when he caught a great white in the bay. Jesus, Mary, and Joseph, it's a miracle my mom didn't get eaten, sucked out to sea, or drowned. Maybe this is why my mom has no fear? Nerves of steel, that one. She would have made a great naval commander on a nuclear submarine were the choice available to her.

Tony and the great white.

HALUSKI (FRIED CABBAGE AND NOODLES), THE #1 COMFORT FOOD IN POLAND

SERVES 4

HOMEMADE NOODLES*

2 cups all-purpose flour, and more for sticking if needed (optional) and dusting

1 teaspoon salt, and more for salting cooking water

4 large eggs, room temperature

1 tablespoon olive oil

* If you don't want to make homemade noodles, use 12 ounces dry noodles.

FRIED CABBAGE

8 slices thick bacon, cut into ½-inch pieces

1 large onion, peeled and diced

3 tablespoons unsalted butter

1 head green cabbage, sliced into ½-inch-thick pieces

½ cup dry white wine

¼ teaspoon crushed caraway seeds

1 teaspoon salt, and more for salting cooking water

2 teaspoons freshly ground black pepper

2 teaspoons green chile powder or crushed red pepper (optional)

TO MAKE THE HOMEMADE NOODLES

1. Combine the flour and salt in a large bowl. Create a well in the center of the flour, and crack the eggs into the well. Add the olive oil and 1 tablespoon warm water to the well. Mix until well incorporated. If the dough is sticking to the bowl, add more flour until it can form a ball.

2. Let the dough sit in the bowl, covered with a damp paper towel, for 10 minutes.

3. Generously flour a work table, and dust the dough with flour. Knead the dough until it is still soft but does not stick to the table. Add more flour during this process if it's too sticky.

4. Roll the dough to about ⅛ inch thick. Noodles will plump a little when boiled, so roll thinner than desired. Do not roll too tightly, as you don't want the dough to stick to itself. Cut the rolled dough into ¼-inch pieces.

5. Unwrap the noodles carefully so that the dough doesn't stick to itself. Lay the noodles out on the floured table, and then cut them to your desired length.

6. Fill a large pot with salted water, and bring to a boil. Add the noodles, and cook until they float to the top of the water.

TO MAKE THE FRIED CABBAGE

1. Cook the bacon in a large nonstick skillet until crispy. Remove and place on a paper-towel-lined plate, leaving the bacon grease in the skillet.

2. Add the onion to the bacon grease, and cook until it begins to soften, about 2 minutes.

3. If you are using dry noodles and not homemade, bring a large pot of salted water to a boil. Add the noodles and cook according to the directions on the package. When they are done, drain and place in a large bowl with the butter.

4. Add the cabbage to the skillet with the bacon grease, and cook until tender and browned, about 15 minutes, stirring as it cooks down.

5. Deglaze the skillet with white wine, and then add the caraway seeds, salt, pepper, and green chile powder.

6. Mix the cabbage and bacon into the noodles, and then serve.

I was in a relationship. My life with Wayne was a learning experience and not one that ever gave me a sense of belonging.

One clue that we weren't a good fit should have been that he was allergic to mustard. I only found out after I nearly killed him, when my sister Lisa, who flew across the country to spend Thanksgiving with me, helped me make my brand-new recipe for roasted turkey. I was still working on what would become my traditional recipes, and I had just found one that sounded amazing. Coat the turkey inside and out with a spice rub based in Dijon mustard. It was a theme. We made Dijon salad dressing and sautéed mustard greens as a side. Then we spent the meal watching him suck down bottles of Benadryl, with me, my sister, and a few guests feeling guilty, quietly eating that delicious turkey. I should have known then that this relationship was destined for ruin, but I digress.

The only redeeming factor of this relationship was that he had introduced me to his old friends Bob and Noni, LA screenwriters, when they had come to Santa Fe on vacation. We instantly hit it off. When I decided it was time to go "make my mark," he called them and let them know I was arriving. I had never been to LA before, and they were eager to help in any way they could once I got there.

Through word of mouth in our small but tight acting community in Santa Fe, I had found a room in a house in the valley. "Oh, yeah, my friend is leaving this room he has been renting. It's a quiet house, and the lady who owns it is super nice," the friend of a friend assured me. I called the number and introduced myself to her, and the deal was sealed.

Wayne drove me and my stuff to LA, and we fought the whole way. Fun trip. As soon as we finally approached the city limits after the extremely long thirteen-hour drive, the clutch on my car went out. We somehow rolled into a Toyota dealership. He offered to help me pay for repairs, but I instinctively knew that would become another noose in the relationship, so I dug out my way-overused credit card. We had a long wait ahead of us.

"Oh, yeah," the man at the front desk grumbled. "There is a monastery museum not far from here. It's kinda interesting. Here's a cab number."

"Oh, that's okay. Just tell us where it is. We can walk. We are ex–New Yorkers," Wayne interjected before I might take the number, moths flying everywhere.

"*What?*" The mechanic's craggy face sparked up. "You can't walk that far. It's five blocks from here. No one walks in LA." Rubbing my lucky charm, I was praying this wasn't an omen as we walked to the monastery. I never felt like I belonged in New York, and I was praying I would feel better in LA.

Many hours later, with the clutch fixed and Wayne gone, I finally arrived at the house and met my new LA roommate. The first thing I noticed was the tacked-up old magazine picture of Van Gogh's vase of sunflowers. I thought, *I can replace that with a real framed picture*, and I touched it gently to see if there was a nail hole behind it. Instead I found a hole. A real hole. Like the wall had been punched. I replaced the crinkled page and felt scared. That's when I called Bob and Noni to tell them a little about the blue room, trying to seem nonchalant.

"We'll be there in about thirty minutes," Bob said quickly, hearing the bit of my anxiety that I let slip out. I sat on the edge of the bed and waited, pondering the blue carpet. I hadn't known that the kind of area rug you usually see only in bathrooms in front of a toilet, made of polyester shiny-blue shag with a plastic foam backing, could be made large enough to cover an entire room. Who knew?

My friends arrived, and we hugged like long-lost buds. "Can we see your room?" Noni asked politely. "Sure. It's . . . blue," I tried to say cheerily. I led them through the house to this new room of mine. Noni walked in and swallowed a gasp.

"Well, you're right. It *is* blue. Are you okay with it?"

"Oh yeah," I assured them, trying to sound confident. "I probably won't even be here much, with auditions and classes and all," I added, as much to reassure myself as her.

They left after a bit and immediately called Wayne. They were traumatized by all the blue and wondered if they should offer me a space in their home. "You can ask her. Ask her to cook for you too. You won't regret it." This response always surprised me, because God knows, he nearly did regret it when I almost killed him with the mustard turkey.

From that moment on, I belonged. In their home, in their kitchen, in their lives. I was only supposed to be there for three months, but I ended up staying with them for a year, and we have been best friends ever since. They eventually walked me down the aisle when I met and married David, the love of my life.

I look back on that time and understand that their friendship set me on the path to finding and honing a sense of belonging. I offer it to all those who enter our home, and I believe both Lisa and I want nothing more than for those who join us in these uncertain times to feel that same sense of belonging when they invite Corona Kitchen into theirs.

Bob and Noni.

"I Don't Have Time for That" Two-Day Beef Bourguignon

SERVES 6

3 slices thick pancetta, cubed

4 pounds boneless beef chuck roast or bone-in short ribs, cubed

1 bottle Syrah or Rhône blend red wine

2 cups beef stock (homemade is best if you have it)

¼ cup tamari sauce

¼ cup all-purpose flour

Sea salt, to taste

Freshly ground black pepper, to taste

1 cup marinara sauce

2 cups pearl onions

5 garlic cloves, 4 finely chopped and 1 minced

3 tablespoons finely chopped fresh thyme and a few fresh thyme sprigs

3 tablespoons finely chopped fresh parsley

3 large carrots, peeled and sliced 1 to 2 inches

3 medium turnips, sliced 2 inches

2 bay leaves

1½ pounds small purple potatoes or the even smaller red or yellow ones

8 ounces cremini mushrooms, sliced with stems attached

3 tablespoons unsalted butter

¼ cup white wine or marsala
1 teaspoon smoked paprika

Basmati rice for 6, cooked, for serving

1. Fry the pancetta in a large cast-iron skillet to crisp. Do not overcook. Then put it in a slow cooker, reserving the droppings.

2. Sear the beef cubes in the pan with the pancetta drippings. Brown on all sides, and then add the beef to the slow cooker, leaving the drippings in the pan.

3. Make a reduction by simmering the beef and pancetta drippings. Add ½ cup red wine and ½ cup beef stock. Scrape the pan to release the meat residue. As the mixture reduces to half, slowly add the tamari, another ½ cup red wine, and another ½ cup beef stock. Then slowly whisk in the flour as it begins to thicken.

4. With a spatula, pour and scrape the entire reduction into the slow cooker. Then add the rest of the wine and the sea salt, pepper, marinara sauce, onions, finely chopped garlic and thyme, parsley, carrots, turnips, bay leaves, the remaining beef stock, and the potatoes to the stew. Stir gently. Cover and cook on your slow cooker's appropriate setting. (Mine is a "low" setting—and it will cook for about 8 hours.)

5. About 20 minutes before the slow cooker is finished, sauté the mushrooms in the butter, white wine, minced garlic, sea salt, and pepper, and add to the stew, incorporating them in gently.

6. Serve over basmati rice.

TIP: Because this will cook for about 8 hours, it's best to start it in the morning. Leftovers can be frozen.

Salmon in Parchment
Tous Ensemble… Toujours Mieux! (All Together… Always Better!)

SERVES 2

3 tablespoons unsalted butter

2 garlic cloves, minced

12 small fingerling potatoes, parboiled to just fork tender

10 baby asparagus stalks or 6 regular asparagus stalks, per parchment, with ends cleaned, or 2 small zucchini, cut into ¼-inch slices on the diagonal

2 (3-ounce) wild-caught salmon fillets

½ teaspoon sea salt

1 lemon, cut into round slices

2 tablespoons chopped fresh parsley

1. Melt the butter in a pan set over medium heat, and then add the garlic for 2 minutes.

2. Place the potatoes in a bowl, and lightly coat them with the butter mixture.

3. Cut 2 sheets of large parchment paper, approximately 15 x 16 inches, so that each will hold 1 fillet in the center and be able to wrap and enclose the fish with potatoes on the side.

4. Place the veggies in the center of the parchment papers and then the salmon on top; add some of the butter and garlic mixture. Sprinkle with salt. Then lay lemon slices across the top of the fish, about 3 slices each, and top each with half the parsley. Add 1 serving of the potatoes on the sides of each fish fillet.

5. Wrap the fish and veggies tightly by pulling the parchment paper up and over the fish and rolling the paper until it closes the fish snugly; then roll in the ends tightly to enclose it all for baking.

6. Carefully lift the packets (you can use a wide spatula) onto a 9 x 13-inch baking pan that holds both packets snugly.

7. Bake the packets for about 20 to 25 minutes, depending on how thick the salmon is. You can use a thermometer to test the fish through the parchment at the 20-minute mark. It should reach an internal temperature of 145°F.

Over the last few years I have had the honor and pleasure of getting to know Nadyne and Joe Bicknell. They are a remarkable couple. They live in Albuquerque and are the parents of Morse, my beloved. There is nothing like being in their big, beautiful backyard at the height of summer, as they are avid gardeners and meticulously attend to their orchard, flowers, herbs, and homegrown vegetables. This spring Morse and I had dinner with them one night when the rose garden happened to be in full bloom. It was spectacular! There are so many natural wonders at their place, like the gorgeously maintained apricot tree in their courtyard that most years has a prolific yield of fruit. Nadyne uses the fruit to make countless jars of the most delicious jam that she shares with friends and family all year long. And they grow so many kinds of mouthwatering tomatoes: Black Krims, Brandywines, Early Girl, Green Zebra, Purple Cherokees, Super Sweet Sungold 100s, and more, planting them in Martha Stewart–level custom boxes in between their fruit trees. They also have Winesap, Braeburn, and Granny Smith apple trees; Bosc, Bartlett, and Asian pears; white and yellow peaches; and a sixty-year-old Rainier cherry tree of their neighbor's that hangs over the side and into their yard that they share. A few weeks ago, Nadyne baked a Rainier cherry pie with her mother's trusted piecrust recipe. It was seriously one of the best pies I have ever eaten in my life. I admire how they always work as a team, with an unspoken language about who does what, year after year, to keep up with the sheer amount of manual labor and planning it takes to grow and harvest all of their bounty. The respect and care they show for one another I find especially endearing. They have been married now for *sixty-four years*. How is that even possible? Why aren't there medals for *that* kind of love and commitment?

It's funny—they actually believe they are slowing down, and when I look at what they do, I am in awe of their tales of what I would classify as extreme outdoor adventures, because I am certain I could not even attempt to do half of what they accomplish in their eighties. They have always been super outdoorsy, and they still actively hunt at their Duck Club in Colorado and go fishing and camping and even telemark skiing! I would have never made it as one of their kids, drama club–nerd–wimp that I was. Morse always says jokingly to me when I feel like turning around in the middle of a hike or when I decline camping for a hotel stay, "Sweetie, I just don't know if you're Bicknell material—but I love you all the same." At this point in my life, I embrace my utter lack of Sporty Spice skills and inability to function without hot water, lattes, and a 5G cell phone. Fortunately for me, there was an aspiring artist inside that Bicknell-raised camper-in-25-below Boy Scout, and Morse became an actor-filmmaker-musician-writer, so we can be namby-pamby pantywaists together!

Case in point: this salmon dish was made from a wild-caught salmon that Nadyne Bicknell caught *by herself* up near Vancouver Island. At eight-four, she won the prize for catching the biggest salmon on the trip! They go every year with the delightful Marti Stockard, their best friend from college at the University of Michigan, and fish to their hearts' content. This is not sissy stuff. You ever try to reel in a deep-water ocean fish that weighs thirty-seven pounds up from thousands of tons of sea water? All I can say is they are both absolute treasures, and I'm so grateful to them for welcoming me into their home and hearts and family with countless amazingly delicious dinners and family stories that are what life is all about.

Nadyne and Joe Bicknell in their rose garden.

LISA'S

Dónde Están Mis Fish Tacos Especiales?

(GF)

FISH

Dash chipotle powder

Dash Tajín chile (Mexican lime-chile seasoning)

¾ teaspoon sea salt

½ teaspoon freshly ground white pepper

2 garlic cloves, chopped

2 large fillets tilapia, red snapper, or cod

Juice of 1 large lime (about ⅓ cup)

3 tablespoons grape-seed oil or other high-temperature oil (such as vegetable oil, coconut oil, or avocado oil)

CREAM SAUCE

½ cup sour cream

Zest of 1 lime

2 tablespoons fresh lime juice

1 teaspoon Tajín chile (Mexican lime-chile seasoning)

⅛ teaspoon sea salt

¼ jalapeño, minced

3 tablespoons green tomatillo salsa*

1 teaspoon chopped fresh cilantro (optional)

*You can buy this or make a homemade version by combining 1 roasted Hatch chile, 2 roasted tomatillos, the juice of ½ a lime, and sea salt, to taste, together in a food processor for a few seconds.

TORTILLAS

1 tablespoon grape-seed oil or other high-temperature cooking oil (such as vegetable oil, coconut oil, or avocado oil)

8 mini corn tortillas (street taco size)

TACO ASSEMBLY

1 cup spicy sauerkraut

½ cup orange cherry tomatoes, quartered

8 tablespoons green tomatillo salsa (use 1 tablespoon per taco)

½ cup cotija cheese, shredded

TO MAKE THE FISH

1. In a medium bowl, combine the chipotle powder, Tajín chile, sea salt, white pepper, and garlic.

2. Season the fillets on both sides using the lime juice first and then the mixed ingredients. Refrigerate for 1 hour.

3. Coat a skillet with grape-seed oil, and panfry the fish in it for about 3 to 4 minutes per side.

4. Remove the fish from the pan, and set aside.

TO MAKE THE CREAM SAUCE

1. Mix all ingredients for the cream sauce together well, and then cover and refrigerate.

TO PREPARE THE TORTILLAS

1. In an oiled skillet set over medium heat, cook the tortillas on each side for about 45 seconds per side.

TO ASSEMBLE THE TACOS

1. Shred the fish with a fork.

2. Fill the cooked tortillas with the shredded fish and then, in order, sauerkraut, tomatoes, green tomatillo salsa, and cream sauce. Sprinkle with cheese.

When I was pregnant with both kids, I was lucky to have found a nanny to help raise them while I worked in TV. Her name was Queta. She was and is a wonderful woman, and I love her so much. I'm honestly not sure how I could have been a full-time working mother without her. I know what a luxury it was to have her in our lives. She was a terrific chef too. She came from a family who owned a restaurant in Puebla, a city in southeast Mexico known for its rich culinary history and, most notably, for being the birthplace of mole poblano. Some days I would come home late, and Queta would have made fresh tortillas and roasted tomato salsa and already be starting to cook her famous mole. She taught the kids how to cook, and she knew the fine art of sauces.

She loved to laugh, and for eight years she dedicated her life to the kids and me. She had to leave her own family to survive. I cannot imagine the amount of strength, bravery, and love for her children that enabled her to do that. We talked about it a lot. I understood what she had given up and that she was now giving that love to my family to provide for hers. It's so wrong that a person would have to make that sacrifice. She saved me at a time when I didn't even know what was amiss. She knew, though. I could see it in her eyes. She saw me crying night after night for no reason and would comfort me. I thought it stemmed from the exhaustion of working and child-rearing, but it wasn't. It was loneliness. She stayed with me because she wanted to help another mother in a loveless marriage. I was lost, and she saw the complicated weaving I had gotten myself into. And yet, I was in deep denial and had convinced myself that everything was *fine*, and if there were problems, I made a vow that I could and would make the marriage work, damn it. She knew all too well how difficult it would be for me to leave, because she had experienced the same thing in Mexico, having fled her ex-husband. So we made a pact to save each other.

It's shocking the obvious things we won't admit to ourselves. The things we know to be true that we keep unsaid and buried for years. Well, the truth always comes out. Eventually. I'm so glad that Queta remarried and is in love with a man who adores her. She gave me some of the best years of her life to help raise these children, whom I know she loved like her own. She still asks about them all the time. We got to revel in the joy of them together as babies and toddlers. She taught them how to speak Spanish. She taught them manners, and she taught them about food and culture. She protected them when I could not be there. I will never forget her and her capacity for love and compassion.

Queta and Seamus.

DEBRIANNA'S

KNOCK YOUR SOCKS OFF ROASTED ZUCCHINI LASAGNA

SERVES 6 TO 8

2 or 3 large zucchini or eggplant (about 1½ pounds), or more if skipping the noodles

5 tablespoons olive oil

1½ teaspoons kosher salt

½ teaspoon freshly ground black pepper

1 tablespoon tomato paste

3 garlic cloves, minced

4 sausage links or 1 teaspoon ground fennel seeds

½ cup red wine

3 cups tomato sauce (see Debrianna's sauce, page 144, or Lisa's sauce, page 142, or use your favorite store-bought brand)

1½ cups ricotta

8-ounce container mascarpone

¼ cup chopped fresh basil

¼ cup chopped fresh parsley

1 tablespoon finely chopped fresh thyme

1 (16-ounce) box no-boil lasagna noodles (optional; you will not use the whole box)

3 cups freshly shredded cheese (Merlot BellaVitano, Pecorino Toscano, or Asiago works well)

8 ounces fresh mozzarella (packed in water)

¼ cup goat cheese (optional)

1. Set oven racks in upper part of oven, and then preheat oven to 400°F.

2. Cut the ends off the zucchini and discard. Cut the remainder of each in half crosswise and then in half lengthwise, creating slices about ¼ inch thick.

3. Pour 2 tablespoons olive oil into 2 rimmed baking sheets, and spread evenly. Arrange the zucchini slices in a single layer on the sheets, turning once to coat with olive oil. Sprinkle each sheet with ¼ teaspoon salt and ¼ teaspoon pepper. Roast until the slices sizzle and begin to brown, 12 to 15 minutes.

4. Meanwhile, set a medium saucepan over high heat, and add the remaining 1 tablespoon olive oil. Once heated, add the tomato paste. Cook for 1 minute, and then add 2 of the minced garlic cloves and cook for another minute. If using sausage, remove from casing and brown it in the saucepan, breaking it up into small pieces and then removing and setting aside. If not using sausage, add the fennel seeds.

5. Carefully add the red wine to deglaze the pan, and cook for 1 minute; then add the tomato sauce. Salt to taste. Simmer, covered, until ready to use, adding back the sausage if using.

6. Combine the ricotta, mascarpone, herbs, and remaining garlic and salt and pepper to taste.

7. Remove the zucchini when done, and let cool a bit.

8 Spread 1 cup of the tomato sauce on the bottom of an 11 x 7-inch (or 6- to 8-cup) baking dish.

9. Coat the noodles with some of the shredded cheese on 1 side, and lay them in the bottom of the pan with the cheese side facing up. Place them tightly together but not overlapping. You will likely need to break noodles to fit the pan; don't worry if they don't fit exactly, as they will absorb the excess liquid and expand.

10. Arrange half the cooked zucchini slices on top of the noodles in a solid layer, and again close together. Spoon 1 cup tomato sauce on top, and then add a layer of shredded cheese. Top with the remaining zucchini, some more of the cheese, and then some of the sauce. Do this until the zucchini is fully used. If using noodles, coat 1 side with cheese and add to the top layer, cheese side up; then top with more sauce. Add the mozzarella to the top layer.

11. Cover tightly with foil, and bake on the middle rack for 20 minutes; then remove the foil and bake until the sauce is bubbling and the cheese is golden, about 40 minutes more.

TIP: It's fun to roast your own garden tomatoes in the oven with minced garlic, olive oil, and salt and then purée them to make the tomato sauce.

FOR THE LOVE OF 40 CLOVES OF GARLIC CHICKEN

GF

SERVES 4

4 pounds whole chicken

2 to 3 tablespoons kosher salt

¼ cup (½ stick) salted butter, room temperature, and more to coat the skillet

2 tablespoons chopped fresh rosemary

2 tablespoons chopped fresh thyme

½ teaspoon freshly ground black pepper, and more to taste (optional)

Zest of ½ lemon

½ lemon, quartered

1 (3-pound) bag of small fingerling potatoes

Olive oil for lightly coating the potatoes

40 garlic cloves (about 3 heads), peeled

½ cup dry white wine

1½ cups chicken broth

2 tablespoons unsalted butter, cold

Juice of ½ lemon

1. Coat the chicken in salt, and let it sit in the refrigerator for 1 to 24 hours. Bring the chicken to room temperature before baking by patting it dry and letting it sit, unrefrigerated, for 1 hour.

2. Preheat oven to 425°F.

3. In a bowl, mix the salted butter with the fresh herbs, pepper, and lemon zest.

4. With your fingers, ease the skin away from the chicken, and spread some of the butter mixture inside. Spread the rest of the butter on the outside, all over the chicken. Sprinkle on additional black pepper if desired. Put the lemon quarters in the cavity.

5. Coat the potatoes lightly in olive oil, and then rub a cast-iron skillet or baking dish with salted butter and place the potatoes, garlic, and chicken, breast side up, in it. If desired, tie the drumsticks together with twine. Organize the garlic around the chicken.

6. Roast the chicken and potatoes for 1 hour, basting with pan juices and a little of the chicken stock every 15 to 30 minutes, until the juices run clear when the meaty part of a thigh is pricked with a skewer or knife or the chicken reaches 160°F.

7. Remove the chicken, garlic, and potatoes, placing them in one bowl and reserving the juices in another bowl.

8. Set the skillet over medium-high heat. Add the wine to deglaze the pan, and scrape the browned bits from the bottom. Let cook until reduced by half, and then add the pan juices and the chicken broth. Boil until reduced to about ¾ cup.

9. Remove the skillet from the heat, and add the unsalted butter to help thicken the gravy. Stir in the lemon juice, and season with salt and pepper.

10. Plate the chicken on a serving platter, and spoon some of the gravy on it prior to serving.

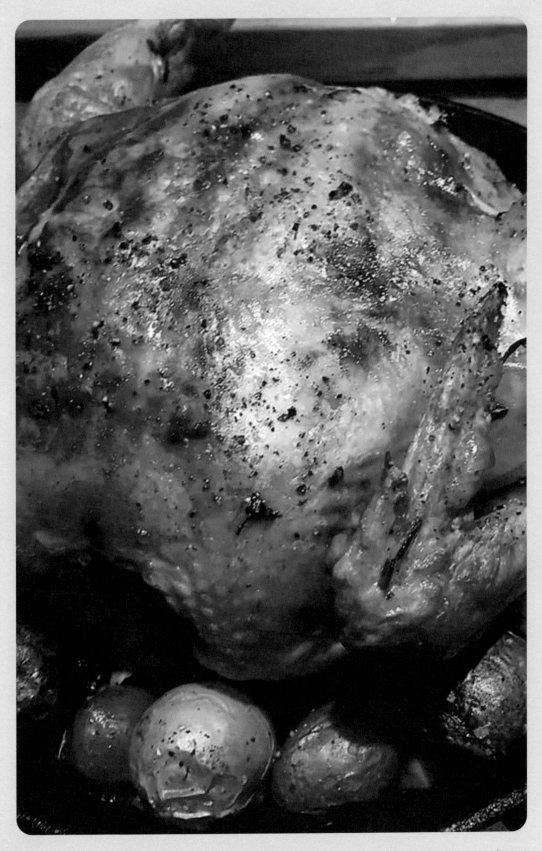

MAKE YOUR OWN DAMN RAMEN

SERVES 2

4 teaspoons sesame oil

3 garlic cloves, minced

2 teaspoons minced fresh ginger

3 tablespoons black soy sauce

¼ cup mirin
(sweet rice wine for cooking)

4 cups chicken or roasted
vegetable stock

5 dried shiitake mushrooms,
soaked in water (reserve
the water)

3 to 4 bird's eye chiles
(depending on your
tolerance for heat)

Kosher salt, to taste

2 large eggs

1 large shallot, sliced

5 fresh cremini
mushrooms, sliced

1 cup cooked chicken, beef,
or shrimp (optional; leftovers
work great)

1 cup frozen spinach or broccoli

2 (3-ounce) packs dried
ramen noodles

Freshly ground black
pepper, to taste

1. Set a large pot over medium heat, and add 2 teaspoons sesame oil. Cook until shimmering. Add the garlic and ginger, and cook for a few minutes until softened. Add the soy sauce and mirin, and stir to combine. Cook for another minute.

2. Add the stock, cover, and bring to a boil. Remove the lid and let simmer, uncovered, for 5 minutes; then add the dried shiitake mushrooms and soaking water, taking care not to add any grit if there is any. Add the chiles and simmer gently for another 10 minutes, and then season with salt.

3. Fill a pot with enough water to cover the eggs, and then bring to a boil. Gently lower the eggs (still cold from the fridge) into the boiling water, and then simmer for 7 minutes to achieve a slightly runny yoke or 8 minutes if you prefer a soft, set-up yoke.

4. Fill a large bowl with ice water. Transfer the eggs to the ice bath to stop the cooking process. Wait at least 5 minutes or until cool enough to handle the eggs, and then carefully peel away the shells and slice in half. Set aside until ready to serve.

5. Sauté the shallot in remaining 2 teaspoons of sesame oil until crispy, and gently sauté the cremini mushrooms for 2 minutes. Slice the chicken into thin pieces, and then set it aside.

6. Add the frozen spinach to the stock. When nearly done, add the ramen noodles to the boiling stock. Cook until soft, about 2 to 3 minutes.

7. Divide the noodles into 2 large bowls. Add the sliced chicken and then the ramen broth. Top with the shallot slices and the soft-boiled eggs sliced in half. Serve immediately.

SPINACH AND MUSHROOM CRÊPES

SERVES 6 TO 8 (WITH 10 SMALL OR 7 LARGE CRÊPES)

CRÊPE BATTER

2 eggs

1 cup whole milk

1 cup all-purpose flour

3 tablespoons melted unsalted butter, slightly cooled (hot butter will scramble and cook the eggs)

½ teaspoon salt

1 tablespoon finely chopped fresh herbs of choice, such as parsley, chives, or tarragon (optional)

SPINACH AND MUSHROOM FILLING

7 tablespoons unsalted butter

1 shallot, minced

2 pounds baby portobello, cremini, or button mushrooms, or a mix, sliced

2 teaspoons and 1 pinch HH Rancho Moraga Salt or sea salt

½ teaspoon ground cayenne pepper (optional)

4 tablespoons all-purpose flour

2 cups whole milk

1 cup heavy cream

Pinch freshly ground black pepper

¼ teaspoon freshly grated nutmeg

10 ounces fresh spinach

¾ cup grated Gruyère, Jarlsberg, or Swiss

½ cup grated Havarti or Monterey Jack

¼ cup freshly grated Parmesan

TO MAKE THE CRÊPE BATTER

1. Combine all batter ingredients in a food processor until smooth, about 20 to 30 seconds. If you don't have a food processor, use a hand mixer or whisk and beat until smooth.

2. Pour into a bowl, and refrigerate for at least 30 minutes.

TO MAKE THE SPINACH AND MUSHROOM FILLING

1. In a large frying pan set over medium heat, warm 5 tablespoons butter, and then add the shallot.

2. Add the mushrooms, 2 teaspoons salt, and cayenne pepper, and cook 6 to 8 minutes over medium-high heat. Then transfer to a bowl.

3. Add remaining 2 tablespoons butter to the frying pan (no need to clean), and then reduce heat to low. Add the flour, and whisk until it becomes a paste. The color should be very light (tan). If the sides of the pan or the color starts browning, turn down the heat.

4. Slowly add the milk, and start to whisk the butter and flour mixture to combine it. There will be lumps, so keep whisking and they will start to blend into the milk. Whisk over low heat for 3 minutes, and then add the heavy cream and continue to whisk for another 5 minutes.

5. Add pinches of salt and pepper, and the nutmeg. Turn up the heat to cook over medium heat until small bubbles begin to appear on the sides of the pan. Once you see the bubbles, turn off the heat immediately.

6. With the heat off, add the spinach and fold it into the sauce. As it begins to wilt, add the cooked mushrooms and any liquid from their bowl. Slowly fold the mushrooms and their liquid into the sauce.

7. Add the cheeses, and slowly mix them into the sauce. Keep the mixture in the pan with the heat off while you make the crêpes.

TO MAKE THE CRÊPES

1. Remove the batter from the refrigerator (it should have been there for at least 30 minutes).

2. Heat a crêpe pan over medium heat; if it begins to smoke, it's too hot. Once the pan is warm, use a ladle to pour ½ to 1 cup batter into the pan, depending on its size. It should be a thin layer.
Start by pouring it in the middle, and then pick up the pan by its handle and slowly move it side to side in a circular motion so the batter travels to all edges of the pan. Too much batter and it will spill over the edge, too little and it will not cover the pan and make an even crêpe. This takes some practice, so be patient and keep trying.

3. Cook the crêpes until light golden brown, about 2 minutes; then, using a rubber spatula, flip and cook the other side until light golden brown and slightly crisp on the edges, 30 seconds to 1 minute.

4. When the crêpes are done cooking, set them on a large plate. Place a paper towel in between each crêpe so they don't stick together.

5. Continue making crêpes until you have used all of the batter.

TO ASSEMBLE THE CRÊPES

1. Preheat oven to 350°F.

2. Spread a large spoonful of filling over the bottom of a ceramic or glass baking dish.

3. Add ½ to ¾ cup filling in a line about 2 inches from the sides. Roll the crêpes onto themselves, like a cigar or burrito, but not too tight. Place the rolled crêpes in the baking dish.

4. Pour any remaining filling sauce over the crêpes in the baking dish.

5. Bake until the crêpes are golden brown on top and the filling is bubbling in the dish, about 30 to 35 minutes.

TIP: You will need a nonstick pan, preferably a shallow crêpe pan. Serves well paired with a California chardonnay or pinot noir.

Rack of Lamb with Herb Honey Glaze

SERVES 4

1¾ to 2 pounds rack of lamb, frenched

Salt, to taste

Freshly ground black pepper, to taste

2 tablespoons grape-seed oil or olive oil

8 medium garlic cloves, whole but smashed

1 tablespoon HH Herbal Glaze Herb Infused Honey or mix of 1 tablespoon honey and ½ tablespoon blend of dried rosemary, dried thyme, and dried mint

1 small fresh mint sprig, finely chopped, for finishing

1 small fresh rosemary sprig, finely chopped, for finishing

Roasted potatoes or rice for serving (optional)

1. Preheat oven to 450°F.

2. Liberally season the rack of lamb with salt and pepper.

3. Set a 12-inch cast-iron skillet over medium-high heat, and add the grape-seed oil.

4. Using tongs, place the rack of lamb fat side down. Sear until golden brown, about 6 to 8 minutes, and then use the tongs to flip and sear all other sides of the rack for an additional 6 to 8 minutes.

5. Turn the lamb fat-side up and add the garlic, and then place the lamb in the oven. For medium-rare, roast until a thermometer reads 130°F in the center, 12 to 14 minutes.

6. Remove the lamb from the oven (be careful, as the skillet will be hot), and allow it to rest on the stovetop. Add 1 more pinch of salt to the lamb.

7. Turn oven to broil.

8. With a spoon, spread the HH Herbal Glaze Herb Infused Honey or honey and dried herbs liberally over the top and sides of the lamb.

9. Place the skillet back in the oven for 1 to 2 minutes, keeping an eye on it to make sure it doesn't start smoking. It should bubble but not burn.

10. Remove the lamb skillet, and let it rest for 5 minutes before slicing it into chops (slicing between the bones). Take a spoonful of sauce from the bottom of the skillet, and drizzle over the top of the lamb chops on a plate or platter.

11. Lightly sprinkle mint and rosemary over the meat and side dish of roasted potatoes or rice.

TIP: The honey glaze can be made with any herb you like with lamb, including rosemary, thyme, chives, lemon basil, or mint.

PASTA CARBONARA

SERVES 3 TO 4

4 tablespoons butter, room temperature (allow to sit unrefrigerated for about 1 hour prior to using)

4 egg yolks

1 cup Parmigiano-Reggiano, grated

1 tablespoon half-and-half (optional)

Freshly ground black pepper, to taste

Salt, to taste, and more for salting cooking water

Pancetta (ideally use thick-cut slices), cut into bite-size pieces

1 (16-ounce) box linguine or other pasta of choice*

* Manu recommends a thicker noodle, like linguine or bucatini, over a spaghetti noodle, as the thicker noodles do not stick together.

1. Set water to boil for cooking the pasta.

2. Place the butter in a bowl, and then add the egg yolks, cheese, and salt and pepper, to taste. Whip with a fork until a meringue-like consistency is reached. If the mixture needs to be loosened, add 1 tablespoon half-and-half.

3. Toast the pancetta in a pan set over medium-low heat until it is crisp and lightly browned. Once crisp, drain off the fat, and pat dry with a paper towel.

4. Salt the boiling water with ½ a kitchen spoonful of salt, and then add the linguine and allow to cook. When the pasta is half-cooked, mix the cheese mixture again and ensure a consistent texture.

5. Drain the pasta, reserving the pasta water, and then add the noodles to the bowl with the cheese. Top with the pancetta, and mix thoroughly.

6. Add roughly ¼ cup pasta water to the pasta, sauce, and pancetta mix to prevent the pasta from sticking or congealing.

ROASTED SPAGHETTI SQUASH WITH HEIRLOOM CHERRY TOMATOES

SERVES 2

1 medium spaghetti squash

2 teaspoons olive oil

1 cup heirloom cherry tomatoes, halved

2 garlic cloves, minced

Salt, to taste

Freshly ground black pepper, to taste

¼ lemon

5 large basil leaves, rolled lengthwise and cut into thin strips, for finishing

1. Preheat oven to 350°F.

2. With a large kitchen knife, carefully cut the spaghetti squash in half lengthwise. Take a spoon and scrape out the seeds of each half. Place on a baking sheet cut side down. Take a fork, and puncture the outside of the squash 3 to 4 times on each side. Cook for 30 to 35 minutes or until the fork is able to easily penetrate the outside shell. Do not overcook, as the squash will get mushy.

3. Ten minutes before the squash is finished cooking, heat the olive oil in a medium sauté pan set over medium heat, and then add the cherry tomatoes. Cook for 2 minutes, and then add the garlic, ⅛ cup water, and salt and pepper. Squeeze the lemon into the pan. Cook until the tomatoes are soft and start to separate from their skins; then turn off the heat, add the basil, stir, and cover to keep warm.

4. Remove the squash with an oven mitt. Turn the squash over and hold it still with the mitted hand. Take a fork and scrape the inside of the squash. If it's cooked correctly, it will look like spaghetti. While the shredded squash is still in the skin, season with salt and pepper.

5. Spoon the shredded squash onto a plate, and spoon the ingredients in the sauté pan over the squash. Garnish with fresh basil and lemon.

KARL FRISCH'S

NEW YORK STRIP STEAK (SOUS VIDE*) WITH WHITE TRUFFLE BUTTER

SERVES 2

Two (8- to 10-ounce)
New York strip steaks

4 teaspoons fleur de sel

2 teaspoons freshly ground
black pepper

2 tablespoons white
truffle butter

1 tablespoon cooking oil
(optional)

1. Remove the steaks from their packaging, wrap them in cheese cloth, and place them in the refrigerator on a wire rack for 3 to 4 days to partially dehydrate them.

2. Set a sous vide machine to 130°F. Remove the steaks from the refrigerator, and remove the cheese cloth.

3. Season each steak with 2 teaspoons fleur de sel and ½ teaspoon pepper.

4. Place 1 tablespoon white truffle butter on each steak.

5. Seal the steaks in a sous vide–safe bag using a food-saving air removal device, or use a large zip-top bag and the air displacement method.** Make sure the bag is securely closed.

6. Once the sous vide machine reaches 130°F, submerge the bag of steaks into the water bath. Let the sous vide machine cook the steaks for 1 hour to 90 minutes. When the steaks are cooked, remove them from the water bath and the sous vide bag.

7. Sear the steaks using either a kitchen torch on each side of the steak until desired crust is achieved, or preheat a cast-iron skillet over medium-high heat and add 1 tablespoon neutral cooking oil, and as soon as the oil begins to smoke, sear each side of the steak.

8. Serve immediately. Since the steaks were cooked using a sous vide, they do not need to rest.

* You will need a sous vide machine for this recipe.

** The internet offers great tutorials on the air displacement method.

FRIENDSHIP CHILI

SERVES 4 TO 6

1 tablespoon olive oil

½ onion, peeled and diced

1 green bell pepper, diced

3 yellow squash, cut as desired

3 garlic cloves, chopped

2 (15.5-ounce) cans black beans, pinto beans, or red beans, drained

1 small can of corn

1 (8-ounce) can diced tomatoes

1 (16-ounce) can crushed tomatoes

1 (3.65-ounce) box Carroll Shelby's Chili Kit or a general chile spice mix: chile powder, garlic powder, onion powder, paprika, cumin, black pepper, salt—all in equal amounts or to taste

TOPPINGS (OPTIONAL)

Sour cream for finishing

Cheddar cheese, for finishing

Oyster crackers, for finishing

Green onions, for finishing

1. In a large pot, heat the olive oil and sweat down the onion, green pepper, and squash for 4 minutes; then add the garlic and cook for 1 minute.

2. Toss in the beans, corn, and tomatoes and stir. Add the chile seasonings and 1 cup water, and bring to a simmer for 15 minutes.

3. Finish with the toppings.

Szechuan Chicken or Tofu

SERVES 4

SAUCE

1 cup soy sauce

1 cup cooking sherry

3 tablespoons organic apple cider vinegar

3 tablespoons maple syrup

3 teaspoons sesame oil

1½ to 2 tablespoons chile paste with garlic (if you like your sauce extra spicy, you can add another ½ to 1 tablespoon chile paste with garlic)

Arrowroot or cornstarch for thickening

CHICKEN OR TOFU

2 large heads broccoli

1 bunch green scallions

6 to 8 eggs

1 cup olive oil, and more for cooking the tofu if using (optional)

1 to 2 cups rice, cooked

2 to 3 pounds chicken breasts and/or extra-firm tofu

1. Prepare the sauce by combining all of its ingredients and 3 tablespoons water in a large jar and shaking vigorously.

2. Cut the stalks from the broccoli, and then chop it into bite-size pieces.

3. Chop the green scallions, and then place them in a bowl.

4. Break the eggs into a large bowl, and mix well.

5. Cut the chicken breasts into short, thin strips and/or slice the tofu into strips. If using tofu, fry the strips until they are lightly browned, and then cut into short, thin strips. Place the chicken and/or tofu in the bowl with the egg batter and stir well.

6. Pour the olive oil into a wok (or a large stainless-steel frying pan) that is a minimum of 17 inches, cover, and set over heat. Once the oil is hot, pour in the chicken and/or tofu, cover, and fry, stirring frequently.

7. Steam the broccoli in a steamer.

8. When the chicken and/or tofu is fried to a light brown, drain the oil from the wok, and place it over low heat. Add the steamed broccoli and green scallions.

9. Vigorously shake the jar of sauce, and then pour the sauce over the ingredients in the wok. Cook over a low heat, stirring until the sauce starts to thicken and coats the other ingredients.

10. Serve over rice.

Orange-Tomato Spiced Chicken

SERVES 2

4 chicken thighs and legs

Salt, to taste

Freshly ground black pepper, to taste

2 tablespoons canola oil

2 medium onions, peeled and sliced

1 teaspoon tomato paste

1 tablespoon freshly ground cumin

1 tablespoon cumin seeds (optional)

1 teaspoon ground coriander

1 teaspoon paprika

¼ teaspoon ground cinnamon

¼ teaspoon grated fresh ginger

¼ teaspoon cayenne pepper

1 tablespoon orange zest

1 cup freshly squeezed orange juice

1 tablespoon freshly squeezed lemon juice

1 cup diced canned tomatoes

1 cup chickpeas, cooked or canned

1½ cups chicken stock

¼ cup extra-virgin olive oil

2 tablespoons chopped fresh parsley for finishing

½ cup almonds, sliced and toasted for finishing

Couscous for serving

1. Season the chicken well with salt and pepper, and then place it in a heavy-bottomed stockpot set over medium-high heat; sear it in the canola oil until golden brown on both sides. Remove the chicken from the pot and set aside.

2. Pour excess fat from the pot, and add the onions. Sauté over medium heat until caramelized and rich brown.

3. Add the tomato paste, and cook 1 to 2 minutes until the paste turns from red to brown. Stir in the cumin, cumin seeds, coriander, paprika, cinnamon, ginger, cayenne, and orange zest, and quickly cook until fragrant and dry.

4. Add the orange and lemon juices, simmering until the liquid is reduced by half. Add the diced tomatoes, chickpeas, and stock. Return the chicken to the pot, and simmer gently until the chicken is cooked through and the sauce is thick, at least 1 hour.

5. Stir in the olive oil, and season with salt and pepper to taste.

6. Divide the chicken and sauce into 4 bowls, and garnish with parsley and toasted almonds. Serve with couscous.

ELTON FOSTER'S

Louisiana Chicken Thighs, Pork Sausage, and Mushroom Jambalaya

SERVES 8

12 skin-on, bone-in chicken thighs

Kosher salt, to taste

2 tablespoons freshly ground black pepper, or to taste

1 tablespoon cayenne pepper, or to taste

½ cup grape-seed, peanut, or avocado oil or other high-heat oil

1 large yellow onion, peeled and finely diced

3 to 4 celery ribs, finely diced

1 large green bell pepper, finely diced

½ medium red bell pepper, finely diced

¼ cup Chef Paul Prudhomme Salt Free Magic Seasoning (or comparable salt-free Cajun or creole seasoning such as Tony Chachere's or Zatarain's), or more to taste, and more for finishing

½ tablespoon ground white pepper

1 pound Cajun-style, hickory-, or applewood-smoked pork sausage, sliced into small rounds

1 quart raw button mushrooms, chopped (or, if available, dried porcini,* reconstituted and chopped, reserving 1 cup of strained liquid)

8 large garlic cloves, minced

1 stick Irish butter from grass-fed cows

4 cups jasmine rice or other long-grain rice

1 (6-ounce) can tomato paste

1 tablespoon fish sauce

4 tablespoons Worcestershire sauce

1 tablespoon poultry seasoning

1 tablespoon ground dried thyme

1 quart and 3 cups homemade (or high-quality, store-bought) chicken stock

1 cup dry white wine

8 large bay leaves

* If using dried mushrooms, substitute 1 cup strained mushroom broth for 1 cup chicken stock.

1. Preheat oven to 350°F.

2. Liberally season the chicken thighs on all sides with salt, pepper, and cayenne.

3. Place the chicken thighs and cooking oil in a large (8-quart or greater) enamel cast-iron casserole dish or Dutch oven, and sear all sides of the chicken. Remove and set aside.

4. Sauté the Louisiana "trinity"—the onion, celery, and bell peppers—in the oil and rendered fat of the chicken. Liberally sprinkle with Cajun seasoning, salt, pepper, white pepper, and cayenne. Fold in the sliced sausage.

5. In a separate skillet, sauté the mushrooms and garlic in 1 tablespoon butter, being careful not to brown the garlic, and then add both to the dish with the Louisiana trinity.

6. Add the rice, tomato paste, 2 tablespoons butter, and a splash of oil to the skillet with the mushrooms and garlic, and sauté until the rice is almost opaque and the tomato paste is darkened and incorporated. Add the fish sauce and Worcestershire sauce, and then transfer to the dish with the sausage and mix.

7. Add remaining seasonings, stock, and wine until rice is just barely covered with the liquid, along with the remaining butter, placing it directly on the sausage and the rice, and spacing evenly.

8. Add chicken thighs, skin side up, to top of mixture, and sprinkle more Cajun seasoning over skin side.

9. Cover tightly with foil and then a heavy cast-iron lid to form a seal, and bake for approximately 1 hour or until rice is but moist but not soup-like.

Cookies & Cream & Cakes

Desserts

LISA'S

SUNNIER DAYS AHEAD MEYER LEMON SQUARES À LA FRANNY

(V)

MAKES 12 BARS

PASTRY

¾ cup all-purpose flour

⅓ cup powdered sugar

¼ cup cornstarch

½ teaspoon salt

½ teaspoon vanilla extract

½ cup (1 stick) salted butter, frozen and grated

LEMON FILLING

4 eggs

1 cup sugar

¾ cup (3 lemons' worth) freshly squeezed lemon juice

½ cup cornstarch

2 tablespoons all-purpose flour

½ teaspoon salt

Zest of 1 lemon

OTHER

Powdered sugar for dusting

TO MAKE THE PASTRY

1. Pulse all pastry ingredients together in a food processor until a dough ball forms. Remove and carefully press the dough together; then wrap it in plastic wrap, and refrigerate it for 30 minutes.

2. Preheat oven to 325°F.

3. Line a baking pan with parchment paper. (A square 9 x 9-inch pan is ideal, but I used a 10 x 6-inch pan.) It's okay if the parchment paper sticks out; it will help you lift and remove the pastry.

4. Remove the dough from the refrigerator, and place it in the baking pan. Press down on the pastry until it evenly fills the bottom of the pan. Bake until barely golden, 22 to 25 minutes.

5. Remove the pastry, and let cool for at least 1½ hours. Once cool, make the lemon filling.

TO MAKE THE LEMON FILLING

1. Combine all lemon filling ingredients in a bowl, and whisk until frothy and well combined.

2. Pour the filling into the pan with the cooked pastry, and bake for another 22 to 25 minutes, until the lemon is set and jiggles.

3. Remove the lemon bars, and allow them to cool for 1 to 1½ hours. Then refrigerate for a minimum of 1 additional hour.

4. Once the lemon filling is set, remove the pan from the refrigerator, lift the dessert out of the pan, and plate. Dust with powdered sugar, and cut into squares using a sharp knife.

Franny always found time to make delectable treats like lemon squares for special occasions. She also found the time to help with all the ancillary or corollary side jobs a mother can be called to support, such as soccer games, gymnastics, or ballet after school. There was always more to do. When I was five, Mom thought it would be good for me to start ballet lessons, as I was constantly falling down and running into things like a young colt who first finds her legs. A year into it, I was performing as the "marching ballerina" and would debut my first real costume at my first recital. I remember my mother deciding she would sew my ensemble herself (she was and still is an excellent seamstress), and so she and I went to the fabric store to get all of the components. It was the first time I felt tulle, the first time I learned the difference between real silk satin and sateen polyester, the first time my mother dyed my shoes blue marine (but not the last).

Mom stayed up until all hours of the night, working for days, cursing over the sewing machine in the laundry room when she got to the tutu part, and talking to herself. It made us kids chuckle, as we had never experienced our mother swearing. She was a perfectionist, and when the costume was finished, she admitted she was a bit disappointed in her work but thought it would pass. When we got to the theater and all the other kids put on their costumes for the dress rehearsal, theirs were all ill-fitting. Mine seemed like it came from a high-end department store. I love my mom for putting so much care and time into what would wind up being dozens upon dozens of costumes over the years. Living with her when she was designing and sewing was like living with Edith Head, and it was as if my sisters and I were soloists in the Ballet Russe de Monte Carlo, not the Nancy Ann Dance Studio across the street from a strip mall. I haven't thought about that marching ballerina in a long time. I remember having to march. And that the stage floor was surprisingly slippery.

Lisa at age five.

DEBRIANNA'S

Ginger Chocolate Brownie Bite Me's

MAKES 2 DOZEN BITE ME'S

GINGER-INFUSED SUGAR

1½ tablespoons finely grated fresh ginger

1 cup turbinado or demerara sugar

BITE ME'S

¾ cup all-purpose flour

½ cup dark cocoa powder

1 teaspoon baking powder

½ teaspoon kosher salt

8 ounces bittersweet chocolate, broken into pieces

½ cup (1 stick) unsalted butter

8 pieces candied ginger slices, soaked overnight in Lyle's Golden Syrup and thinly sliced crosswise

2 large eggs, room temperature

¼ cup granulated sugar

½ cup brown sugar

1 tablespoon grated fresh ginger

½ teaspoon espresso powder

1½ teaspoons vanilla extract

½ cup bittersweet chocolate chips

½ cup chopped walnuts

TO MAKE THE GINGER-INFUSED SUGAR*

1. Preheat oven to 200°F.

2. Mix the ginger and sugar well, coating the sugar with the grated ginger, and then spread the mixture out on a baking sheet lined with parchment paper.

3. Turn the oven off. Place the baking sheet in the oven, and let the sugar sit for 2 hours or more until dry. It may need breaking up when removed. Store in a jar.

* Hi, this is Lisa. This ginger-infused sugar is the bomb! You will not believe how good it is. Put it on *anything*! I put it on my scones (see page 8). Okay, I'm done now. Bye.

TO MAKE THE BITE ME'S

1. Preheat oven to 350°F.

2. In a medium bowl, combine the flour, cocoa powder, baking powder, and salt, and whisk to combine. Set aside.

3. Combine the bittersweet chocolate pieces and butter in a double boiler. Stir occasionally until completely melted.

4. Remove the bowl from the saucepan, and add the ginger slices and any syrup that clings to the pieces. Stir so it melts into the chocolate and butter. Allow to cool slightly.

5. Place the eggs, granulated sugar, and brown sugar in the bowl of an electric stand mixer. Beat on medium speed to combine, and scrape down the sides. Increase the speed to high and beat until pale and fluffy, about 5 minutes, scraping the bowl as needed. Add the fresh ginger, espresso powder, and vanilla. Beat to combine.

6. Add the cooled chocolate mixture, and beat on medium speed to combine. Add the flour mixture, and beat on low speed until just combined. Remove the bowl from the mixer, scrape the sides, and fold a few times to make sure everything is well combined. Add the bittersweet chocolate chips, walnuts, and chopped ginger pieces, and fold to combine.

7. Refrigerate to tighten the dough, or if you can't wait, make 1-tablespoon scoops onto parchment paper–lined baking sheets, setting them 2 inches apart. Bake until the surface is crinkled and the edges are firm, 8 to 10 minutes, rotating the sheets halfway through.

8. Remove the bite me's, and sprinkle them with a bit of the ginger-infused sugar. Let cool for a few minutes on the baking sheets, and then transfer to a wire rack. The bite me's will keep in an airtight container at room temperature for 3 to 4 days—if they last that long!

"I need to leave this job—it's killing me. Do you know of anything?" I sat across from my longtime friend and begged. If anyone knew of a job opening, she would.

Patrice and I had worked together many times over the years, selling high-end clothing in expensive boutiques. She taught me everything I know about sales, and together we were a powerhouse crack team.

Patrice was the one who taught me to listen, to tease out clues and follow them where they lead. I have made more friends that way, listening and then responding to them. It is a skill I have been eternally grateful to her for in everything I have done since.

"She's crazy!" I wailed to Patrice. "We can never sit! I walk all day on concrete floors, and my back is killing me. Clients have followed me from other galleries, but if it's not 'my day' or 'my turn,' I lose them! And I am *still* making the most money of anyone. Oh my God, I have to get out of there."

"Can you wait a month? I have an idea. Oh, and you look like a wreck. Maybe you should take the month off and recover?"

She was likely right, because I literally couldn't stop talking, the stories tumbling out in a mad torrent, recounting the story of my last workday.

"Well, Debrianna, you sold the 30K painting yesterday," my well-appointed boss announced at 7:59 a.m. to start off one of our crack-of-dawn gallery meetings, without coffee or pastries. She approached, those three-inch spiked heels clanking on the cool concrete from behind me and sending a chill up my spine. "Don't you just love Ann's work?" she said, beaming.

"No," I told her and the entire staff. "No. I really don't." I was already too tired to edit myself.

"What? What do you mean?" she asked, smiling awkwardly.

"I don't. But it's not coming home with me," I said, emboldened by my exhaustion and knowing I was quitting. "It's awful, in my personal opinion. But it isn't hanging in my house, and she is super happy it will be in hers. That's my job. To make the client happy. The money is just a bonus," I said, my sales technique eking out.

"Well," she said, trying to quickly recover from embarrassment, "maybe you can give a presentation to the staff on how you sell?"

"Sure, maybe next week," I replied, knowing I would never do that—why would I, when we didn't share commissions?

As the meeting ended, she leaned in and whispered in my ear, still trying to gain back her ground, "Aren't you glad you don't have to share the commission on that 30K?"

"No," I said, looking directly at her. "No, I'm not. I would actually prefer sharing it."

One month later, as promised, our little crack team was back together. Four years later, the shop closed, and while Patrice went on to another gallery job, I did not. My one-woman show, *The Meatball Chronicles*, was touring the country. I was making plans for performances at the New Orleans Food Festival and in Salt Lake City and London, and then . . . COVID.

Now, with times changed yet again, I am home. Baking, cooking, writing, and with deep gratitude for my friendship with Patrice in my heart daily. I frequently stop by the shop where she works and bring her treats from my kitchen. I know how that simple act can completely lift your day when you're working retail.

These Ginger Chocolate Bite Me's are one of her faves.

Patrice, Debrianna, and Karen sharing dinner.

DON'T TRIFLE WITH ME BERRY TRIFLE

SERVES 4 TO 6

CUSTARD

6 egg yolks

½ cup sugar

1¼ cups whole milk

1¼ cups heavy cream

2 tablespoons pure vanilla extract (or vanilla paste or vanilla bean for extra vanilla flavor)

COULIS

2 cups raspberries

1 tablespoon honey

TRIFLE

2 pints heavy cream

2 tablespoons honey

Sugar, to taste (optional)

1 cup blueberries

1 cup blackberries

1 cup strawberries

1 cup raspberries

10 ladyfinger cookies*

* It's best if you can make your own ladyfingers (traditional ingredient), or you could also use high-end, store-bought madeleines.

TO MAKE THE CUSTARD

1. Preheat oven to 300°F.

2. In a medium bowl, whisk the egg yolks and sugar together. Set aside.

3. In a saucepan, whisk the milk and heavy cream with the vanilla, and then bring to a boil. Turn off the heat after the mixture reaches a boil.

4. Temper (combine the 2 bowls) by adding a little bit at a time of the cream mixture into the egg yolks mixture, whisking constantly to prevent the yolks from turning into scrambled eggs from the hot milk and cream mixture. When everything is incorporated, pour the entire mixture into a large, ceramic custard baking dish or individual ramekins.

5. Place a large baking dish or ramekins into a bain-marie (basically a roasting pan halfway filled with water). This provides the steam in the oven to set the custard. Bake until the custard has formed and solidified, about 30 to 40 minutes.

6. Allow the custard to cool to room temperature, and then cover with plastic wrap and refrigerate.

TO MAKE THE COULIS

1. Place the raspberries in a food processor, and pulse until macerated.

2. Pour the coulis through a sieve to separate the seeds, and then dispose of them.

3. Add the honey to the raspberry coulis, mix well, and refrigerate.

TO ASSEMBLE THE TRIFLE

1. Whip the heavy cream together with the honey, adding sugar to further sweeten if desired, and then refrigerate.

2. Once the custard has cooled to room temperature, been refrigerated for at least 1 hour, and is fully set, you can begin to assemble the trifle. Start by putting a custard layer at the bottom of a large glass bowl or individual glasses. Then layer, alternating berries, the heavy cream and honey mixture, ladyfinger cookies, and custard.

3. When layering has reached the middle of the glass bowl, pour the coulis down the sides to achieve a drip effect all the way to the bottom. You can also set some coulis aside to pour over.

4. Cover and refrigerate for at least 30 minutes. The beauty of this trifle is that you can make it 24 hours in advance, and it still looks amazing and will set beautifully.

TIP: You can use sugar or another sweetener to further sweeten the coulis and heavy cream. I used an incredible orange blossom honey.

ROCK AND ROLL FANTASY: LABNEH PANNA COTTA WITH APRICOT JAM AND WHITE CHOCOLATE PISTACHIO BARK

SERVES 6 TO 8

LABNEH PANNA COTTA

1 (¼-ounce) envelope unflavored gelatin

2 cups plain whole-milk yogurt (not Greek)

1½ cups heavy cream

½ cup granulated sugar

1½ teaspoons vanilla bean paste or 1 vanilla bean, scraped

½ teaspoon orange extract

½ teaspoon fine sea salt

1½ teaspoons orange zest

Coconut oil cooking spray

ORANGE GRANITA

⅔ cup granulated sugar

2 teaspoons orange-flavored liqueur

¼ teaspoon fine sea salt

2 cups freshly squeezed orange juice

4 teaspoons orange zest

APRICOT JAM

8 ounces (about 6 medium) apricots, halved and pitted, or 1¾ cups frozen apricot halves, thawed

½ cup granulated sugar

1½ teaspoons freshly squeezed lemon juice

⅛ teaspoon fine sea salt

WHITE CHOCOLATE TOASTED FENNEL PISTACHIO BARK

½ cup white chocolate chips

½ tablespoon fennel seeds

⅓ cup roughly chopped pistachio meats

TO MAKE THE PANNA COTTA

1. In a small bowl, stir the gelatin and 1½ tablespoons cold water together, and then let stand for 5 minutes.

2. Place the yogurt in a medium bowl.

3. In a small saucepan set over medium-low heat, combine the heavy cream, sugar, vanilla bean paste, orange extract, and sea salt. Cook until steaming, and then remove from the heat.

4. Whisk the gelatin mixture into the cream mixture. Pour through a fine wire-mesh strainer into the bowl with the yogurt, and discard any solids. Whisk until smooth, and then add the orange zest and combine.

5. Lightly grease 8 cups or ramekins with a spray of coconut oil, and then evenly divide the mixture into them. Refrigerate uncovered for at least 8 hours or up to 2 days.

TO MAKE THE ORANGE GRANITA

1. Place the sugar, liqueur, sea salt, and ⅔ cup water in a small saucepan, and stir to combine. Cook over medium-high heat, stirring often, until the sugar is dissolved, about 4 minutes.

2. Pour the mixture into a 13 x 9-inch metal baking pan, and then stir in the orange zest and juice. Freeze, uncovered, until just set (not completely frozen), about 1 hour.

3. Rake through the granita using a fork, breaking up any large chunks.

4. Return the granita to the freezer, and freeze until completely set and frozen, 2 to 3 hours.

5. If storing the granita, transfer to an airtight container, and freeze for up to 2 weeks.

TO MAKE THE APRICOT JAM

1. In a small saucepan, combine the apricots and 2 tablespoons water. Cover and set over medium heat. Cook, stirring often, until the apricots are softened, about 5 minutes.

2. Stir in the sugar and then cook, uncovered, stirring often and mashing the apricots with the back of a spoon, until the sugar melts and the mixture has thickened and reduced to about 1 cup, 10 to 15 minutes. To check the jam, do the spoon test: put a wooden spoon in the jam and drag your finger across the back of the spoon—if you can see the trail of your finger, then it's done.

3. Remove the jam from the heat, and stir in the lemon juice and sea salt. Then let it cool to room temperature, about 1 hour.

4. The jam can be stored chilled in an airtight container for up to 1 week.

TO MAKE THE WHITE CHOCOLATE BARK

1. Use a double boiler to melt the white chocolate chips. While they are melting, toast the fennel seeds. Let cool and crush slightly.

2. Add the fennel seeds and pistachios to the melted chocolate.

3. Spread the mixture onto a baking sheet lined with parchment paper, and refrigerate until set, about 1 hour.

TO ASSEMBLE THE DESSERT

1. Place 1 tablespoon apricot jam on a small serving dish. Spread the jam into a circle.

2. Run a small offset spatula around the edges of the panna cotta.

3. Dip the bottoms of the ramekins in hot water for a few seconds until the panna cotta is loosened. Invert the panna cotta onto the jam.

4. Spoon granita next to the panna cotta.

5. Break up pieces of bark, and sprinkle the chopped white chocolate over the granita.

6. Serve immediately. Reserve remaining granita and jam for another use.

TIP: Any or all of these components can be made for dessert. Together they're spectacular! If you don't want to make the bark, serve with chopped pistachios and shaved white chocolate.

Inspired by a recipe by Lena Sareini in
Food & Wine

IF YOU CAN DO THIS, YOU CAN DO ANYTHING TARTE TATIN

SERVES 6 TO 8

APPLES

5 or 6 apples,* sliced

Juice of 1 lemon

¼ cup granulated sugar

Zest of 1 lemon

* I used local Winesaps fresh from the trees of Nadyne and Joe Bicknell. You can also use Granny Smiths or Honeycrisps. Make sure the apples are really firm; otherwise they will turn to mush.

ROUGH PUFF PASTRY*

½ cup (1 stick) salted butter, frozen and grated

1 cup all-purpose flour

½ teaspoon salt

½ teaspoon freshly squeezed lemon juice

* If you would rather not make your own puff pastry, you can buy amazing, premade frozen puff pastry at your local market. This recipe is a "rough" puff.

OTHER INGREDIENTS

All-purpose flour for dusting

Whipped cream for serving (optional)

Vanilla ice cream for serving (optional)

CARAMEL

1 cup granulated sugar

½ cup (1 stick) unsalted butter

½ teaspoon sea salt

1 teaspoon vanilla extract

TO PREPARE THE APPLES

1. In a large bowl, combine the apples, lemon juice, and sugar, and turn over well with the juice.

2. Cover tightly with plastic wrap and refrigerate, occasionally turning the apples over with the juice and sugar. They can stay in the fridge until you are ready to use them.

3. Meanwhile, make the puff pastry. When the dough is finished, do not turn the juice over the apples again, as it will have drained to the bottom of the bowl, and that's what you want. Leave the juice there; otherwise the caramel is going to get too juicy later.

TO MAKE THE "ROUGH" PUFF PASTRY

1. Combine all puff pastry ingredients and 5 tablespoons ice-cold water in a bowl, and then form the dough into a loose ball—it will just barely hold together. Cover tightly in plastic wrap, and form it into a disc. Refrigerate for 30 minutes.

2. Remove the dough from the fridge, unwrap, and spread it on a lightly floured surface. Using a rolling pin, roll the dough into a rectangle, and then shape it with a metal dough scraper, rolling it flat at different angles. After a few rolls, fold it like a letter going into an envelope, each side folding in and then folding over together. Rewrap it with plastic wrap, and refrigerate for 35 minutes.

3. Repeat step 2 four times. After the fifth time, place the dough in the refrigerator. Once cold again, it will be ready for the tarte. The dough can last a couple days in the fridge if necessary.

TIP: Before you make this legit puff pastry, you must prep the apples and refrigerate them. Some people prefer halves or rounds. I choose to peel and quarter them, making sure there are no seeds or seed pod areas on the apples, so that they can lie flat with the rounded side up in the pan later. If you want to make a "classic" puff pastry and not the "rough" puff, repeat step 2 eight times!

TO MAKE THE CARAMEL AND TARTE

1. Preheat oven to 400°F. Lightly dust the rolling area and rolling pin with flour.

2. Remove the apples from the fridge, uncover, and place next to where you're going to be cooking the caramel.

3. Heat the sugar in a 10-inch cast-iron pan set over medium-high heat, stirring constantly. Add the butter, sea salt, and vanilla. As it cooks, the color should turn to a light brown and the mixture should caramelize. Keep stirring nonstop to avoid burning. A beautiful caramel consistency will be achieved after about 15 minutes. Once reached, turn off the heat.

4. Start arranging the apples with their round sides down into the pan. Cover the entire surface area, and try to fit them all in snugly. There could be a couple layers.

5. Retrieve the dough from the fridge, and roll it out on the lightly floured surface. Continue to roll until the dough is an 11-inch square or similarly sized rectangle.

6. Cover the apples in the pan with the dough, and tuck in the sides all the way down. With a sharp knife, make 4 slit vents on the top, and then put the tarte in the oven to bake until golden brown, about 25 to 30 minutes. It's helpful to place a baking sheet lined with parchment paper underneath the cast-iron pan while the tarte is baking to catch drips and keep a clean oven.

7. Remove the tarte from the oven, and cover with a large flat plate. Flip it over so that the tarte removes itself and the apples are now on top of the pastry on the platter. If some of the apples stick, take them out with a spatula, and place them on top of the dish. Use potholders, as the bubbling-hot caramel can burn.

8. Serve immediately with whipped cream, vanilla ice cream, or as is.

TIP: Start this early in the morning, as it takes many hours. Also, everything must remain cold while making the dough. If you have a marble countertop, use it. If you have a metal rolling pin, use it—you can even freeze it to keep it super cold while rolling. Make sure to freeze the bowl for a bit before you mix the dough so it stays cold too. I used a metal masher to combine the initial dough ball instead of my fingers because I didn't want my body heat to warm the butter. All this prep makes the difference between getting those gorgeous flaky layers and not.

This dish is beyond delicious when eaten immediately out of the oven. The longer you wait, the more the caramel soaks into the pastry.

DEBRIANNA'S

LONGING FOR APRICOT ALMOND SHORTBREAD AND LIVE THEATER

MAKES 24 BARS

1¾ cups all-purpose flour

¼ cup almond flour

1 teaspoon baking powder

¼ teaspoon salt

1 cup (2 sticks) unsalted butter, softened, and more for buttering the baking dish

1 cup sugar

2 large egg yolks

½ teaspoon pure vanilla extract

¾ cup apricot jam (see Debrianna's recipe, page 215)

1 cup sliced almonds

1. Preheat oven to 350°F.

2. In a medium bowl, whisk together the flours, baking powder, and salt.

3. In another medium bowl, beat the butter and sugar at a low speed until combined, and then beat in the egg yolks and vanilla. Add the ingredients in the first bowl, and beat at a low speed until a soft dough forms.

4. Split the dough into 2 logs. Wrap the dough logs in plastic wrap, and refrigerate until firm, at least 1 hour.

5. Butter an 8½ x 11-inch glass baking dish. Working over the baking dish, coarsely shred 1 log of dough on the large holes of a box grater, evenly distributing the dough in the baking dish. Do not pat or press the dough.

6. Using a spoon, dollop the jam over the dough, and gently spread it in an even layer. Grate the second log on top.

7. Using a rubber spatula, tuck in any shreds of dough sticking to the sides of the baking dish to prevent them from burning. Sprinkle the almond slices on top.

8. Bake the shortbread on the bottom rack of the oven, covering it with foil halfway through. The shortbread is done when the pastry is golden all over, after about 35 minutes. Let cool completely, and then cut into 24 bars.

Debrianna and her dad, Al, at the Face of the '80s contest.

Apricots are my favorite summer fruit. In New Mexico, it is such a blessing to have them ripen. The only way we get them is if Mother Nature spares us the nearly inevitable spring frost. As the days begin to get long, sunny, and warm and all gardeners feel the tug to plant, I start to itch for them, but those of us who have lived here long enough know it's best to wait, just wait. We can all see the trees popping, and the apricot trees are the first ones out. White flowers with brownish-red centers, inviting the spring and summer to edge toward us. Still, my better angels know to wait.

Often the frost comes with a fierce spring wind that won't allow even the heartiest gardener to cover the tender blossoms. Once, I found a big sheet and was able to cast it over the top of my smallish tree, and the wind caught it and threatened to pull the entire thing out by the roots, flying it up like a hot-air balloon. It's quite a trick to save the sweet apricots. Nonetheless, I keep trying, reinventing common household items, looking for help where none may be visible, except for the digging, the reimagining. This internal insistence, my refusal to give in, was how my career started.

From my quiet upstate New York apartment, I had seen an ad in the trades for a "Face of the '80s" contest. I thought that entering this competition might help catapult me into the city that scared the bejesus out of me—one that struck me as noisy, complicated, and dangerous. I was determined to overcome my fears, so I went ahead and filled out the application. I had been successful as a model in my small state of Connecticut, but now it was time to face my fears and move to New York City.

There were the typical categories—swimsuits and evening gowns. Sure. How was I going to pay for an evening gown good enough for this competition? I had been supplementing my local modeling gig income by working in an exclusive fabric shop in New Paltz, New York. On the days when I wasn't pounding the pavements of Manhattan, I was learning advanced tailoring from a French seamstress at the shop. And that provided my answer: I'd make one!

I scoured the fine stores of Fifth Avenue until I found a gown I thought I could replicate. Conjuring my best rich young woman imitation, I told the salesclerk I was just "trying it on" as I entered the private dressing rooms, which were larger than the bedroom in my apartment. Seeing myself from three sides in the mirrors, I pulled out my measuring tape and small notepad and wrote careful notes on design and seam allowances, all the while calmly and politely turning down assistance from anyone who offered. I was sure I'd get caught by my third trip to "try on" the same gown.

It was a black silk faille gown with a back scoop that went to just below the waist, with rhinestones spaced over the entirety. Smart, sophisticated, and sexy in a subtle way. I knew I could re-create the pattern, which was exactly what I did. And I won that contest.

I often think of that accomplishment of mind over matter when I am tugging at the roots of my plants or trying to think of a way to outsmart the frost. I haven't done that yet, but don't count me out. It may just happen one spring. Until then, I am grateful for my big freezer and a way to save the apricots that do show up.

Chipper AF Coconut Macaroons Dipped in Chocolate

MAKES APPROXIMATELY 16 MACAROONS

4 egg whites

1½ cups turbinado sugar

2 big pinches sea salt

2 tablespoons vanilla extract

5 cups shredded unsweetened coconut

2 cups dark chocolate chips (I recommend a high cacao percentage of 60 to 80)

1. Preheat oven to 325°F.

2. Place the egg whites in a bowl, and whisk until frothy, stopping just before they start to form peaks. Add the sugar, sea salt, vanilla, and coconut, and incorporate well.

3. Scoop the dough into tablespoon-size mounds, and place them on a baking sheet lined with parchment paper. They will not spread out while baking, so you can fit quite a few. Have a bowl of cold water nearby to rinse hands when shaping mounds into pyramid-like shapes.

4. Bake until golden brown, about 17 minutes, rotating the sheet halfway through baking. Then remove the macaroons from the oven, let them stand for several minutes, and transfer them to a cooling rack.

5. Melt the chocolate chips in a double boiler set over low heat. Stir constantly, and do not overcook. You can use a standard pot with several inches of boiling water and a steel mixing bowl over it to melt the chocolate if you don't have a double boiler.

6. Dip the macaroons in the melted chocolate and then place them back on the rack to cool. Once cooled, refrigerate for several hours.

TIP: These can be stored in an airtight container for 1 week or frozen. #betterthanamoundsbarbyfar.

DEBRIANNA'S

GOOD FOR YOU! ZUCCHINI, OATMEAL, CHOCOLATE CHIP, WALNUT COOKIES

MAKES ABOUT 2 DOZEN COOKIES

COOKIES

1½ cups shredded zucchini

1½ cups old-fashioned whole rolled oats

½ cup all-purpose flour

½ cup whole wheat flour

½ cup shredded coconut, unsweetened

½ teaspoon baking soda

½ teaspoon salt

1 teaspoon ground cinnamon

¼ teaspoon freshly grated nutmeg

½ cup (1 stick) unsalted butter, softened

¾ cup packed dark or light brown sugar

¼ cup granulated sugar

1 large egg, room temperature

1 tablespoon pure maple syrup or honey

1½ teaspoons pure vanilla extract

1 cup dark chocolate chips

½ cup chopped walnuts

LEMON GOAT CHEESE FROSTING

½ cup (1 stick) unsalted butter, room temperature

½ cup goat cheese, room temperature

Zest of ½ lemon

¼ teaspoon freshly squeezed lemon juice

½ teaspoon vanilla extract

1½ cups confectioners' sugar

TO MAKE THE COOKIES

1. Blot any excess water from the zucchini using a clean kitchen towel or paper towel.

2. In a medium bowl, whisk together the oats, flours, coconut, baking soda, salt, cinnamon, and nutmeg. Set aside.

3. In a separate bowl, cream the butter and both sugars together on medium speed until smooth, about 2 minutes.

4. Add the egg to the oats mixture, and mix on high speed until combined, scraping down the sides and bottom of the bowl.

5. Add the maple syrup and vanilla, and mix on high until combined.

6. Add the ingredients from step 2 and the zucchini to the wet ingredients; then mix on low speed until combined. While still on low speed, beat in the chocolate chips and walnuts.

7. Cover and chill the dough for at least 2 hours (and up to 4 days) in the refrigerator. If chilling for longer than a few hours, allow to sit at room temperature for at least 30 minutes before baking, because the dough will be hard. You can also make the cookie balls and freeze them for baking later.

8. When ready to bake, preheat oven to 350°F.

9. Scoop or roll the cookie dough in a heaping 1 tablespoon of dough per cookie onto baking sheets lined with parchment paper or silicone baking mats. Place 2 inches apart, and bake until lightly browned on the sides and bottom, 15 to 20 minutes. The centers will look very soft, so be sure the cookies are lightly browned elsewhere.

10. Remove the cookies from the oven, and cool on the baking sheets for 5 minutes before transferring to a wire rack to cool completely.

TO MAKE THE LEMON GOAT CHEESE FROSTING AND ICE THE COOKIES

1. Beat together the butter, goat cheese, lemon zest and juice, and vanilla, and then whisk in the confectioners' sugar. Refrigerate until ready to use on cooled cookies.

2. When you are ready to frost the cookies, remove the frosting from the fridge and frost a few cookies at a time so they don't get too soft from the moisture. Frost the tops of the cookies if eating individually or the center of the cookies if stacking.

LISA'S

QUEEN FOR A DAY THREE-LAYER CHOCOLATE MOUSSE

MAKES 10 SERVINGS IN SMALLER GLASSWARE
OR 6 TO 8 SERVINGS IN MEDIUM-SIZE GLASSES

DARK CHOCOLATE LAYER

8 ounces bittersweet chocolate chips (63 percent cacao)

8 ounces organic mini marshmallows*

1 tablespoon Kahlúa or Cointreau

¼ cup whole milk

MOCHA LAYER

8 ounces milk chocolate or semisweet chocolate chips (I used Guittard semisweet)

8 ounces organic mini marshmallows*

1 to 2 tablespoons instant coffee

¼ cup whole milk

WHIPPED CREAM

2 pints heavy cream

1 tablespoon turbinado sugar

1 teaspoon vanilla extract

OTHER INGREDIENTS

Raspberries for finishing

Dark chocolate shavings for finishing

* These should be made with cane sugar, not high-fructose corn syrup. If you can't find mini ones, tear the big ones into quarters.

TO MAKE THE DARK CHOCOLATE LAYER (FIRST LAYER)

1. Melt the ingredients for the dark chocolate layer in a double boiler set over medium-low heat, stirring constantly.

2. When entirely melted, let cool to room temperature. Stir often to cool evenly.

3. Once cooled, place in a glass bowl in the refrigerator for about 15 minutes.

TO MAKE THE MOCHA LAYER (SECOND LAYER)

1. Melt the ingredients for the mocha layer in a double boiler set over medium-low heat, stirring constantly.

2. When entirely melted, let cool to room temperature. Stir often to cool evenly.

3. Once cooled, place in a glass bowl in the refrigerator for about 15 minutes.

TO MAKE THE WHIPPED CREAM (THIRD LAYER) AND ASSEMBLE THE MOUSSE

1. Whip all ingredients for the whipped cream together with a hand mixer or standing mixer until it just becomes stiff. Be careful not to overwhip, stopping before it's butter-like.

2. Remove the bowl with the first layer from the fridge, and gently fold ⅓ of the whipped cream into it.

3. Spoon 2 tablespoons of the first layer with the whipped cream mixed into it into all serving glasses. Refrigerate serving glasses for 5 minutes to set.

4. Remove the glasses and the bowl with the second layer from the fridge, and gently fold another ⅓ of the whipped cream into it. Spoon 2 tablespoons of the second layer with the whipped cream mixed into it into all serving glasses. Refrigerate the serving glasses for another 5 minutes to set.

5. Remove the glasses, and put a third layer of whipped cream on top. Wrap tightly with plastic wrap, and place back in the fridge for at least 1 hour or overnight.

6. Prior to serving, top with fresh raspberries and dark chocolate shavings.

TIP: If you don't have a lot of time and want to make only one layer, choose either mocha or chocolate and save a portion of the whipped cream for the top.

DEBRIANNA'S

That's Amazeballs! Cardamom Coffee Cake Cookies (Say That Really Fast)

MAKES 3 DOZEN COOKIES

TOPPING

½ teaspoon ground cinnamon

1½ teaspoons ground cardamom

½ cup turbinado sugar

COOKIES

2 cups all-purpose flour, and more if needed

½ cup walnuts, finely ground

½ teaspoon baking powder

¼ teaspoon baking soda

½ teaspoon ground cardamom

½ teaspoon salt

1 scant cup granulated sugar

⅓ cup unsalted butter, room temperature

1 large egg

½ cup crème fraîche

½ teaspoon vanilla extract

1. Grease baking sheets or line with parchment paper.,

2. Combine the ingredients for the topping in a small bowl and then set it aside.

3. In a medium bowl, whisk together the flour, walnuts, baking powder, baking soda, cardamom, and salt. Set aside.

4. Using an electric mixer with a paddle, cream the sugar and butter well. Add the egg, crème fraîche, and vanilla, and mix on low until combined. With the mixer still on low, gradually add the flour mixture until a soft dough forms. You may need to slowly add more flour to make a smooth but not sticky dough.

5. Refrigerate the dough until it is well chilled, at least 1 hour.

6. Preheat oven to 375°F.

7. Scoop heaping teaspoons of dough, and dip them into the sugar mixture. Place the coated dough scoops 2 inches apart on a baking sheet, and bake until lightly golden, about 8 to 10 minutes.

8. Sprinkle the cookies with the sugar topping, and let them cool for 2 minutes on the sheet before cooling on a rack.

My dear friend Patrice would start playing holiday songs in October. As we approached October of the lockdown, thinking of it made me miss her and my boss-friend, Karen. The three of us worked together at the Karen Melfi Collection jewelry shop, showing up daily in our self-styled "uniforms" of long black leather vests, dripping with KMC signature brown and black diamonds in 22K gold and wearing our hand-painted angel combat boots. Those boots caused me to name us the Angel Squad, which is how we were infamously known in jewelry retail sales. Tucked in the corner of 225 Canyon Road, the wee shop was only slightly larger than my bedroom, but it overflowed with queenly 22K gold and hand-forged bobbles. Our bathroom was barely large enough to turn around in, but we were lucky to have one, as many shops in the art district, often reconfigured from large compounds, do not. Our miniature office, a reformed closet, doubled as a place to wrap gifts and eventually became known as my "camping kitchen," basically because it was the only space that had a plug that wouldn't short out the entire building—a common occurrence, as the shop was located on the east side of our four-hundred-year-old town. The door had been removed for easy access and replaced with rich brown floor-length drapes.

"Mmm, it must be lunchtime. What smells so good?" People would drop by the shop to see what I was "cooking" in my mini hot pot. By bringing fresh veggies, my mini dark-wood chopping board from Germany, an egg, and a jar of organic Better Than Bouillon chicken stock, I could whip up a soup that rivaled anything we could get from the restaurants up the road. My mini hot pot doubled as a serving bowl, so out I would pop from behind the chic silk damask curtains, the aroma sneaking out ahead of me, and voilà! Lunch was served.

On days when we needed a treat and I had not brought in something baked at home, Karen, my generous-beyond-imagination boss, would hand me cash. Then she'd give me the look, and I knew what I had to do: drive to Dulce, our favorite bakery, and return with "that coffee cake." I'd bring back a super-size slice of cardamom coffee cake that we could split among the three of us and give a small piece of to our neighbor gallerist, John.

That sour cream coffee cake was a giant of cinnamon swirls and tender crumbs exploding in a glorious sensation that could only come from the cardamom. It was like nothing we could get anywhere else. My only dread was that she would shoot me the look on a Sunday when the bakery was closed. The thought of that cardamom taste would then linger all day and would require my leaving early the following Monday morning to stop and pick up a piece on my way to work.

Then COVID changed everything. We said goodbye to Dulce, one of the myriad businesses that shuttered (although thankfully would later reopen under new ownership–and still offer the cake!), to the joy of "camping" in the office and to the utter delight of getting to look for cardamom coffee cake. I miss all of them every day. Truthfully, part of me didn't even want to try to replicate that cake because I wanted it to maintain that special place in my heart—that sense of joy that made a workday seem like play. Instead, I decided to try to replicate that taste, that feeling, in what is most familiar to me: cookies. These cookies are my personal ode to Karen and Patrice and the bakery that gave us so much pleasure in our corner of paradise at 225 Canyon. Please wear your best jewelry when you enjoy them.

Debrianna, Karen, and Patrice in their angel boots.

DEBRIANNA'S

Salted Tahini Chocolate Chip Pecan Cookies Win the Day!

MAKES ABOUT 20 COOKIES

½ cup (1 stick) unsalted butter, softened

½ cup tahini, well stirred

½ cup granulated sugar

½ cup packed light brown sugar

1 large egg, room temperature

1 large egg yolk, room temperature

1 teaspoon vanilla extract

½ cup and 2 tablespoons all-purpose flour

½ cup almond flour

¾ teaspoon baking soda

1 teaspoon kosher salt

2 cups bittersweet chocolate chips

½ cup chopped pecans or walnuts

Flaky sea salt or vanilla salt, to taste

1. In a large bowl, beat the butter, tahini, and sugars together with an electric mixer on medium speed until fluffy. Scrape down the sides. Add the egg, egg yolk, and vanilla, and mix until combined, making sure the eggs are fully incorporated.

2. In a small bowl, whisk together the flours, baking soda, and salt. Add the dry ingredients to the wet until just combined, and then add the chocolate chips and nuts. Do not overmix. Cover the dough and refrigerate overnight.

3. Preheat oven to 325°F.

4. On 2 baking sheets lined with parchment paper or silicone baking mats, place rounds of dough (about 1½ inches wide for small cookies) 3 inches apart. Bake 1 sheet at a time, placed on the middle rack of the oven, and turn the baking sheets midway through baking. The cookies are done when golden brown around the edges but still pale in the center, after about 12 minutes. Large cookies will take a bit longer.

5. Remove the cookies from the oven, and sprinkle with sea salt. Allow to cool on the baking sheet.

6. The cookies will keep for 2 or 3 days at room temperature but are best the same day they're baked. The unbaked dough can be refrigerated for up to 1 week or frozen for up to 2 months.

TIP: If you want to make these gluten-free, substitute the ½ cup and 2 tablespoons all-purpose flour for GF flour. I like Flour Farm brand.

"Those cookies were amazing. Thank you so much for thinking of me!" my beautiful neighbor Aimee said. Aimee is the best neighbor. Thoughtful, kind, and an essential worker—a term we never had to use in daily vernacular until 2020. She is a hospice nurse who worked throughout the crazy, dangerous days of the pandemic, showing up with her sweetheart self for patients every day. I wanted to say thank-you to her, for her spirit. And as she is a gluten-free gal, it was my mission to make a delicious gluten-free cookie. So I perused the internet and my cookbooks, putting on my "hunting" mask and searching for the best ingredients and conjuring up ways to replace allergy-ridden flour with something equally tasty.

I settled on good old-fashioned chocolate chip cookies: the comfort cookie of all comfort cookies. But I wanted to step them up, like a hug in every bite. That's how I wanted her to feel when she eats them. Hugged. Not masked.

I bought several kinds of gluten-free flours and read ingredients lists carefully. They vary a lot. Some have coconut flour nestled in the list, while other use garbanzo flour. I looked for just the right one and decided to use almond flour to incorporate its sweet flavor into the cookies. Not wanting the cookies to be ordinary, I perked up when I spotted tahini in an ingredients list. That sparked something in me. Not peanut butter, but tahini! Brilliant. It would add to the complexity of the batter. And I wasn't even tempted to use plain ol' semisweets; instead, I opened my go-to bag of Ghirardelli dark chips. They are larger in size, not cloying with sugar, and have the full taste of cocoa—heavenly!

"I am so glad you liked them," I said over my masked shoulder on one of our Saturday walks together. We try to catch up and get some outside exercise time in and, when required during COVID, figured out a way to be together while six feet apart and safe. "I thought the salt really added something to the chocolate chips. Not an ordinary cookie for you, my friend. I gave it a lot of thought, and when I came across tahini as an ingredient, I was really excited."

"*Tahini?* There was *tahini* in them?" She looked kind of panicked.

"Yes. . . . Why?"

"Oh my God! I am so allergic to sesame seeds!" I nearly passed out when she said this. I had no idea anyone could be allergic to sesame seeds.

"Oh no! But you ate them?"

"Yes, I did," she said and smiled. "I did eat them, and they were amazing. Only you could make me tahini chocolate chip cookies and I would never know it!" She looked delighted with all the color returning to her face—and mine!

The best-ever Salted Tahini Chocolate Chip Pecan Cookies won the day.

Debrianna and her best neighbor, Aimee.

DEBRIANNA'S

Wanna Be an Italian *Lemon-y Snicket* Ricotta Cookies

MAKES ABOUT 2 DOZEN COOKIES

COOKIES

2 cups gluten-free flour

3 tablespoons almond flour

1 teaspoon baking soda

¼ teaspoon salt

½ cup (1 stick) unsalted butter, room temperature

2 teaspoons lemon zest

¾ cup sugar

1 cup ricotta

½ teaspoon freshly squeezed lemon juice

2½ teaspoons vanilla extract

1 large egg, room temperature

GLAZE

1½ cups confectioners' sugar

½ teaspoon lemon zest

Freshly squeezed lemon juice enough to make a thick glaze)

1. In a medium bowl, whisk together the flours, baking soda, and salt. Set aside.

2. In a mixing bowl with a paddle attachment set to medium-high speed, cream together the butter, lemon zest, and sugar until pale and fluffy.

3. Add the ricotta, lemon juice, and vanilla, and mix on low speed until combined, scraping the sides of the bowl if necessary. With the mixer still on low speed, slowly add the ingredients from step 1 until combined.

4. Cover and refrigerate for at least 2 hours.

5. Preheat oven to 350°F, and line baking sheets with parchment paper.

6. Scoop dough into balls using a heaping teaspoon and flatten gently, placing 2 inches apart. Bake the dough in the center of the oven until golden, about 12 to 15 minutes.

7. Remove the dough from the oven and let cool.

8. Make the lemon glaze by combining its ingredients. Start with 1 teaspoon of lemon juice, and continue adding until the glaze is thick.

9. Dip the cookies in the lemon glaze prior to serving.

LISA'S

CATHOLIC GUILT-FREE
ANGEL FOOD BIRTHDAY CAKE

MAKES ABOUT 12 SERVINGS

1 cup cake flour

½ teaspoon salt

12 egg whites

1 teaspoon cream of tartar

1¼ cups superfine sugar*

1 teaspoon lemon zest

2 teaspoons vanilla extract

Whipped cream for finishing (optional)

Berries of choice for finishing (optional)

* If you don't have superfine sugar, grind regular sugar in a food processor for 30 seconds.

1. Preheat oven to 350°F.

2. Sift the flour and salt in a large bowl, and then set aside.

3. Using a large electric mixer or hand mixer, begin to beat the egg whites on medium speed. After 2 to 3 minutes, add the cream of tartar and keep beating, and then slowly add the superfine sugar and lemon zest. Keep beating for another 3 to 4 minutes, and then add the vanilla while continuing to beat. When the egg whites appear to have stiff peaks (like meringue), take the bowl off the mixer and fold in the flour slowly with a spatula. Be careful not to overmix.

4. Spoon the batter into an angel food cake pan—do not grease the pan. Cut through the batter gently with a spatula to remove bubbles and then even out the top of the cake. Bake 40 to 45 minutes. When you remove the cake, the top should spring back to the touch.

5. Immediately cool the cake for 1 hour by inverting it. After an hour, remove it from the angel food cake pan by carefully taking a thin, sharp knife and going around the cake and the hole of the pan to loosen it. Then gently remove it and place it on a cake platter.

6. Either cut the cake in half with a serrated knife and spread a generous amount of whipped cream and berries and then stack the other half back on the top, or cover the entire outside of the cake with whipped cream and berries.

TIP: A buttercream frosting with a bit of lemon juice or coconut shavings can work well in place of the whipped cream and berries.

Seamus, my youngest, is going to be fourteen in three days. That in itself is a mindblower. Always an inquisitive, curious, bright person, he never ceases to amaze me. A silver lining of quarantine was the gift of more time to get to know Sea as a teenager. He can always make me laugh—the kid possesses a true talent for comedic timing, as well as a passion for outer space, science, technology, music, gaming, and film. He has grown into a compassionate, caring, and brilliant young man. I love him to bits, and he happens to enjoy our family classic: angel food cake.

I have been eating this cake since as far back as I can remember. My mother, Franny, was and is an avid baker and terrific cook. A young bride of the Kennedy era, she was also the perfect hostess for her dashing husband, who was the heir to a table-grape-growing dynasty in central California. However, her life was not the life she originally intended. She had wanted to have a career in medicine, perhaps orthopedics or sports medicine, and she ended up in an arranged marriage that would elevate her family's relatively recent Croatian immigrant status. She dropped out of college when my father proposed to her in her junior year, and they got married. They had me nine months after their wedding night. They had both been good Catholic virgins, and they always did the right thing.

But my dad's family controlled almost every aspect of their lives, so around my fifth birthday, my mother gave my father an ultimatum: either we would leave the town where this dysfunctional family of his ruled their lives and strike out on their own, or she was out of there. My dad, in a spectacular singular moment of loving my mom more than his family of origin, moved us from the Central Valley of California to the Central Coast and decided to begin anew their life together. He would grow wine grapes and start a winery. And he proceeded to pioneer an entire wine-grape-growing industry there. But he worked all the time, and as a result he and my mother grew apart. My mom gave birth to three daughters by the age of twenty-seven. She became a celebrated housewife and mother, a member of the country club, and played tennis. She took dance lessons to learn the hustle. At times, she seemed bored when not reading her favorite novel or packing for an international business trip with my dad. But there were some things that truly excited her, like the absolute delight she expressed when the monthly *Gourmet* magazine would arrive. I fondly remember looking over the pages of delicious food photos with her and the articles that accompanied them in a sunny nook of the house. She couldn't wait to try out a new recipe. My mom seemed to be on a personal quest to improve herself, be it serving some daring new cuisine, wearing the latest fashions, or taking French classes at the local college. She had many friends who looked up to her, and I realized early on that she gave up having a career to raise us. We kids were her focus, and she put everything she had into our lives. And every time she made this cake, she made it as if she had been commissioned to bake it for the Queen of England. It would be spectacular every birthday. That was pure love.

Seamus on his fourteenth birthday.

DEBRIANNA'S

"LOVE THE ONE YOU'RE WITH" WEDDING COOKIES

(V) (GF)

MAKES APPROXIMATELY 3 DOZEN COOKIES

1 cup (2 sticks) unsalted butter, room temperature

½ teaspoon vanilla extract

⅛ cup triple sec

½ cup confectioners' sugar, and more for rolling the dough

2 cups gluten-free flour (I like Flour Farm brand for this recipe, but use what you love)

½ teaspoon xanthan gum if the flour does not have it

¼ teaspoon salt

1 cup finely chopped walnuts or pecans

Dark chocolate chips (optional)

Zest of 1 orange

1. Preheat oven to 400°F.

2. Cream the butter, vanilla, triple sec, zest, and confectioners' sugar.

3. Add the flour, xanthan gum if you need it, salt, and walnuts, and combine until the dough holds together.

4. Shape the dough into 1-inch balls. If you want, you can tuck a couple chocolate chips in their centers. Place the balls on a baking sheet lined with parchment paper, and freeze for 5 minutes. Remove from freezer, and bake until set but not brown, 10 to 12 minutes.

5. Let the cookies cool for 5 minutes, and then roll in powdered sugar. Roll again when the cookies are cool. Store in an airtight container.

My heart is my hearth. However, on the occasion of my wedding, I did not cook. I planned the event of my life top to bottom, but I did not cook. I asked everyone else to do that. Hence, the lasagna bake-off wedding.

The rules of the contest were simple. The dish was required to be in a 9 x 13-inch pan, with the ingredients listed. The lasagna was to be brought to the big pink castle on the hill, otherwise known as the Scottish Rite Temple, by noon on the day. We asked the entries to be submitted a month before the wedding so we could be sure there would be enough food. The caterer, my friend the Italian chef–restaurant owner Lino, would be the judge. He would serve the lasagnas with an antipasto that we designed together.

The guests came from far and wide—almost every person we invited showed up. Everyone except my maid of honor. "I can't! I can't do it. I don't want to ruin your day," my closest friend, Susan, sobbed.

"What are you talking about? How could you ruin my day? Jesus, Susan, what are you saying? Oh . . . my God . . . the wedding is in two weeks!"

I had asked her to be my maid of honor a year before the date, knowing she would want to plan, maybe even lose some weight, the bane of her existence. I thought I'd give her a date far enough out so that if she was serious, it might help her accomplish her long-held goal. She'd have a year to plan for her disabled daughter's care. That way, she could spend time with me and recognize this hard-earned day, where I would have no parents standing with me. Where she, my longest friend in the universe, could stand in for my broken family. She was the friend who had been by my side for so many harsh breakups and who had picked me up off the floor and taken me to the divorce lawyer. She is the woman who'd moved in with me when we thought it was possible an ex-boyfriend had a gun, the woman who had seen me just days before I ran away from my familial home in Connecticut. She got me my first waitressing job. She had watched this long-awaited romance bud into the truest love of my life. She'd had a year to find a dress and make it work, to be a part of my joy instead of always my pain, a year to plan and prepare to be there.

And she ditched.

"I can't. I can't do it! You can find someone else. There are a lot of people you can call. I'm sorry. I just can't," she cried through broken words and promises, and then she hung up. I was numb. Susan, of all the people in my life. I couldn't believe it. My beloved fiancé, the man I had waited for all my life, walked into the room, took one look at me, and somehow knew.

"What's wrong? Did she back out?"

"Yes, she did. How did you know?"

"I don't know. I just didn't think she'd do it."

My mind reeled, and all the years flipped back like dominoes falling across the decades. At this point, I had two weeks before everyone arrived, and I was putting the finishing touches on my wedding gown. I was organizing for one hundred people, and my best friend canceled for reasons I still to this day cannot fathom.

My next dearest friend, who oddly is also named Sue, often called me from New York to share in the planning details. She was known affectionately as Shoe Sue to distinguish her from Susan, because we had met many years before while modeling for Calvin Klein footwear. We had stayed fast friends over the years, despite the distance between us when I moved to New Mexico.

Shoe Sue and Debrianna on Debrianna's wedding day.

"I'll be there," she said without hesitation.

"You can't, I know you can't—it's too fast. What would you do with Kayla?"

"I'm coming," she said in her firm, don't-fuck-with-me Shoe Sue way. "I'll be there the day before. What color dress do I need?"

And that was that. Shoe Sue arrived the day before the wedding, dress bag slung over her shoulder, and took charge, laughing all the way. She was there in every way, guiding me through the family challenges of my sisters, organizing the one photograph we have of all of us together as adults before my dear sister, Lisa, died a few years later. This photo, the moment we put our heads together at my wedding, is one I will always cherish.

GLASS HALF FULL FAMILY BAKLAVA

MAKES ABOUT 30 PIECES

BAKLAVA

7 cups ground walnuts or pistachio meats or mix of both

½ cup granulated sugar

½ cup brown sugar

1 teaspoon lemon zest

Juice of 1 lemon

1 teaspoon orange zest

¼ teaspoon freshly grated nutmeg

1 pound salted butter, melted

1 pound phyllo dough or 2 boxes (36 sheets) store-bought

¼ teaspoon sea salt

1 teaspoon vanilla extract

30 whole cloves (1 for each piece of baklava)

HONEY SYRUP

2 cups granulated sugar

1 pound honey

1. Preheat oven to 300°F.

2. In a large bowl, thoroughly mix the walnuts, sugars, lemon zest and juice, orange zest, and nutmeg, and then set aside.

3. Use the butter to baste the bottom and sides of a 10 x 15-inch baking pan.

4. Brush 1 side of the phyllo dough sheets with butter, and then create 7 layers of sheets in the pan.

5. Sprinkle ⅓ of the walnut mixture on the seventh layer, and then add 4 layers of phyllo dough, buttering each and then giving each a light coating of the nut mixture. Add the remaining phyllo sheets with just butter.

6. Cut the baklava into diamond shapes, and then insert a whole clove in the center of each piece.

7. Bake for 80 minutes.

8. While the baklava is baking, prepare the syrup by boiling the sugar, honey, and 1 cup water over high heat until it reaches a medium-thick syrup consistency. Remove from heat and allow to cool.

9. When the baklava is ready, pour the syrup over it. When all the syrup is absorbed, cut through and place diamond shapes in individual paper muffin cups. It is best to pour cooled syrup over hot baklava.

This delicious baklava recipe is from my maternal great-grandma, Mary Papatone. She gave it to my Great-Aunt Georgia, who then gave it to my Nana, who wrote in her cookbook, "This one good."

Lisa's great-grandmother Marija Plese Papatone in the 1920s.

OPTIMISTIC MOOD-ALTERING CHOCOLATE CUSTARD WITH SEA SALT CARAMEL AND WHIPPED CREAM

SERVES 6 TO 7

CHOCOLATE CUSTARD

8 ounces bittersweet chocolate (I used Lindt 70 percent cocoa), broken into small pieces

1¾ cups heavy cream

½ cup whole milk

1½ teaspoons instant coffee or espresso (I used Mount Hagen)

1 teaspoon pure vanilla extract

⅛ teaspoon sea salt, and more for finishing

6 large egg yolks

2½ tablespoons sugar

Berries of choice for serving (optional)

WHIPPED CREAM

2 cups heavy cream

1 teaspoon vanilla extract

1 tablespoon vanilla sugar

SEA SALT CARAMEL

½ cup brown sugar

1 teaspoon sea salt

¼ cup salted butter

¼ cup heavy cream

2 teaspoons vanilla extract

TO MAKE THE SEA SALT CARAMEL

1. In a saucepan, combine all ingredients for the caramel, and set over medium heat. Whisk constantly until the mixture has bubbled for about 4 minutes and reached a caramel color.

2. Remove from heat and cool to room temp; then pour into an airtight container, and set aside until ready to serve.

TO MAKE THE CHOCOLATE CUSTARD

1. Halfway fill a baking dish with water, and then place the dish in the oven. Preheat oven to 325°F, warming the dish as it heats so that it will be hot when you place the ramekins in.

2. Place the chocolate in a medium bowl.

3. In a saucepan, combine the heavy cream, milk, coffee, vanilla, and sea salt, and set over medium heat. Turn off the heat just before it begins to boil, and pour the mixture over the chocolate. Whisk until well incorporated, and then set aside to cool off a bit—it will still be warm when ready to use.

4. In another bowl, whisk the egg yolks and sugar together until well blended.

5. Using a semi-fine sieve to remove any egg debris, gradually strain this egg/sugar mixture into a bowl with a pouring spout or an extra-large Pyrex measuring cup.

6. Slowly add this strained mixture to the warm chocolate (step 3) to finish making the custard. Do not combine too fast, as you don't want to cook the eggs.

7. Pour the chocolate custard mixture into ramekins, and wrap each in foil. Place in the bain-marie of hot water that is in the oven. You want the hot water to reach the halfway mark on the ramekin. Bake for 30 minutes.

8. Remove from oven, and immediately remove foil tops. Let cool for a few minutes in the bain-marie. As soon as you can take the custards out of the water, let them cool on a rack. When room temperature, cover with plastic wrap and refrigerate for a minimum of 4 hours. I refrigerated the custards overnight and they were perfect. They can stay in the fridge for up to 2 days.

TO MAKE THE WHIPPED CREAM

1. Combine cream, vanilla, and vanilla sugar in a large mixing bowl, and beat with a hand mixer until stiff peaks form.

2. When ready to serve the custards, top with a hefty dollop of sea salt caramel, freshly whipped cream, and perhaps accompanied by your favorite berries.

LISA'S

WHO'S BETTER THAN US? NEW YORK FOREST BERRIES CHEESECAKE

Ⓥ

SERVES 6 TO 8

CRUST

1¾ cups all-purpose flour, and more for dusting the pan

½ cup light brown sugar

¼ teaspoon salt

¾ cup (1½ sticks) salted butter, cut into small pieces and chilled, and more for pan and parchment paper

2 large egg yolks

1 teaspoon vanilla extract

⅓ cup apricot jam (page 215)

FILLING

9 ounces cream cheese, room temperature

1 cup cottage cheese (large curd), room temperature

¾ cup light brown sugar

¼ teaspoon salt

Dash ground cinnamon

Dash freshly grated nutmeg

2 large eggs

This is a riff on a recipe from Dorie Greenspan's cookbook *Baking: From My Home to Yours.*

1. In a mixing bowl, use a hand mixer to combine the flour, sugar, salt, and butter until the mixture resembles coarse meal.

2. In a separate bowl, whisk the egg yolks and vanilla, and then add them to the flour mixture. Combine until the dough comes together. Do not let it form into a ball.

3. Wrap the dough in plastic wrap and refrigerate for 20 minutes. Remove and roll out to the full circumference of a 9-inch springform pan. Butter and lightly flour the pan, and then press the rolled dough evenly into it. The dough should come up about 1½ to 2 inches from the sides. Refrigerate for another 30 minutes.

4. Preheat oven to 375°F.

5. Butter a piece of parchment paper on 1 side, and cover the crust with the buttered side. Cover with some kind of weight (like dry rice, beans, or pie weights), and bake for 20 minutes. Remove from the oven, take the weight and parchment paper off, and put the crust back in the oven to bake until golden brown, 4 to 6 more minutes.

6. Remove from oven and let cool. Lower the oven temperature to 350°F.

7. Warm the jam and then spread it over the bottom of the crust. Set aside.

8. To make the filling, mix the cream cheese and cottage cheese together with a hand mixer for 2 minutes or until you have a creamy finish. Add the sugar, salt, and spices and mix on high for another minute. Add the eggs. Keep mixing and scraping the bowl as needed for a couple more minutes, until you have a satiny filling. Pour the filling over the jam.

9. Bake 60 to 70 minutes. Check with oven light on. Make sure the filling does not jiggle.

10. Transfer the springform pan to a cooling rack, and cool to room temperature. The cheesecake will decompress.

11. Chill the tart at least 2 to 4 hours. To serve, loosen the crust from the sides of the pan with a sharp spatula or bendable knife and then remove the cheesecake. Add berries or make a coulis (see Lisa's Don't Trifle with Me Berry Trifle on page 212), or dust with confectioners' sugar.

TIP: When you don't want the full-on New York cheesecake classic, this will do the trick. You could also adapt this recipe to make a chocolate or coconut cheesecake or use another jam flavor to make a lemon or raspberry cheesecake, for example. Truth be told, I could eat an entire cheesecake if left alone with one.

My stepdad, Stan, pretty much loves two things: classical ballet and New York cheesecake—okay, three things—and my mother, Franny. Okay, four things—it always tickles him to toast with the words "Who's better than us?" after a really great meal my mom has made for the family.

A couple years ago, on the night Stan lay in a hospital bed in the emergency room after suffering a stroke, we were, for some reason, talking about Mikhail Baryshnikov. It was a very intense night, and thank God he recovered completely and lived to tell the tale. As I sat there with him in the darkened room when we were both super scared and he couldn't sleep, the first thing to come to mind that might calm him down was Misha and his ballet roles we both admired. So I started musing about one of the greatest ballet dancers of all time. As a youth, I was so inspired by Baryshnikov. My ballet friends and I worshipped him. He defected to the US from the USSR in 1977 ("I need artistic freedom") just as my friends and I were coming of age in our training and he was simply sensational and took the world by storm. I have seen him perform in both classical and modern dances many times over the years, as has Stan.

Misha was one of the greatest dancers in history, but it was not only his technique and artistry that made him legendary, it was his capacity for emotional connection to his partner and to the audience. "I do not try to dance better than anyone else. I only try to dance better than myself," he once said. Many times I was moved to tears watching him perform. And I never made it far enough in ballet to be able to dance anywhere near him. But I have to say it always gives me a small, secret thrill that he happened to marry a woman named Lisa.

I am so grateful that Stan made it through that fateful dark night of the soul. It made me think about how much he has meant to me in my life. He has been a stand-up man and a compassionate father figure, and he has been so good to my mom. I cherish the laughs we have had and our countless debates over classic movies, actors, and film scripts. COVID has been so difficult. It's an especially frightening thing if you have health issues. I feel like I missed out on a year with my mom and Stan. It is unconscionable how many families have lost loved ones to COVID. It is a devastating number. History will not be kind to Forty-Five and the rest of his GOP fascist death cult sycophants. Absolutely shameful.

Seamus, Ronan, Lisa, Franny, and Stan at Thanksgiving.

DAVID FERGUSON'S

(v)

WE ARE THE CHAMPIONS PIE

SERVES 8 TO 10

CRUST

9 ounces gingersnaps

5 tablespoons butter

BITTER ORANGE CURD

Zest and juice of 4 Seville oranges (or ½ cup and 1 tablespoon regular orange juice, ¼ cup lime juice, and 2 tablespoons orange zest), and more zest for finishing (optional)

½ cup sugar

5 eggs (3 whole and 2 yolks only)

10 tablespoons (1¼ sticks) butter, cut into cubes

FILLING

2 sticks butter, softened

½ cups sugar

1 teaspoon vanilla

1 cup whipping cream (unsweetened), beaten into soft peaks

TOPPING

1 cup cream

⅓ cup sugar

Orange or lemon zest for finishing (optional)

This is a combination of two recipes, Nigella Lawson's Bitter Orange Tart and Sally McKinney's French Silk Pie.

1. Pulse the gingersnaps in a food processor until crumbled, and then add the butter and pulse until the mixture looks like dark, wet soil. Press it into a deep 9-inch pie dish, and refrigerate to chill for at least 2 hours until firm.

2. Combine the orange zest and juice, sugar, eggs, yolks, and cubed butter in a saucepan, and heat, stirring constantly, until thickened. Set aside and allow to cool to room temperature.

3. Whip the butter and sugar for the filling together in a mixer bowl or with a hand mixer on medium speed until fluffy (at least 2 minutes). Add the vanilla, and whip an additional 30 seconds. Reduce mixer to medium-low speed, and pour in orange curd until thoroughly blended.

4. Gently fold in unsweetened whipped cream and pour into gingersnap crust. Chill for at least 4 hours.

5. Whip 1 cup cream with ⅓ cup sugar, and spread over chilled pie. Garnish with orange or lemon zest.

Been Gaslit One Too Many Times $Fake Billionaire$ Shortbread Bars

MAKES APPROXIMATELY 12 BARS
IN AN 8 X 8-INCH PAN 3 INCHES DEEP

SHORTBREAD CRUST

¼ cup sugar

¼ cup brown sugar

½ cup (1 stick) salted butter

1 egg yolk or 1 tablespoon coconut oil

½ teaspoon vanilla extract

½ teaspoon sea salt

1⅛ cups all-purpose flour

PEANUT BUTTER FUDGE LAYER

1 cup chunky peanut butter

4 tablespoons salted butter

1⅛ cups powdered sugar

1 teaspoon vanilla extract

2 tablespoons heavy cream, and more if needed (optional)

MARSHMALLOW LAYER

1½ cups mini marshmallows (use ones made with cane sugar)

1 tablespoon salted butter

Dash sea salt

2 tablespoons heavy cream

CHOCOLATE TOP LAYER (GANACHE)

1 cup chocolate chips (I used Ghirardelli 60 percent cacao)

½ cup heavy cream

½ teaspoon vanilla extract

½ teaspoon sea salt

COCONUT TOPPING

¾ cup unsweetened shredded coconut

TO MAKE THE SHORTBREAD CRUST

1. Preheat oven to 350°F.

2. In a mixing bowl, combine the shortbread crust ingredients. Mix, but don't overmix.

3. Line a baking pan with parchment paper, and then spread the dough in even lines in it. Prick the dough with a fork.

4. Bake until golden brown, about 25 to 30 minutes.

5. Remove the crust from the oven, and allow it to cool for at least 30 minutes.

TO MAKE THE PEANUT BUTTER FUDGE LAYER

1. In a mixing bowl, combine the peanut butter fudge ingredients. You may need to add a bit more heavy cream depending on the consistency of the peanut butter. The fudge should be able to spread easily and evenly over the shortbread.

2. Refrigerate.

TO MAKE THE MARSHMALLOW LAYER

1. Melt the ingredients for the marshmallow layer in a double boiler.

TO MAKE THE CHOCOLATE TOP LAYER (GANACHE)

1. Melt the chocolate chips in a double boiler.

2. In a mixing bowl, combine the heavy cream, vanilla, and sea salt, and then add the melted chocolate. Whisk together.

TO ASSEMBLE THE BARS

1. Once the shortbread has cooled, add the subsequent layers. Spread the peanut butter fudge layer evenly over the shortbread, and then pour the marshmallow layer over the peanut butter fudge layer and spread across evenly. Refrigerate.

2. Toast the coconut in a cast-iron pan and then set aside.

3. Remove the shortbread from the fridge, and spread the ganache evenly over the marshmallow layer. On top of the ganache layer, sprinkle the toasted coconut.

TIP: Bake the shortbread first, and while it is cooling, work on the other layers. Refrigerate for at least 1 hour, even better 2 hours and they were perfect. Let them sit for 5 minutes after you take them out so that you can easily slice them into bars. They will last in an airtight container in the fridge for several weeks.

LISA'S

WAIT, WHAT? *SHE'S* THE BOSS? STRAWBERRY CREAM PUFFS

MAKES 18 TO 24 CREAM PUFFS

STRAWBERRY PURÉE

¼ cup granulated sugar

1 cup organic strawberries

Zest of ½ lemon

PÂTE À CHOUX

½ cup whole milk

½ cup (1 stick) salted butter

½ teaspoon sea salt

3 teaspoons granulated sugar

1 cup all-purpose flour

4 large eggs

CRÈME CHANTILLY

2 cups heavy cream

2 tablespoons superfine sugar

1 teaspoon vanilla extract

TO MAKE THE STRAWBERRY PURÉE

1. Pulse the sugar in a food processor to make it superfine, and then remove it and set it aside.

2. Reserve some strawberries for plating, and pulse the rest in a food processor (about 25 pulses) to make a purée. Add the superfine sugar and lemon zest.

3. Pour the purée into an airtight container and refrigerate.

TO MAKE THE PÂTE À CHOUX

1. Preheat oven to 400°F.

2. In a medium saucepan, combine the milk, sea salt, butter, sugar, and ½ cup water. Cook over medium heat, whisking constantly. Once the mixture begins to bubble, lower the heat and add the flour.

3. After adding the flour, return the heat to medium and stir constantly, cooking until the mixture resembles a ball and doesn't stick to the sides of the pan. Smoosh the ball into the pan for 1 or 2 minutes to cook the flour a bit more. Then remove the choux from the heat, and transfer it to a mixing bowl. Let it cool for at least 5 to 10 minutes.

4. Add the eggs 1 at a time while whisking by hand or use a standing mixer. Mix well. The choux should have a thickish, frosting-like consistency. Place it in the refrigerator for 10 to 15 minutes.

5. Line a baking sheet with parchment paper, and brush a scant coat of water onto the paper. This will add an element of moisture to the baking process that will help the cream puffs rise. Remove the choux from the refrigerator.

6. Fill either a proper pastry bag with the right size tube attachment for piping or a makeshift one (a zip-top bag that has been pushed into a tall and large enough drinking glass with the plastic edges hanging over the sides) with the choux. Push the dough into the lower corner of the bag, twist the top, and if the bag is makeshift, cut a small hole in the corner. You should be able to create 18 to 24 puff balls on the baking sheet.

7. Dab water with your finger on top of each cream puff, and then brush the egg wash onto each. Pipe the puffs with the choux.

8. Immediately place the baking sheet into the oven, and bake for 10 minutes. Then reduce the heat to 375°F, and bake until well cooked and golden brown, an additional 10 to 15 minutes. Observe the cream puffs through the oven window with the oven light on, but do not open the oven door while they bake. The cream puffs should rise to the size of a baseball or half a baseball.

9. Remove the puffs from the oven, and cool on a baking rack. Repeat the process with the next batch. When all the puffs are baked and on racks to cool, create the filling.

TO MAKE THE FILLING

1. In a mixing bowl, whip together the cream, superfine sugar, and vanilla until you have perfect whipped cream peaks.

2. Gently fold ½ to ¾ (to taste) cup of the prepared strawberry purée into the whipped cream peaks. Make sure to save enough strawberry purée to pour over the cream puffs when serving.

3. Cover the filling with plastic wrap and refrigerate.

TO ASSEMBLE THE CREAM PUFFS

1. Gently cut each puff in half with a serrated knife. They should be hollow.

2. Fill the cream puffs by the spoonful with the crème chantilly.

3. Add fresh strawberries to the plate, and top with the strawberry purée.

"You just have to try this place at least once when in Paris. If you have a command of French, be sure to use it when making a reservation; otherwise they will seat you in the front with all the tourists. If you don't have a command of the language, have your hotel make the call."

I don't remember how we got into Bouillon Julien, but our whole family was there celebrating Heidi and her magna cum laude, and we sat down to dinner at this lavishly elegant table perfectly framed by the opulent artwork and art nouveau paintings above, and we all were in a bit of a daze like it was a dream. Heidi was so happy to finally be able to experience this restaurant with all of us, as she could never afford to go there during her four years at university, and mom was footing the bill.

The very first thing I noticed, from moment one, was that the waiters were the absolute snobbiest, stereotypically condescending French naysayers you could ever imagine. Like, *the worst*. The movie cliché about restaurants in Paris with the classic snob maître d' playing the part where they're putting down the customer with full force was happening right in front of our eyes. Soon, Heidi began to get upset.

No matter how cute we Americans might think we are in the role of clueless, bumbling customers, you never win the maître d' over unless a miracle happens—or, as my mom likes to say, "the universe throws you a bone."

My mother decided to try to get the snobbish waiter who thought we were rubes from 'Merica to be nicer. She ignored him and acted above it all. It must be said that Franny will tend to get slightly British all of a sudden when she feels she needs to go there. So what did she do? She looked this condescending ass of a maître d' in the eye and called his bluff. "Well, sir, we shall have champagne then. For everyone!" Franny, doing her best Marie Antoinette side eye to the plebeian waiters, doubled down and ordered some fine, expensive champagne. The maître d', though, was playing it off like, I know your tactics, *madame*. I was not born *hier*. Then, amid all the Parisian fanfare of the champagne ceremony, with the silver bucket of ice, the crisp linens, the lyrical hand gestures, etc., just as he was about to twist the cork and pour champagne into my mother's flute while still donning his best *I so have better things to do with my time and life* look, he popped the cork for what was probably the three millionth time in his life, and the glorious Épernay champagne gods decided that this particular cork at this day and time would not come out smoothly. The cork burst off and—*bam!*—he accidentally spilled champagne all over my mother's beautiful white suit. The guy was *mortifié*, and, of course, Franny did her classic "British" distaste face, playing the part of the customer with the ruined suit. Other touristy people noticed from across the room as well as the chic locals next to us, who were all looking at him like, *You've got to be kidding. Note to self, never coming here again. They can't even pour champagne.*

The spill was a serious problem—instant karma—and launched a 180-degree attitude adjustment. The next thing you know, he was bringing us free dessert! He was speaking French with Heidi and me, and he wanted to know where we all came from in America. He *loved* that my dad is a winemaker from California. I don't think I have ever witnessed such an abrupt about-face in my life. So in the end, we all toasted to Heidi, to life, and to France. "*Vive la France!*" we all exclaimed over and over. The maître d' toasted with us and literally hugged us while we said our goodbyes as we sauntered out the door into the beautiful summer night in the 10th arrondissement on Rue du Faubourg Saint-Denis. And BTW, Mom gave the maître d' a big American FU tip (FYI, restaurant workers are on salary in France and a tip is not required on restaurant bills) just to piss him off! Nothing like having the last laugh. That's my mother. Most importantly, though, we had magnificent profiteroles for dessert, like the ones from this recipe. They were perfectly baked, warm, fluffy, and buttery. And the waiters poured the most gorgeous melted chocolate over them.

Heidi in Paris.

NANA'S

CARAMEL APPLE MAKE-UP CAKE

(V)

SERVES 8 TO 10

CAKE

1½ cups (3 sticks) salted butter, melted, and more for greasing the pan

3 cups all-purpose flour, and more for dusting the pan

2 teaspoons vanilla extract

½ cup grape-seed oil or other neutral vegetable oil or coconut oil

3 eggs

1 cup brown sugar

1 cup granulated sugar

1 teaspoon baking soda

1 teaspoon sea salt

2 teaspoons ground cinnamon

½ teaspoon freshly grated nutmeg

Zest of 1 lemon

1 cup chopped walnuts or pecans

3½ cups peeled, chopped apples (I used Honeycrisp)

1 cup golden raisins

CARAMEL SAUCE

½ cup brown sugar

1 teaspoon sea salt

¼ cup salted butter

¼ cup heavy cream

2 teaspoons vanilla extract

TO MAKE THE CAKE

1. Preheat oven to 350°F.

2. Grease a standard 10-inch (12-cup) Bundt pan thoroughly with butter, and then dust with flour. Set aside.

3. With a hand mixer, combine all the wet ingredients for the cake in a large bowl. Add the dry ingredients for the cake except the flour, walnuts, apples, and raisins. Mix to incorporate.

4. Add the flour by the cupful. With a large spoon, mix in the walnuts, apples, and raisins.

5. With large spoonfuls, transfer the batter to the pan, and even out the top with a spatula.

6. Bake for about 75 minutes. Keep the oven light on, and check occasionally. Check doneness by piercing with a clean knife or toothpick.

7. Remove the cake, and let cool 5 to 10 minutes while you are making the caramel sauce.

TO MAKE THE CARAMEL SAUCE

1. In a saucepan, combine all caramel sauce ingredients, and set over medium heat.

2. Whisk constantly until the mixture starts to bubble. Remove the mixture from the heat once it is a caramel brown, after about 4 minutes of bubbling.

TO SERVE

1. Place a cake plate on top of the Bundt pan and turn the cake and plate upside down in one fell swoop so the cake rests on top of the cake platter. It should remove itself quite easily. Then take a long wooden skewer, and make holes in the top of the cake so that the caramel will fill the holes as you drizzle over it.

2. Glaze the cake while it is still warm, using the caramel sauce.

3. Leave the cake out to cool at room temperature for a ½ hour, and then slice and serve.

TIP: Depending on your sweet tooth, you could double the caramel sauce recipe and have maximum caramel to both cover the cake adequately and have extra in a bowl to spoon on top of each slice when serving it later. This is also a great dessert to be accompanied by ice cream or whipped cream. Please note: it will be all gone in 2 days. Tops.

Baby Lisa and her Nana.

Rose Petal Honey Ice Cream

MAKES 1 QUART

2 cups heavy cream

1 cup whole milk

1 teaspoon vanilla extract

3 tablespoons HH Rose Petal Herb Infused Honey or plain honey and 1 teaspoon dried crushed roses

Pinch sea salt

FLAVOR OPTIONS (OPTIONAL)

Additional honey (warm to 85°F to 90°F and then drizzle on the finished ice cream. It will harden and make a marble effect throughout the ice cream.)

Chocolate

Caramel

Fresh rose petals, chopped

Chopped nuts like pistachios, macadamia nuts, or cashews

Fresh berries or pineapple

Chocolate chips, colored sprinkles, or other festive treats

1. In medium saucepan set over medium heat, combine the heavy cream, milk, vanilla, honey, and sea salt. Stir until the honey has dissolved. Do not let boil.

2. Remove the mixture from the heat, and transfer to a bowl or large glass mason jar. Cool to room temperature and then refrigerate until cold, at least 1 hour. The mixture must be cold before it goes into an ice cream maker.

3. Pour the mixture into the canister of an ice cream maker. Process according to the manufacturer's instructions.

4. When the ice cream is finished churning, add flavor option if using.

5. Serve immediately, or transfer to a freezer-safe container and keep frozen until ready to serve.

PENINA MEISELS'S

Almond Cake

SERVES 8

1 cup unsalted butter, cubed, room temperature, and more for greasing the pan

¾ cup sugar

8 ounces almond paste*

¼ cup coconut flour

¾ cup almond flour

1½ teaspoons baking powder

¾ teaspoon salt

1 teaspoon vanilla extract

1 teaspoon almond extract

6 large eggs, room temperature

*TO MAKE THE ALMOND PASTE

4 ounces whole blanched almonds

4 ounces powdered sugar

Almond extract to taste (start with ¼ teaspoon)

1 egg white, well beaten

1. Preheat oven to 325°F. Grease a 9-inch cake or springform pan with butter, dust it with flour, and tap out any excess. Line the bottom of the pan with a round of parchment paper.

2. In the bowl of a food processor, grind the sugar, almond paste, and coconut flour until the almond paste is finely ground and the mixture resembles sand.

3. In a small bowl, whisk together the almond flour, baking powder, and salt.

4. Once the almond paste is completely broken up, add the cubes of butter and the vanilla and almond extracts; then process until the batter is very smooth and fluffy.

5. Add the eggs, 1 at a time, processing a bit before the next addition. (You may wish to open the machine and scrape the sides down to make sure the eggs are getting fully incorporated.) After you add all the eggs, the mixture may look curdled. Don't worry; it'll come back together after the next step.

6. Add half the almond flour mixture, and pulse the machine a few times; then add the rest, pulsing the machine until the dry ingredients are just incorporated, but do not overmix. (You can also transfer the batter to a bowl and mix the dry ingredients in, which ensures they get incorporated evenly and you don't overbeat the batter.)

7. Scrape the batter into the prepared cake pan, and bake the cake for 45 to 60 minutes, or until the top is deep brown and feels set when you press in the center.

8. Remove the cake from the oven, and run a sharp or serrated knife around the perimeter, loosening the cake from the sides of the pan. Let the cake cool completely in the pan. Once cool, tap the cake out of the pan, remove the parchment paper, and set on a cake plate until ready to serve.

TO MAKE THE ALMOND PASTE

1. Place almonds and sugar in a food processor and process until it is the consistency of almond flour.

2. Add the almond extract and then pulse and taste. Add more if needed. Then add a tablespoon of the egg white. Pulse 5 to 6 times. If it is not starting to ball around the blade, add an additional teaspoon, and pulse again. Keep adding until it comes together around the blade.

3. Wrap in plastic wrap and refrigerate until ready to use. Can be made several days ahead of time and will keep for a week refrigerated.

TIP: This cake will keep for 4 days at room temperature, well wrapped. It can also be frozen for up to 2 months.

GRACE GOMEZ LAPSYS'S

LEMON PISTACHIO TORTE SANS RIVAL

SERVES 6 TO 8

CREAM FILLING

1 (.25 ounces) packet unflavored gelatin

⅓ cup and 1 tablespoon heavy cream, cold

⅔ cup confectioners' sugar

1 tablespoon vanilla paste or extract

7 ounces plain yogurt

6 ounces light sour cream

DACQUOISE

2 cups pistachio meats, roasted

1 cup cane sugar

3 tablespoons potato starch

10 large egg whites, room temperature

¼ cup confectioners' sugar

LEMON CHOCOLATE MOUSSE

¾ teaspoon unflavored gelatin

2 egg yolks

1½ tablespoons sugar

3½ tablespoons whole milk

¾ cups heavy cream

5 ounces white chocolate callets or chips

1 to 2 drops lemon essential oil or 1 to 2 teaspoons lemon extract,* to taste

* Lemon zest will do, as well. Add lemon zest to the cream the night before, and then strain before using.

OTHER INGREDIENTS

Lemon peels for finishing

Pistachio meats for finishing

MAKE THE CREAM FILLING

1. Prepare the gelatin by placing the contents of the packet and 4 tablespoons water in a small, microwave-safe bowl. Let stand until thick, 3 to 5 minutes.

2. Heat the gelatin in the microwave for about 5 seconds. Keep heating in 5-second increments until the gelatin is liquid.

3. In a stand mixer, whisk the heavy cream, sugar, and vanilla on low until combined. Then increase the speed to high, beating the cream mixture until soft peaks form, and add the liquid gelatin to the cream mixture in a constant, thin stream while the mixer is beating. Continue whisking until stiff peaks emerge, about 2 to 3 minutes. Add the yogurt and sour cream, and whisk again to combine.

4. Cover and place mixture in the fridge until ready to use.

MAKE THE DACQUOISE

1. Preheat oven to 350°F. Line a half sheet pan with parchment paper.

2. Using a blender or food processor, grind the pistachios, sugar, and potato starch. Pulse to create fine crumbs, about 15 to 20 seconds, depending on the power of your machine; be careful not to turn it into a nut paste. Set aside.

3. Using a stand mixer with a whisk attachment, whisk the egg whites until foamy. Slowly add the confectioners' sugar to create stiff peaks.

4. Using a rubber spatula, gently fold the nut mixture into the egg mixture, adding little by little so as not to deflate the dacquoise. Transfer the mixture onto a prepared half sheet pan. Use an offset spatula to spread evenly.

5. Bake for 20 minutes or until golden brown; it is ready when a toothpick inserted in the center comes out clean. Let cool before cutting.

ASSEMBLE THE CAKE

1. Invert the dacquoise onto a cutting board, and gently remove the parchment paper. Cut in 3 equal parts lengthwise.

2. Spread half of the cream filling onto 1 of the cut layers. Cover the filling with a second layer of dacquoise. Spread the other half of the cream filling on top of the second layer. Place the last cut layer on top of the filling. Chill in the refrigerator.

TIP: If preparing ahead of time, wrap in plastic wrap or parchment paper and freeze.

LEMON CHOCOLATE MOUSSE

1. Cover the gelatin with 1 tablespoon of water, allowing it to bloom. Set aside.

2. Whisk the egg yolks with the sugar until combined and light in color.

3. In a small saucepan, heat the milk and bloomed gelatin until it just comes to a boil. The gelatin *should* be dissolved at this point. Pour half the milk into the egg and sugar mixture, and whisk together. Pour the milk, egg, and sugar mixture into the remaining milk in the saucepan. Cook over low heat until mixture thickens and holds shape on the back of a spoon.

4. Meanwhile, beat heavy cream to stiff peaks.

5. Place the chocolate in a medium mixing bowl. Using a strainer, pour the milk mixture over the chocolate, and mix until incorporated. Microwave 10 to 15 seconds at a time if white chocolate is still solid. Add extract or essential oil. Allow to cool to room temperature.

6. Fold the heavy cream into the chocolate mixture.

FINAL ASSEMBLY

1. Remove chilled cake, trim as desired, and frost with the chocolate mousse, covering the entire cake evenly.

2. Freeze and garnish with thinly sliced, twisted lemons and crushed pistachios.

TIP: Each component can be prepared ahead of time and assembled on the day the torte will be served. The chocolate mousse can be a stand-alone dessert, placed in small dessert cups or goblets garnished with nut brittles or pralines. I've also made this with wild orange essential oil, served in a dessert glass layered with crushed hazelnut brittle with a candied orange on top.

PINK VELVET CAKE

SERVES 8

PINK VELVET CAKE

½ cup unsalted butter, softened, and more for buttering the cake pans

¼ cup freshly squeezed beet juice

1 cup peeled and grated beet

½ cup buttermilk

1 tablespoon white wine vinegar

2 tablespoons freshly squeezed lemon juice

1 tablespoon vanilla extract

1 cup cassava flour

3 tablespoons cocoa powder (natural, not Dutch-process)

2 teaspoons baking powder

1 teaspoon cream of tartar

1 teaspoon sea salt

1½ cups blanched almond flour

½ cup avocado oil

2 cups organic sugar

3 large eggs

WHITE CHOCOLATE ERMINE FROSTING

6 tablespoons cassava flour

1½ cup whole milk or nondairy milk (such as coconut or almond milk)

¼ teaspoon sea salt

3 ounces white chocolate, melted

12 tablespoons (1½ sticks) unsalted butter, softened

1 cup sugar

1 teaspoon vanilla extract

TO MAKE THE CAKE

1. Preheat oven to 350°F. Butter two 8-inch cake pans, and line the bottom of the pans with parchment paper.

2. Add the beet juice and grated beets into a blender, and blend into a purée.

3. Add the buttermilk, white wine vinegar, lemon juice, and vanilla to the beet purée, and blend until well combined. Set aside.

4. Using a sieve, sift together the cassava flour, cocoa powder, baking powder, cream of tartar, and sea salt. Whisk in the almond flour, and then set aside.

5. Using a standing mixer or hand-held mixer, cream together the softened butter and oil until smooth.

6. Add the sugar, and continue beating for another 2 minutes.

7. Add the eggs, 1 at a time, blending well after each addition.

8. Alternate adding flour mixture then beet purée into the batter. Beat well after each addition, and end with beet purée.

9. Pour the batter into prepared cake pans, and bake for 35 to 40 minutes or until a toothpick inserted in the center of the cake comes out clean.

10. Cool the cakes for 15 minutes, and then run a butter knife carefully around the edge and invert.

11. Frost with white chocolate ermine frosting.

TO MAKE THE WHITE CHOCOLATE ERMINE FROSTING

1. Whisk together the cassava flour, milk, and sea salt over medium heat until smooth and thickened like a roux. Remove from heat and transfer to a bowl. Allow to cool.

2. In a double boiler, melt the white chocolate and set aside to cool slightly.

3. Using a stand mixer or hand-held mixer, beat the softened butter and sugar together for about 5 minutes.

4. Add the cooled roux mixture by the spoonful, beating well after each addition. The frosting will be thicker but may also look somewhat broken. Don't worry; keep mixing.

5. Add the vanilla, followed by the melted white chocolate and continue mixing.

6. The frosting may be soft at this point, so chill for 30 minutes and then mix again until you have a frosting-like consistency.

TIP: The neat thing about this frosting is that you can troubleshoot it fairly easily. If you leave it in the fridge too long, take it out and leave it at room temperature until it softens enough to mix easily. Then, mix it really well.

PATRICIA MEDINA'S

CARROT CAKE

Ⓥ

SERVES 8 TO 10

CARROT CAKE

2 cups and 1 tablespoon all-purpose flour, and more for flouring the pan

1½ cups canola oil, and more for greasing the pan

2 cups sugar

1¼ teaspoons baking soda

¼ teaspoon salt

2 teaspoons ground cinnamon

5 large eggs

3 cups packed finely grated carrots

½ cup unsweetened coconut

1 (8-ounce) can or 1 cup crushed pineapple, drained

½ cup chopped walnuts or pecans, and more, finely chopped, for finishing

CREAM CHEESE FROSTING

2 (8-ounce) packages full-fat cream cheese, softened

½ cup (1 stick) unsalted butter

1½ cups powdered sugar, and more if desired

Zest from 1 medium orange

3 tablespoons fresh orange juice or pineapple juice

1 teaspoon vanilla

TO MAKE THE CARROT CAKE

1. Preheat oven to 350°F. Grease and flour three 8- or 9-inch round cake pans, and line with parchment paper.

2. Mix the flour, sugar, baking soda, salt, and cinnamon in a large bowl. If using a stand mixer, mix on low speed.

3. Add the canola oil, and mix for 1 minute.

4. Add the eggs, 1 at a time, and beat for 30 seconds after the addition of each egg.

5. Add the carrots, coconut, and drained crushed pineapple, and mix at low speed. Fold in the nuts.

6. Pour the batter evenly into the 3 pans. Bake for 20 to 25 minutes or until a toothpick inserted in the middle comes out clean.

7. Allow to cool on wire racks for 10 minutes. Remove cakes from the pans onto wire racks, and cool completely before frosting.

8. After frosting, decorate the sides and top of the cake with the nuts.

TO MAKE THE CREAM CHEESE FROSTING

1. Using the whip attachment for your mixer, beat the cream cheese and butter together until light and fluffy.

2. Add the powdered sugar, and whip on low speed. Add the orange zest, juice, and vanilla. Whip some more until the frosting is spreadable. Add more powdered sugar incrementally if desired for added sweetness.

PUMPKIN PIE

SERVES 6 TO 8

1 cup candied yams, drained (plain canned yams are okay if you can't find candied yams)

1 cup heavy cream

1 cup whole milk

5 large eggs (3 whole and 2 yolks only)

1 teaspoon vanilla extract

1 (15-ounce) can pumpkin purée

¾ cup granulated sugar

¼ cup maple syrup

½ teaspoon ground cinnamon

3 teaspoons grated fresh ginger

¼ teaspoon freshly grated nutmeg

1 teaspoon salt

1 standard 9-inch piecrust, blind-baked, warmed

1. Preheat oven to 400°F.

2. Press the candied yams through a ricer.

3. Whisk the cream, milk, eggs, egg yolks, and vanilla in a mixing bowl and set aside.

4. Combine the pumpkin purée, yams, sugar, maple syrup, cinnamon, ginger, nutmeg, and salt in a saucepan. Simmer over medium heat for 15 to 20 minutes, stirring almost constantly, until thickened and shiny. Remove from heat, stir in the cream mixture, and then press the mixture through a fine-mesh sieve.

5. Pour the filling into the warmed piecrust.

6. Bake at 400°F for 10 minutes; then lower the oven temperature to 300°F and bake for another 20 to 35 minutes, until the edges of the pie are set and a thermometer measures the pie's temperature at 175°F.

LIVING MAGIC PIECRUST

(V)

MAKES ONE SINGLE-CRUST 9-INCH PIE

1 cup all-purpose white flour, and 3 tablespoons for rolling out the dough

¾ cup (1½ sticks) unsalted butter

3 generous pinches salt

> The alchemy of cooking something never ceases to amaze me, whatever it is. And so it is with piecrust. How is it that a cup of flour, some butter, salt, and a bit of water can end up as a flaky crust inspiring oohs and ahhs? Every time my surprise is my reward, and I'm quite sure that I'll never tire of that magical feeling.

1. With a chef's knife, cut the butter into tiny cubes about the size of peas, and then place them into a bowl.

2. Add the flour and salt.

3. Start working the butter into the flour and the flour into the butter, squeezing the dry ingredients into the fat with your fingers and the palms of your hand. It should come together and become yellowy in small, ropey chunks.

4. Start slowly adding ¼ cup cold water. Pour about a third of the water in, being careful to distribute it evenly around the bowl. Work the water into the dough, and then add the next third of the water. Repeat until you've poured the entire ¼ cup in.

5. Start pushing the dough together into a sphere just larger than a baseball. You want it to hold together, but just barely. If it refuses to hold together, you'll need to add a bit more very cold water, but the less the better.

6. The dough ball should be mottled throughout with yellow concentrations of butter that haven't fully integrated with the flour. Work the ball in your hands, pushing on those buttery lodes with the palms of your hands and spreading them out and into the dough. This is called fraisage, and it's the final phase of crafting an exquisite crust. Don't eliminate those splotches—just spread them out a bit. And if you miss a few of these buttery masses, don't obsess. Life is imperfect, just like a perfect pâte brisée (piecrust). More to the point, it's imperative that you not overwork the dough. Touch it as little as possible.

7. Shape the dough into a disc about 6 inches in diameter and 2 inches thick. Wrap it in cellophane, and put it in the refrigerator to let it rest.

Bar Snacks, Cocktails, & Mocktails

LISA'S

WHENEVER THIS DIP SHOWS UP IT'S A PARTY ARTICHOKE DIP

Ⓥ

SERVES 4

1 (18-ounce) jar marinated artichoke hearts, drained and chopped

Zest and juice of 1 lemon

5 ounces creamy goat cheese

⅓ cup whipped cream cheese

1 cup lemon-infused mayonnaise or regular mayonnaise with juice of ½ lemon

2 teaspoons minced fresh dill

2 garlic cloves, minced

Sea salt, to taste

Freshly ground black pepper, to taste

1 large bunch (about 3 cups) spinach, roughly chopped, or 1 (16-ounce) package frozen spinach, defrosted and drained of excess water

1⅓ cups fresh bread crumbs (I used toasted baguette heels mixed with 2 tablespoons olive oil), ⅓ cup reserved for topping

1⅓ cups freshly grated Parmesan, ⅓ cup reserved for topping

8 baby scallions (green part of stalks only), finely chopped

2 teaspoons roasted Hatch green chile, finely chopped

1 tablespoon unsalted butter, and more for greasing the baking dish and topping

1. Preheat oven to 375°F.

2. Combine all ingredients, except those for topping, by pulsing together a few times in a food processor or mixing together by hand in a large bowl. Do not overmix.

3. Butter a baking dish, and then transfer the mixture to it. Top with Parmesan and then the bread crumbs and then small pats of butter.

4. Bake until golden brown, about 40 minutes.

5. Serve hot.

TIP: Slice and serve with toasted baguette, fresh veggies, crackers, or pita bread.

So Divine Maple Nut Caramel Corn

MAKES 1 BIG BOWL (APPROXIMATELY 22 CUPS)
OF CARAMEL CORN—BUT YOU WILL WISH YOU HAD MORE!

SPICE MIX

½ teaspoon dry mustard

½ teaspoon ground
cayenne pepper

½ teaspoon five-spice powder

¼ teaspoon baking soda

½ teaspoon sea salt, or
more to taste

CORN

6 tablespoons coconut oil

⅔ cup popcorn kernels

1 cup pecans, toasted

4 strips bacon, cooked
and chopped

1 cup maple syrup

¾ cup (1½ sticks)
unsalted butter

1 tablespoon bourbon

⅔ cup light brown sugar

½ teaspoon vanilla extract

1. Preheat oven to 300°F, and line a rimmed baking sheet with parchment paper or use a silicone baking sheet.

2. Combine all spice mix ingredients.

3. In a large pot with a tight-fitting lid, heat the coconut oil and 3 popcorn kernels over medium-high heat. When the kernels pop, add the remaining kernels, lower the heat to medium-low, and crack the lid open a sliver, facing the opening away from you, to release steam. Cook, shaking the pot occasionally, until the popping stops.

4. Place the popcorn in a heatproof bowl, removing any unpopped kernels. Add the pecans and bacon, and mix to combine.

5. In a medium pot, bring the maple syrup, butter, bourbon, and brown sugar to a boil. Cook, stirring constantly, until the butter and sugar have melted (the mixture should be foamy) and the mixture reaches 240°F on an instant-read thermometer. Remove from heat.

6. Carefully stir in the vanilla and spice mix. (The mixture may bubble up.)

7. Immediately pour the hot syrup over the popcorn mixture, and use a spatula to mix well.

8. Scrape the popcorn onto the prepared baking sheet, creating 1 layer. Bake, rotating the pan after 15 minutes, for 25 to 35 minutes. It is done when you can remove a piece of the popcorn, and after letting it cool for about 1 minute, it's crisp when you bite into it.

9. Taste and sprinkle lightly with more sea salt if desired. Let cool before serving.

* Hi, this is Lisa again. I just asked Debrianna to please make this for us right now as we edit the book. We need it!

"TAKE A CHANCE ON ME" FIVE-SPICE CHICKEN WINGS

SERVES 4

Nonstick cooking spray

2½ tablespoons baking powder

½ teaspoon salt

2 teaspoons five-spice powder

4½ pounds chicken wings

SAUCE

½ cup ketchup

¼ cup gochujang sauce

¼ cup rice vinegar

3 garlic cloves, minced

2 teaspoons grated fresh ginger

2 tablespoons soy sauce

1 teaspoon toasted sesame oil

1 teaspoon five-spice powder

2 teaspoons fish sauce

1. Preheat oven to 400°F.

2. Line baking sheets with parchment paper, and spray with nonstick cooking spray.*

3. In a large plastic bag, mix the baking powder, salt, and five-spice powder. Add the chicken wings, and coat them in the powder mix.

4. Arrange the wings on the baking sheets, and then bake for 40 minutes, rotating the pans about halfway through and turning the wings.

5. Add all ingredients for the sauce to a small saucepan, and simmer over medium-high heat for 3 to 5 minutes to combine the flavors.

6. Serve the wings with the sauce to dip or coat in advance of serving.

* If you have wire oven racks, you can spray them with the nonstick spray and then place the wings on them instead of using baking sheets. If placing directly on wire racks, no need to rotate in step 4.

We grew up on food stamps. That truth pops out of my mouth, and it still stings. Not because we were poor, but because of how we were treated for being poor. I remember when I noticed that sting for the first time. We were in the checkout line at our local market, and my mom had toilet paper on the black conveyor belt heading toward the blond cashier, whose hair was piled high up on her head. The cashier looked straight at my mom and said, "You can't buy paper goods with food stamps. Just food. Toilet paper isn't food."

My mom became deeply irritated and said, "It is just as necessary as food is for my family. It *should* be allowed."

The cashier pulled the toilet paper off the conveyor belt and said, "It's not allowed. You'll need cash. Separate the paper goods out."

My mom turned to me and, trying to hide her pain with pride, said, "Pull out the paper stuff. Put them back in the cart. We can't afford them today."

Looking back, I wonder if that thoughtless act made that woman feel dignified, as she stole our dignity from us in that moment. She taught me what it felt like to be shamed in public for something I did not do or ask for. We did not "feel" poor in our home most times. We felt creative. We used whatever we had in the fridge and made phenomenal lunches and dinners. We made our own bread on Sundays for weekly sandwiches, never using the ever popular and tasteless Wonder Bread. We baked our own cookies for snacks, although we got one box of some packaged treat like Little Debbie or Yodels, which were gone by Monday afternoon. Oddly enough, stuff like that was allowed to be bought on food stamps. I never liked them, though. They tasted of bland sugar and air and had none of the complex tastes that arise from grinding cardamom seeds, adding star anise, using soft brown sugar and real butter—things we regularly experimented with in our homemade desserts.

As I put that moment into the context of my life, I often muse upon the resurgence of "comfort food." I sometimes feel that blush of first shame when I see "Homemade Chicken Potpie" on a menu or whole restaurant chains devoted to chicken wings. We used to use the wings to make stock for soup; I now know it is because they are the cheapest part of the chicken. What I remember most is that I loved to eat the wings after they boiled in the pot, filled with aromatics, the tender meat softly falling off the bone. My mom would put the pile in a bowl after straining out the broth—now a trendy item known as "bone broth"—and we would all gather around the biggest yellow Pyrex bowl we had, pull out the bones, and return some of the meat to the soup, with some of the tender sweetness being eaten right then and there.

Today we have wings of all kinds, served as the food attraction of Super Bowl Sunday parties and other festivities. When I feel that blush, the kind of sting that never leaves you once you feel that branding as a child, I like to rebrand myself and just say that we were merely ahead of our time.

Denice, Debrianna, Donna, and Lisa at Christmas.

JEN WEGE'S

VEGAN AVOCADO CREMA DIP

SERVES 2 TO 4

2 large ripe avocados

⅔ cup full-fat coconut cream

⅔ cup cilantro leaves

1 tablespoon freshly squeezed lemon or lime juice

½ teaspoon salt, or to taste

1. Blend all ingredients and 1 tablespoon water together in a blender or food processor until smooth and creamy. Add extra water and blend again if thinner consistency is desired.

TIP: This dip is great for topping tacos, sandwiches, wraps, and burgers but also works well as a salad dressing, vegetable dip, or yummy sauce. It's always best to make the crema just before you want to use it. You can store leftovers in an airtight container and press a piece of plastic wrap over the top of the crema to prevent oxidation.

EMILY SWANTNER'S

PIMENTO CHEESE

MAKES ABOUT 5 CUPS

1 cup mayonnaise (preferably Best Foods or Hellmann's)

2 tablespoons Durkee Famous Sandwich & Salad Sauce

2 tablespoons hot-and-sweet mustard

2 tablespoons heavy cream or half-and-half

A few dashes Tabasco, or to taste

½ teaspoon curry powder

Seasoned salt (such as Lawry's), to taste

Freshly ground black pepper, to taste

2 cups grated sharp cheddar cheese

2 cups grated Monterey Jack cheese with jalapeños

2 cups grated smoked Gouda

1 (8-ounce) jar grated piquillo peppers, drained and sliced, or 2 (4-ounce) jars pimentos, drained

½ cup toasted pecans, coarsely chopped (optional)

1. In a medium mixing bowl, whisk together the mayonnaise, Durkee's sauce, hot-and-sweet mustard, heavy cream, Tabasco, and curry powder. Season with seasoned salt and pepper.

2. Add the 3 cheeses, piquillo peppers, and pecans to the mayonnaise mixture, and mix together with a wooden spoon. If the mixture is too stiff, add a little more cream. Taste for seasoning, and add more seasoned salt and pepper if desired.

3. Chill 1 hour before serving. Serve with your favorite crackers or crostini.

TIP: I sometimes like to make toast points for the pimento cheese. To do so, use Very Thin white Pepperidge Farm bread. Remove the crust from 2 sides of each piece of bread, and cut them in half diagonally. Spray with butter-flavored cooking spray, and let crisp in a 250°F oven for about 20 minutes. Allow to cool before serving.

DEBRIANNA'S

ONE OF THE GOOD WHITE RUSSIANS MILKSHAKE

SERVES 1

1½ ounces vodka (optional)

2 ounces Kahlúa, coffee liqueur, or coffee syrup* (for a mocktail version)

1 cup vanilla ice cream (I used Peekaboo's Organic Vanilla with Hidden Zucchini)

2 ounces half-and-half or whole milk

FOR THE RIM

¼ cup chocolate chips, melted

¼ cup nuts of choice, finely chopped

* To make coffee syrup, combine equal parts sugar and extra-strong brewed coffee in a medium saucepan, stirring to dissolve the sugar. Lower the heat and simmer for 10 minutes, and then let cool. Keeps in the refrigerator for up to 1 month.

COCKTAIL VERSION

1. Chill a tall highball glass.

2. In a blender, combine the vodka, Kahlúa, ice cream, and half-and-half.

3. Mix the melted chocolate and chopped nuts in a bowl wider than the glass's rim.

4. Dip the edge of the glass in the chocolate and nuts to coat the rim. Fill the glass with the blended drink.

MOCKTAIL VERSION

1. Follow the instructions for the cocktail, but skip the vodka and replace the Kahlúa with coffee syrup.

When You Need to Go to Mexico in Your Mind Watermelon Margaritas

(VG) (GF)

SERVES 4 TO 6

RIM MIX

¼ cup sea salt

Zest of ½ lime

Zest of 1 mandarin orange

1 teaspoon finely chopped fresh mint

½ teaspoon Chimayo red chile powder

1 lime wedge

COCKTAIL OR MOCKTAIL

5 cups seedless watermelon, cubed and frozen for at least 6 hours, and 1 slice for finishing

1 cup top-shelf tequila (optional; I used Hornitos Silver)

½ cup fresh lime juice

¼ cup orange simple syrup (use mandarin orange juice and orange zest to make a simple syrup)

½ cup lime or blood orange sparkling water (I used lime S.Pellegrino) or 1½ cups for mocktail version

Fresh mint for finishing

COCKTAIL VERSION

1. On a flat plate, combine the ingredients for the rim mix except the lime wedge. Mix with a spoon.

2. Squeeze the lime wedge around the entire rim of the glass. Turn the glass upside down, and dip the rim in the rim mixture to coat it.

3. Combine all cocktail ingredients in a blender. Blend until the mixture looks like a slushy.

4. Pour the cocktail into the glass with the dipped rim. Garnish with a watermelon slice and fresh mint.

MOCKTAIL VERSION

1. Follow the instructions for the cocktail, but omit the tequila and use an additional cup of sparkling water for a total of 1½ cups.

DEBRIANNA'S

HALLELUJAH, GEORGIA! BOURBON ROASTED PEACH SMASH

 VG GF

SERVES 1

2 tablespoons brown sugar

1 peach, halved with pit removed

2 ounces bourbon or club soda

1 ounce chamomile-tea simple syrup or 2 ounces for mocktail version

3 fresh mint leaves and 1 fresh mint sprig for finishing

Raspberries for finishing

Club soda or good ginger beer for topping

This drink was created to celebrate the Senate wins in Georgia in 2020!

COCKTAIL VERSION

1. Add the brown sugar and 2 tablespoons water to a small frying pan set over high heat. Bring to a boil, add the peach halves, and then reduce heat to simmer. Cover and cook until peach halves caramelize and are cooked through, about 20 minutes.

2. Remove from heat and let cool.

3. Add caramelized peaches, any juice from the pan, the bourbon, and the chamomile-tea simple syrup to a shaker, and muddle the mixture.

4. Add 2 ice cubes and shake well.

5. Strain the mixture into a rocks glass or mason jar over ice.

6. Garnish with a few mint leaves, the mint sprig, and fresh raspberries. Top with club soda.

MOCKTAIL VERSION

1. Follow the instructions for the cocktail, but add club soda to the peach smash instead of the bourbon, and use 2 ounces of simple syrup instead of 1 ounce.

DANCE LIKE NOBODY'S WATCHING THISTLE IN THE PECK

FENNEL GINGER SYRUP

Makes about 6 ounces

½ cup cubed fennel (use ½-inch pieces cut from ½ small bulb)

½ cup sugar

⅓ cup chopped fresh ginger

COCKTAIL OR MOCKTAIL

3 fresh basil leaves, and 1 fresh basil sprig for finishing

1¾ ounces fresh lime juice

2 ounces bourbon or good ginger ale or club soda, and more ginger ale or club soda for topping (if making the mocktail)

> This is adapted from a recipe in *Food & Wine*, but we made a ginger fennel syrup, adding ginger to the drink, which makes it totally different.

SERVES 1

TO MAKE THE FENNEL GINGER SYRUP

1. In a saucepan, boil ½ cup water.

2. Remove the pan from the heat, and add the fennel. Let steep for 6 minutes, and then remove and discard the fennel.

3. Add the sugar to the saucepan and bring to a boil, stirring until dissolved.

4. Add the ginger and simmer over very low heat for 30 minutes.

5. Remove from heat and drain the ginger. Let cool, and then transfer the syrup to a jar.

6. Refrigerate for up to 2 weeks.

COCKTAIL VERSION

1. In a cocktail shaker, muddle the basil leaves with 1½ ounces of the fennel ginger syrup.

2. Add the lime juice and bourbon, and then fill the shaker with ice and shake well.

3. Fine-strain into a chilled rocks glass with a large ice cube, and garnish with the basil sprig.

MOCKTAIL VERSION

1. Follow the instructions for the cocktail, but substitute the bourbon for a good ginger ale or club soda, and take care to avoid shaking.

2. Use additional ginger ale or club soda to top off the muddled mix in the serving glass.

LISA'S

(VG) (GF)

LOVE YOUR MAMA—AND MAKE FRANNY'S CLASSIC SANGRIA OLÉ!

SERVES 10

4 blood oranges
(reserve 2 to slice for garnishes)

1 lemon

1 lime

1 Honeycrisp apple

1 nectarine or white peach

1 cup green grapes, halved

1 cup raspberries

1 cup blackberries

½ cup blueberries

1 bottle Spanish rioja or
other low-tannin red wine
or red grape juice or alcohol-
free "wine"

2 tablespoons maple syrup

1 cup Cointreau or orange
simple syrup

Flavored seltzer for topping
(for mocktail version)

COCKTAIL VERSION

1. Juice 2 of the blood oranges, and then thinly slice all remaining fruit except the berries. Slice in corresponding half-moon shapes, and then place the cut fruit and the whole berries in a pitcher.

2. Add the rioja, then the maple syrup, then the Cointreau. Mix very gently with a wooden spoon. Refrigerate pitcher for a minimum of 1 hour.

3. When ready to serve, spoon ample fruit that is soaked with the sangria into clear glasses. Add blood orange slices for garnish, then the ice and the sangria.

MOCKTAIL VERSION

1. Follow the instructions for the cocktail, but substitute the wine for red grape juice or use an alcohol-free "wine," and substitute the Cointreau for orange simple syrup. Top each glass with a flavored seltzer (such as raspberry lime).

When I am in the waking hours of my day, most of my conscious thought considers the loss to society, to science and to art because women were not given the equality and opportunity they deserved and were instead pretty much forced to live in our societal stations rough-hewn from the fashion magazines and housework and child-rearing. When I take pause to think of how many people have gone crazy from the inequalities, the drug addiction and suicides from not being able to live their best life because there were so few choices, and when I consider the magnitude of this same scenario of discrimination toward people of color, indigenous people, anyone other than a white male, I want to cry and never stop.

My mother could have been anything. She could have done anything she set her mind to. She had dreams, but she knew she could only dream. She was and is clever, a terrific conversationalist and storyteller. This became a strength of hers when my dad needed a wife who could hold her own at cocktail parties. She could never appear smarter than the men, even though she was smarter than all of them! My mom was and is a self-taught admirer of art and aesthetic and has been her entire life. She even painted, and while no one thought anything of her paintings, they were stunning. It was a cute "hobby."

In 1961, her grandfather Tony recognized her need to feed her soul and invited her and her younger brother and two cousins to Europe to see the great cities and experience a grand tour of culture. The only reason she got to go was that her grandfather didn't see her as just a girl. She had a brain and they had a solid connection, one he did not have with her younger brothers. She was so excited about this trip. Finally a chance to explore and breathe in the work of the masters. When she walked up to the *Mona Lisa* in the Louvre for the first time, she studied it without the plexiglass. People could still touch it back then, she said. In my baby book she wrote, "Lisa, named after the Mona Lisa and Christmas Noel."

Franny always encouraged me and my sisters to reach our full potential—and we did because of her.

One time when I was in Singapore, I took up a suggestion from Franny to have Singapore slings at the Raffles Hotel. It was 1997 and they were twenty-five dollars each—a fortune at the time. But she was right. Damn, if that wasn't the best cocktail!

One thing for sure about my mother is that whenever we went anywhere we always ate at the best restaurants and drank at the best bars to get the full experience. But it must also be noted that she is, at times, prone to constructive criticism with really unattainably high standards. If you ever receive a rare compliment from her, be sure to know whatever you did must have been exceptional in her eyes. I hope she likes this cookbook. This sangria is an ode to my mother: classically crafted with the best ingredients and sure to delight in its complexity and flavor, just like her.

Franny circa 1969.

SPECTACULAR DARK AND STORMY

SERVES 1

¼ lime, quartered

Dash Angostura bitters

Drop vanilla extract

Fresh mint leaves

2 ounces black rum (such as Goslings or Myers's dark rum) or apple cider or vanilla seltzer for mocktail

1 ounce light rum (such as Mount Gay's Eclipse) or apple cider or vanilla seltzer for mocktail

Ginger beer (such as Q or Fever-Tree) for topping

¼ teaspoon grated fresh ginger for mocktail (optional)

From Lisa's brilliant brother-in-law, Steven Rossan—a.k.a. Sister Steven

COCKTAIL VERSION

1. Add the lime, bitters, vanilla, and torn mint leaves to a cocktail shaker, and muddle well. Add ice. Continue to muddle, crack the ice a bit, and then add the rum.

2. Cover and shake well.

3. Using a strainer, pour the cocktail over rocks into a low glass tumbler, filling ¾ of the glass.

4. Add ginger beer to top, and garnish with the whole mint leaf.

MOCKTAIL VERSION

1. Follow the instructions for the cocktail, but replace the rum with apple cider or vanilla seltzer.

2. Add ¼ teaspoon of grated fresh ginger to the muddle if desired.

While my sister Heidi and bro-in-law Steven visited during the monsoon season, they guest-hosted Corona Kitchen for cocktail-mocktail night with Steven's infamous Dark and Stormy, and we all reminisced about their wedding and how he became Sister Steven.

Heidi and Steven's wedding was the epitome of the classic family wedding and was held at Franny's house eight years ago. Everyone came together to make something special happen for them to celebrate their love. The wedding was for the family as well as this darling couple starting a new life together. Seeing them get married was so moving.

Steven said to me, "You become a man when you have a child." They had this beautiful baby together, Luka Jai, before they got married. They were in their forties. They knew who they were and what they wanted out of life. They had found each other. Music was incorporated through it all. On the night of their wedding, we danced the night away in a Croatian dance party USA extravaganza, and the food was incredible. Franny had a gigantic tent erected with a parquet floor in a field next to the house. And what a table of treats: prosciutto, cheeses, nuts, fig jam, beautiful fruit, and outstanding wine from Dad's vineyard.

But the loveliest thing of all was the heartfelt wedding ceremony overlooking the gorgeous view of the Galisteo Basin in Santa Fe. It was sunset, and when Steven brought out his guitar as part of his vows and crooned ever so softly, "You're my best friend until the end," there was not a dry eye in the house. Steven is one of the most caring, intelligent, and funny people on planet Earth. He "gets" the Lucas sisterhood vibe completely—and that is unusual for any man. He instantly found a family with ours, and we welcomed him with open arms. I love him like a sister.

HAD A HELLUVA WEEK BLOODY MARY

SERVES 1 WITH A TALL DRINK

1 cup tomato juice or tomato-based vegetable juice

2 dashes Worcestershire sauce

4 dashes hot sauce

1 teaspoon sea salt, and more for topping

5 cranks freshly ground pepper, and more for topping

2 tablespoons freshly squeezed lemon juice

½ teaspoon horseradish

¼ teaspoon smoked paprika

1 tablespoon brine from pepperoncini

½ teaspoon celery seeds or ground coriander

2 ounces of your favorite vodka (I used Grey Goose)

Garnishes of choice (see below)

GARNISH IDEAS

Grape tomatoes

Castelvetrano olives

Pepperoncini

Flat pretzels

Stalk celery with leaves

Shrimp

Dill pickles

Pickled asparagus

Bacon

Grilled artichoke hearts

Keep vodka in the freezer beforehand. Have ice cubes ready.

COCKTAIL VERSION

1. Whisk all ingredients except vodka and garnishes together in a medium bowl.

2. Pour tomato mix and vodka into a shaker with a few cubes of ice. Shake well, and then strain into a tall glass over ice.

3. Add sea salt and pepper to the top of the drink; then create edible garnishes on skewers, and top the drink with the skewers.

MOCKTAIL VERSION

1. Follow the directions for the cocktail but skip the vodka.

TIP: There is an endless number of garnishes that could work here. We've even seen Bloody Marys with mini sliders, BBQ shrimp, or chicken wings!

I'll never understand why some people don't like Hillary Clinton. Is it because she is a strong woman and always the smartest person in the room? Is it because Barack Obama declared she was the most qualified person to ever run for president of the United States? Is it because she dared to think she could be an astronaut when she was a little girl, even though no woman had ever been one before? Is it so wrong to dedicate your entire life to upholding the concept of creating a more perfect union, one that is ever evolving, changing, and progressing, and to push our representatives to make this country better and more equal for all? Apparently so, as she threatened a lot of men in a way they didn't like. I am grateful for her lifelong service to this country, to women, and to children. She has inspired me to let even the most difficult things go, as well as shown me that people can grow and change and learn. She made mistakes, a lot of them. She picked herself up and reflected, pivoted, and rolled with it. She never gives up and continues to serve the country she loves and believes in so much, as well as the world at large, despite all of the hideous lies and harassment she undeservedly receives. Who else could ever have that much strength and grace to rise above the unbelievably harsh, judgmental, misinformed microscope that has become US politics?

If someone had told me at ten years old that this was the way life was going to be, that we would still not have an equal rights amendment in 2023, I would have never believed them. When I was a kid, the whole world around me seemed to be on this wave of change, and it was exhilarating. I loved challenging my elementary school teachers in gender politics. It led to my questioning authority and the authenticity of what we were taught in high school. I knew it couldn't be only white men who invented everything. If this reaction is what happens when you give women an education, well then no wonder some men are afraid. I wrote this on the morning I voted for Hillary with both kids in tow at the polls in 2016:

Dressed in a white suit as a nod to suffragettes, I voted with my kids today. It feels like the dawn of a new era. I cannot contain my excitement. We will finally break the Presidential glass ceiling. Representation is everything. And so this day really belongs to my children, Ronan and Sea, as well as my nieces and nephews, Jack, Bella Francesca, Luka, and Izzy. These kids represent all Americans and they are the future of this nation, here long after we are gone. They deserve the greatest hope for the best life and all that is equal, decent, and fair, with all the rights and freedoms as is befitting to citizens of the United States in a democracy.

And then it all went to hell when Forty-Five got elected. I will never get over this monster getting into the White House instead of her. I still believe what I wrote that day, and I am so thankful for Joe Biden and Kamala Harris. It's going to be a long road toward recovery, systemic and fundamental mindset changes, and healing. We are lost as a nation, but I have to have faith we will find our way to a better world.

LISA'S

IMPATIENT FOR ITALIA ORANGE CONTRATTINIS

SERVES 1

4 oranges slices

2 ounces blood orange soda
(use a dry sparkling soda), or
5 ounces for mocktail version

3 ounces sparkling white
wine (I used Moscato d'Asti),
or 2 tablespoons orange
bitters (I used Angostura) for
mocktail version

4 ounces Contratto
Aperitif, or 3 ounces freshly
squeezed orange juice for
mocktail version

Drizzle orange blossom honey

Small orange zest "strings" and
1 wide slice orange zest

COCKTAIL VERSION

1. In a white wine glass, add ice cubes or crushed ice and
orange slices.

2. Add the soda, wine, Contratto Aperitif, honey, and zest, incorporating some zest strings and placing the zest slice on top.

MOCKTAIL VERSION

1. Follow the instructions for the cocktail, but use 5 ounces soda
instead of 2, replace the wine with 2 tablespoons orange bitters,
and replace the Contratto Aperitif with 3 ounces freshly squeezed
orange juice.

TIP: This is a wonderfully refreshing and delicious orange drink for a
summer night. My wine glasses were on the larger side; if yours are
smaller, cut the recipe in half.

505 COLLINS

SERVES 1

SAGE SYRUP

1 cup sugar

8 fresh sage leaves

COCKTAIL OR MOCKTAIL

1½ ounces Wheeler's Western Dry Gin or other dry gin or 2 ounces fresh lemonade for mocktail

2 tablespoons freshly squeezed lemon juice

2 ounces soda water or lemon S.Pellegrino (for mocktail version) for topping

Lemon slices for finishing

Marasca cherries for finishing

TO MAKE THE SAGE SYRUP

1. In a small saucepan, combine 1 cup water with the sugar. Bring to a slow boil, and then turn off the heat.

2. Stir in the sage leaves and let steep for 5 minutes.

3. Drain out sage and store in the fridge.

COCKTAIL VERSION

1. Combine the gin, lemon juice, and 1 ounce of the sage syrup in a glass, and mix well. Drain over ice into a collins glass.

2. Top with soda water, and garnish with the lemon slices and cherries.

MOCKTAIL VERSION

1. Follow the instructions for the cocktail version, but replace the gin with 2 ounces fresh lemonade and the soda water with lemon S.Pellegrino.

LISA AND DEBRIANNA'S

WE WISH YOU A MERRY MERRY GIN FIZZ

SERVES 1

3 marasca cherries

4 tablespoons top-shelf gin (we use Wheeler's Western Dry Gin) or lemonade for mocktail version

1½ tablespoons freshly squeezed lemon juice

1 tablespoon maple syrup or marasca cherry syrup

¼ teaspoon lemon zest

1 egg white (dry powder or fresh egg)

Lemon seltzer for topping

1 fresh rosemary sprig for finishing

COCKTAIL VERSION

1. In a rocks glass, muddle the cherries.

2. In a shaker or mason jar with a lid, combine the gin, lemon juice, maple syrup, lemon zest, and egg white. Shake well for a good 15 seconds.

3. Fill the shaker with ice, and shake for another 30 seconds.

4. Strain into the rocks glass, and top with the seltzer. As the egg white separates, a cherry-pink fizz will be produced. Garnish with the sprig of rosemary.

MOCKTAIL VERSION

1. Follow the instructions for the cocktail, but substitute lemonade for the gin.

TIP: Two tablespoons aquafaba (the liquid from a can of chickpeas) can be used in place of the egg white.

WHEW, THAT WAS CLOSE BLUE WAVE COCKTAIL

SERVES 1

BLUEBERRY SYRUP

2 cups sugar

½ vanilla bean (optional)

3 cups blueberries

COCKTAIL OR MOCKTAIL

2 pinches baking soda

1 large fresh sage leaf, and more for finishing

15 blueberries

2 ounces bourbon

4 ounces hard cider, or apple cider for mocktail version

Ginger ale for topping mocktail version (optional)

1 apple slice for finishing

1 fresh lavender sprig for finishing

TO MAKE THE BLUEBERRY SYRUP

1. Add all ingredients for the syrup and 2 cups water to a small saucepan, and bring to a boil.

2. Simmer for 15 minutes, and then strain into a jar.

TIP: The syrup is excellent on pancakes and for other uses. Add zest of 1 lemon to the syrup when not using it for a blue cocktail; otherwise, the acid in the lemon will not give you a true blue color. You could also use the mashed blueberries as a jam.

COCKTAIL VERSION

1. In a large bowl, add the baking soda to 1½ ounces of the blueberry syrup. Add slowly as it may bubble. It should turn blue.

2. In a shaker, muddle the sage leaf and blueberries. Add the syrup mixture, bourbon, and ice, and shake.

3. Strain into a glass with ice. Add the hard cider and garnish with the apple slice, lavender sprig, and sage leaves.

MOCKTAIL VERSION

1. Follow the instructions for the cocktail, but substitute apple cider for the hard cider and top with a good ginger ale before garnishing.

Hillary lost. She *lost*. It felt impossible, a catastrophe of monumental proportions.

Earlier, when we'd walked into the Democratic headquarters on Cerrillos Road in Santa Fe, it was filled with excitement and the smell of New Mexico. Chiles were joyfully circling the room on paper plates. The anticipation from my elders, the women who had worked for decades to witness the first woman president of the United States, was palpable. While we still weren't, and even today aren't, receiving equal rights or equal pay for equal work, at least the path to getting these seemed clearer. The glass ceiling that has protected the myriad men who have ruled this country since its inception seemed as though it might soon be shattered.

I was alone election night. My husband was at his biggest show of the year at the Philadelphia Museum of Art. The patrons there were sharing their excitement in the City of Brotherly Love. *Brotherly* love. Instead we were talking by cell phone in anticipation as each state's results came in and calling each other every fifteen minutes. I was with my "sisters" who had campaigned with me: women who have campaigned for decades in races small and large, silver-haired women who have phone-banked and door-knocked with me and many others before me, for this race and prior ones. But this race was different. The first woman would be president of our nation. My heart was so full, it felt as if I could reach in and touch it, hold it in my hand and tell it, "You will be treated equally. It will happen *tonight*."

I ran into my dear friend Tanya. I was somewhat surprised to see her there, as she was a Bernie supporter and this battle had been vicious, but her fiancé is transgender, and I knew Tanya knew the importance of the night. If the monster on the GOP ticket won, not only would women be the targets of his hideous behavior, but LGBTQ+ people would be at risk too. Winning this race was essential, and Hillary's win would be life-affirming—who wouldn't want to see that?

As states were called, cheers erupted as well as some groans. David and I were calling each other, and Tanya was on the phone with her love, who was in Maine. The excitement started to wane as states got called for him who shall not be named. Then the numbness began. The packed room began to open—people were leaving. I looked around for Mary Ellen, my dear friend who has worked for women's rights since she was old enough to breathe, and saw she was gone. She had left with her partner, Judy. The sadness was sitting on top of a deep anxiety, and I couldn't find a set of eyes to look to for an answer. *How could this be happening?*

I found Tanya again, and she appeared stricken. She had her love on the phone, and he was starting to cry. I called David, and he didn't say anything when he answered. I could hear his breathing. Then I could hear my heart beating through my chest. It seemed like everything else went quiet.

Soon Tanya and I were somehow standing in the parking lot, looking through the glass of the Democratic headquarters and at the TV monitors. We were seeing the impossible electoral numbers glaring at us. Pennsylvania, Michigan . . . We held hands. When the fate of our nation seemed sealed, we fell into one another, both of us sobbing.

Somehow I got home, and somehow I made it to work the next morning. But I couldn't stop crying—or sobbing. The tears came on my way to work, in the bathroom while at work, on my way home from work. I cried for three months straight, enveloped by a crushing grief.

I felt the nation had no idea what it had just done. But I knew. I had grown up with this kind of monster, and the last thing you should ever do is give money or power to malignant narcissism like this, and certainly not both.

I didn't know where I would be when it came time to watch the 2020 election results. I only planned on being exhausted from working to make sure it would be a night we could be proud of as we saw the first woman stand as vice president. And it worked out. We got there. Biden and Harris. Equality is on the horizon.

Debrianna and David, activists.

MESQUITE MANHATTAN

SERVES 1

2 ounces Colkegan Single Malt Whiskey or ginger ale for mocktail version

1 ounce sweet vermouth or lemon-lime seltzer for mocktail version

2 dashes Angostura bitters or ½ ounce grenadine for mocktail version

A few Luxardo cherries or marasca cherries for finishing

COCKTAIL VERSION

1. Combine all ingredients, except cherries, over ice in a mixing glass.

2. Stir until ice cold, and then strain into a chilled coupe.

3. Garnish with the Luxardo cherries.

MOCKTAIL VERSION

1. Follow the instructions for the cocktail version, but replace all alcohol with 2 ounces ginger ale, 1 ounce lemon-lime seltzer, and ½ ounce grenadine over ice. Then add the cherries.

Ode to Santa Fe Spirits: We decided to include these AMAZING spirits from SFS. They are unique to our hometown of Santa Fe because they use locally sourced ingredients that capture a spectacular flavor like no other. Of course, you can always substitute with another brand.

Apple Brandy Sour

SERVES 1

1½ ounces Santa Fe Spirits Apple Brandy or apple cider for mocktail

2 tablespoons freshly squeezed lemon juice

1 ounce simple syrup

1 egg white

Marasca cherries for finishing

COCKTAIL VERSION

1. Combine all ingredients, except cherries, in a mixing glass, and shake vigorously for 10 seconds.

2. Add ice, and shake again.

3. Strain over ice into a collins glass and garnish with a couple marasca cherries.

MOCKTAIL VERSION

1. Follow the instructions for the cocktail version, but replace the apple brandy with apple cider.

Contributing Chefs

HAL SPARKS

FRANGELA

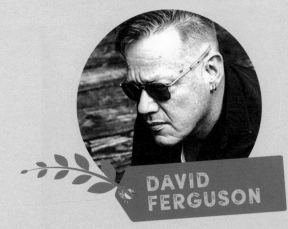

DAVID FERGUSON

YONI MARTEN

ELENA ALLALAY

SANTA FE SPIRITS

KARL FRISCH

DANA GOLDBERG

OLLY

MANU AZZARETTO

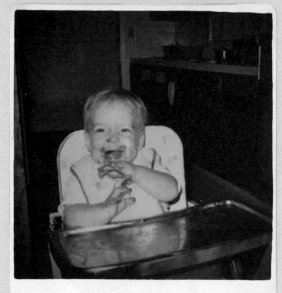

Baby Lisa.

Baby Debrianna.

Acknowledgments

FROM LISA:

My heartfelt love and gratitude go to my nearest and dearest loves: Seamus and Ronan and my new fiancé, Morse. And to the next generation of great cooks in the family, my loving sisters, cousins, niece, and nephews: Hollie, Heidi, Abigail, Emily, Jenny, Tatianna, Peter, Natalie, Eric, Stesha, Anthony, Simone, Rakela, Bella, Jack, Izzy, and Luka. Thanks also to my therapists over the last few years, Leslie Pearlman and Judith Kaplan, who got me through some challenging times, and to all my parental figures: Franny and Stanny, Louis and Jill, Joe and Nadyne. I'm grateful to Sarah Gartner, my better half, for believing in me while giving me the space to do this venture as we develop and produce TV shows and features; Belle Allen, my sister from another mister, whose trusted friendship and support helped me find my voice; and Stephanie Holthaus, my oldest friend, who first ventured into the kitchen with me as we faced our adolescence, *zucchini zircles* and all, and lived to tell the tale. And lastly, the biggest hug to my sweet soul sister, Debrianna; you are the real deal, girlfriend. Kindred spirit and the Thelma to my Louise. *Molte grazie* for your unwavering trust to drive off this Corona Kitchen cliff with me into the beyond. We're still soaring over the canyon with this cookbook! When the fates brought us together all those fourteen years ago, of course it was at a fancy dinner with us randomly seated side by side, and all we could talk about was the food.

FROM DEBRIANNA:

It is with deep gratitude that I want to thank my family, elders, and ancestors who have taught me throughout my life and through the ethers the value and joy of cooking. Food *is* love.

Thank you to all the chefs, far too numerous to name, whose work I have read and whom I have watched since I was a child. They have all, in their way, contributed to this book. Cooking is sharing.

If it were not for Maggie Hanley, this book would have been one long run-on sentence. Thank you, my dear friend.

Bob Tzudiker and Noni White, the blessing of your friendship, love, and support is endless and deeply appreciated. Thank you more than can ever be measured.

I am in forever gratitude to Al Garcia, my coach and dear friend. Al, your guidance, kindness, and love over the years are an immense blessing and gift that keep on giving. A thank-you is not nearly enough.

The ongoing support and love of David Lamb are incalculable. Thank you with all my heart.

To the brilliant performer and writer Ann Randolph, thank you for holding such a beautiful and supportive space during the pandemic for me to write.

Thank you, Jillian Hurley. You are an amazing cheerleader and friend. Your efforts and kindness have never gone unnoticed.

For my Stephanie Miller "clan" and to the great Stephanie Miller, who may not know how much we are indebted to her genius—thank you. Without all of you, I am not sure how I would have gotten through the last four years. You offered truth and laughter so we could make it through to 2021.

Most of all, thank you to Lisa, my sister of the heart, my sister from another mother. My love, admiration, and gratitude for you are endless and ongoing. This endeavor has been life-changing, joyful, and blessed. You are this.

And in such odd ways, thank you to the pandemic, which brought us here, to Corona Kitchen, and to a creative community of beautiful people.

FROM DEBRIANNA AND LISA:

We want to give a massive thank-you beyond the moon to our publishers, Julia Abramoff and Alex Merrill, and their associate editor, Drew Anderla, at Apollo Publishers. They took a chance on our crazy asses, and Julia personally edited our original manuscript, which was only seventy thousand words over! Okay, this isn't helping for us to reveal that fact, but . . . hey, we guess we have a lot to say. And, especially to Julia, who didn't bat an eyelash at letting us be exactly who we are in this book. We love you for that. And to Peter Bussian, who originally suggested that Apollo might want a cookbook and made the introduction. *Thank you, Peter!* Also, we owe Penina Meisels a huge amount of gratitude for taking *gorgeous* photographs and sharing her almond cake recipe, home, and friendship with us, and love to little Watson, who was our special doggie mascot during the shoot. To Hollie Lucas-Alcalay, what can we say, you are literally Wonder Woman. Thank you for being such a rock star on this journey. We love you! Jane Keranen, our fearless assistant, you kept us on track, and we could not have made the deadlines without you! Our fab food stylist, Natalie Drobny, who Zoom styled us over the ethers, thank you! And to all of the special guests on the FB Live *Corona Kitchen* show who contributed recipes for this book: Hal Sparks, Dana Goldberg, Chef Olly Ludwig, Manu Azzaretto, Elena Alcalay, David Ferguson, Frances Collier, Angela V. Shelton, Karl Frisch, and Yoni Marten, thank you for hanging out with us and answering our calls! To Bob Cesca and Buzz Burbank, thanks for inspiring the ravioli and pizza from Debrianna's childhood. To our *Corona Kitchen* superstar recipe contest winners who generously donated their personal recipes included in this book: Peggy Stalkr, Patricia Media, Martha Lazuk Swift, Lauren Slaff, Emily Swantner, Lizette Marx, Jen Wege, Elton Foster, and Grace Gomez Lapsys, *thank you.* And to the fans of the show, what can we say? *You are the best.* Thanks to Be.Live for hosting us on FB—glitches and all. Thanks to Stephanie Miller for prescreening our guests, LOL. To Gennica Lee, thanks for making us look at least fifteen years younger for our photos. Anna Rodgers of Revelry Salon, thank you for your always luscious hair stylings. Thank you, Collin and Leif at Santa Fe Spirits! You were our first sponsors. P.S. Your hooch is the absolute best (funny we didn't have any food sponsors, only alcohol!). And last but certainly not least, to Marty Groothuis, our attorney who is The Man.

SPECIAL THANKS

Special thanks to everyone who supported us in making this cookbook a reality. We love you!

Hollie Lucas-Alcalay, Suzanne Apgar, Lisa Bayne Astor, David Bacharach, Alice Bailey, Nancy Baker, Keely Baribeau, Billie Barthelemy, Donald De Bear, Linda Bearman, Joan Benedetti, Nick Bennett, Denise Betesh, Joseph and Nadyne Bicknell, Morse Bicknell, Monica Di Bisceglie, Sandra Bishop, Jennifer Blau, Dona Bolding, Elsa Bouman, Aviva Bowman, Alec Brown, Timothy Buck, Shawn Burich, Jason Burnham, Lindsay Burt, Valerie Cannon, Beth Chang, Kate Chavez, Sanjiv and Joey Chawla, Robin Cobbey, Sue Cohen, Kathi Collins, MaryEllen Collins, Jodi Conway, Sloan Cunningham, Jewell Dennis, David Dirks, Natalie Drobny, Ellen Dupuy, Scott Eckert, Colleen Eugster, Tracy Feldman, Theodora Fine, Lulu Fitcher, Elton Foster, Danielle Foster-Herbst, Jerry Franklin, Johanna Fredrics, Rebekah Fry, Dawn Galzerano, Laura Gardner, Jill Garelick, Sarah Gartner, Amy Golan, Christina Gopal, Lauren Greenwald, Karen Hall, Margaret Hanley-Welles, Kristi Harter, Maria Hensel, David Hoff, Kelly House, Rachel Hroncich, Jillian Hurley, Claudia Jessup, Jody Johnson, Dedee DeLongpre Johnston, Charlotte Katzenmoyer, Andrea Kepple, Casey Kilduff, Ana Krafchick, Karoli Kuns, Grace Gomez Lapsys, Michael Latham, Barbara Laytham, Vivian Leal, Debbie Lemay, Suet Tieng Lim, Lois Lipman, Michelle London, Carla Lopez, Helen Love, Aimee Lowe, Abigail Lucas, Louis and Jill Lucas, Emily Lucas, Heidi Lucas, Rebecca Lynn, Elsie Maio, Meredith Maldonado, David Manzanares, Andie Manzanares, and Maximino Manzanares,, Lucinda Marker, Linda McDill, Christine McHugh, Donna McKee, Sarah Mease, Patricia Medina, Penina Meisels, Karen Melfi, Bega Metzner, Julia Minasian, Stesha Moore Pavich, Jillian Moul, Mara Leader, Michelle Neels, Vivian Nesbitt, Judith Neugebauer, Kimberly Norberto, Alexandria Olguin, Catherine Oppenheimer, Chrys Papatone, Annette Paskiewicz, Frances Pavich, Michael Pavich, Tatianna Pavich, Joni Pearce, Hilary Pfeifer, Pam Pierce, Gwendolyn Pomeroy, Ken Prokuski, Anne Rabe, Victor Ramirez, Robyn Reede, Rocky Mountain Mike, Ann Roylance, Holly Scheib, Marianne Schneller, Cass and Gerry Schuck, Sheila Seclearr, Trish Siemion, Ariana Spencer, Peggy Stalkr, Jennifer Stennis, Bill Sterchi, June Stoddard, Kelly Stranahan, Martha Lazuk Swift, Susan

Thomson, Nicole Torres Piston, Lynn Tracey, Jeanne Trachta, Judith Tucker, Sharon Tuke, Robert Tzudiker, Alton L. Walpole, Carolyn Wickwire, Daniel Williams, Kevin Williams, Karen and Glenn Williamson, Mark Winne, Susan Wise, Alaina Warren Zachary, and Rosemary Zibart.

Hugs to our fur babies: Cashew, Edgar, Monty, and Walnut.

A percentage of Debrianna and Lisa's profits from the sale of this book will go to World Central Kitchen, https://wck.org, and Planned Parenthood, https://www.plannedparenthood.org.

Debrianna's cats, Cashew and Walnut.

Lisa's dogs, Edgar and Monty.